Received On

D0344751

AUTHENTIC GRAVITAS

Who Stands Out and Why

REBECCA NEWTON, PhD

A TARCHERPERIGEE BOOK

tarcherperigee

An imprint of Penguin Random House LLC
penguinrandomhouse.com

Most TarcherPerigee books are available at special quantity discounts for bulk purchase for sales
promotions, premiums, fund-raising, and educational needs. Special books or book excerpts also can
be created to fit specific needs. For details, write: SpecialMarkets@penguinrandomhouse.com.

Library of Congress Cataloging-in-Publication Data

Names: Newton, Rebecca Lianne, author.
Title: Authentic gravitas : who stands out and why / Rebecca Newton, PhD.
Description: New York : TarcherPerigee, [2019] | Includes bibliographical references and index.
Identifiers: LCCN 2018049580| ISBN 9780143132080 (hardcover) | ISBN 9780525503828 (ebook)
Subjects: LCSH: Self-presentation. | Respect. | Dignity. | Leadership.
Classification: LCC BF697.5.S44 N49 2019 | DDC 155.2--dc23
LC record available at https://lccn.loc.gov/2018049580

Printed in the United States of America
1   3   5   7   9   10   8   6   4   2

Book design by Kristin del Rosario

Some names and identifying characteristics have been changed
to protect the privacy of the individuals involved.

To Saskia, Sam, and Amélie

Thank you for reminding me every day,
in your own little ways,
the power of courage, curiosity,
and most of all,
uncontrollable laughter.

CONTENTS

AUTHENTIC
GRAVITAS

INTRODUCTION

The view from the top-floor meeting room of the London office was spectacular on this remarkably sunny day. Red buses, black cabs, old buildings, bustling sidewalks, and an endless skyline set the scene for my early morning coaching session with a partner of an established professional services firm. After a fairly lengthy discussion about what areas were most important to his personal development, Jonathan leaned in and quietly said to me, "Do you know what I *really* need? I need more..." Seeing his struggle to find the right word, I offered, "Gravitas?" "Yes! I need more gravitas!" he exclaimed, appearing relieved at just being able to pinpoint and label this "thing" he felt was missing from his otherwise successful career.

As an organizational psychologist who has spent twenty years coaching professionals and facilitating leadership development programs, I have had the immense privilege of hearing clients share their most intimate personal development goals. One of the most frequent requests I receive is to help them develop more gravitas. At the same time, there's a palpable sense of disbelief that gravitas is something that is actually obtainable—at least for them. But when we explore further, we discover that it's not standing out in the room for the sake of being noticed that they really want—it's *to be valued*. What they're after is to be respected and trusted, and to be *worthy* of that respect and trust; to stand out for making a positive, significant impact in their immediate sphere of influence. But they want to stand out as themselves, holding true to their own values, rather than pretending to be someone else or simply copying another's style: "I still want to be me."

We've all been in a room with a group of people talking and throwing around their ideas and opinions, discussing and debating the best way forward. Then one person says something and it seems like everyone stops, leans in to listen, and considers what this person is saying. It's as if their opinion carries more weight, or there's some kind of pull toward them in the room that makes everyone take note. They're able to pause midsentence and nobody jumps in to fill the silence. It's not that they're necessarily more senior or experienced, louder or more soft-spoken, more motivating or more somber, more serious or more upbeat than anyone else. Yet their words, their opinions, their ideas carry weight. They have an intangible quality: *There's just something about them.*

Throughout this book, you will meet some truly inspiring leaders and professionals who built authentic gravitas, and you will learn how they did it. We'll look at what gravitas is, what it isn't, and debunk the gravitas myths to discover the surprising truth about who stands out and why. This book is for professionals who want to increase their own gravitas, and for leaders looking to help others around them to grow their gravitas. It matters to me personally because through leadership and professional development programs, and particularly in coaching, I've discovered time and time again that it really matters to my clients. It's often a genuine concern, not necessarily overwhelming, but a consistent niggle—one that they're not always comfortable talking about openly, but that they feel holds them back from having the impact they desire. And they're not sure what to do about it. It can be frustrating, exhausting, even debilitating to experience the quiet burden of feeling that you lack gravitas. This book is designed to empower you (and those you lead) with the knowledge that you can develop gravitas, and to equip you with practical tried-and-true tools to do so. My goal is to break down something that is seemingly intangible into a quality you can develop, while at the same time staying true to you.

Often people feel they have gravitas in their regular working life, the day in, day out interactions with colleagues, clients, and associates they know well, but when giving a speech or presentation, they seem to lose all confidence. It can be extremely disheartening, knowing that in "real life" you're better than how you show up in meetings and presentations. For others, they feel they have gravitas in those big moments, but they may lose it in some of their day-to-day challenges with colleagues. Either way, it's annoying to think, *If only I could just be myself and not lose my cool in those critical moments.* My intention in this book is to help you do just that—to be more of yourself, and as such, to have more authentic gravitas, whether in informal one-on-one conversations with a colleague or in your most formal meetings and presentations. It is possible to intentionally build skills to ensure your best "real self" is coming across—even, or especially, in your most pressure-filled moments.

The insights, ideas, and techniques offered in this book are based on research I conducted with professional development experts and leaders across many industries, and the experiences of thousands of dedicated professionals I've had the incredible opportunity to coach, train, and advise over the past two decades. Among the many stories that fill these pages, we hear from a British consultant, Mehira, on how she tackled the "Trap of Expertise"; Jackson, a disheartened American COO who felt he'd "lost his swagger" during a particularly challenging point in his career—and how he got it back; and a Spanish professional, Juan, who made some small daily changes to increase his authentic gravitas in the midst of a demanding schedule. In this book, you'll find wisdom and ideas gleaned from hundreds of dedicated researchers, particularly in the fields of psychology and organizational behavior. These include findings on psychological stress from a study at a Japanese brewery, American researchers' insights into the extraordinary career success of players in the National Baseball Hall of Fame, a comparison of Chinese and Canadian negotiating techniques, Israeli researchers' study of elite soccer goalkeepers' actions in penalty kicks, an analysis of two thousand firms in Malaysia on which influencing techniques are used by transformational managers, and British researchers' analysis of the relationship between emotions and complex decision-making in the brain.

Here's what the research shows: people with gravitas "lead the room," regardless of their place in the hierarchy; they respect authority but don't wait for a title change to take ownership and make a positive difference. They are able to close the inevitable gap between their intention and their impact. These commitments and behaviors are not reserved for a precious few; authentic gravitas is not restricted to those of a certain age, gender, personality, or any other personal characteristic. In this book, we'll see how even wisdom is something that can be learned (and we'll learn how to do it). We'll look at how to build trust, influence, and authentic gravitas with integrity, through a disciplined commitment to self-leadership, as there is a proven relationship between how we lead ourselves and our ability to lead others. Of course, this work is not always easy, so we'll explore how to manage nerves and negative self-talk, and how to sustain authentic gravitas even when things are hard and amid the reality of a challenging schedule. We'll conclude by discussing the power of genuine collaboration, because having gravitas is not about being an invincible superhero, but rather a "joint adventurer." This requires vulnerability, humility, and risk-taking. We can't get caught up in zero-sum-game thinking—"I can only have more gravitas if you have less." And we're certainly not talking about self-important, self-serving dominance or posturing, or simply being the loudest person in the room. Authentic gravitas means you are respected and trusted, your words carry weight, your ideas are taken seriously, and your contributions are valued, but it also requires you to bring out these qualities in others. You are not only inspiring but inspire greatness in others. As you do this, *people gravitate toward you.*

Ultimately, for the many people I've had the privilege of partnering with on their journey to building gravitas, the most important and empowering moment is not when they learn a new technique or introduce new behaviors (although as we'll see throughout the book, these small changes can make a big difference). It is when they make the necessary initial shift in their mind-set to recognize that in order to have gravitas they don't need to feel confident, but they do need to choose courage. We tend to be critical of ourselves when we don't feel confident or qualified, which perpetuates a negative cycle. But we should regularly be nervous. Stepping out of our comfort zone and stretching ourselves with opportunities that make us somewhat uncomfortable is a requirement for growth. Gravitas is reserved for those who continue to challenge themselves and increase their skill, regardless of whether it feels good in the process. Do not wait to feel confident. Choose to step out and be courageous, and you'll likely find that your confidence grows along the way. Courage precedes confidence.

Many clients *whisper* when sharing that they want more gravitas, as if unsure whether it's something they should actually want. But I think there is greatness in committing to the courage and discipline required to grow in this skill. I am continually inspired by my clients' determination to have a positive impact and add significant value as they navigate their unique professional journey. My wish is that this book will inspire and equip you on yours.

ONE

THE MYTHS OF GRAVITAS

What Authentic Gravitas Is (and What It Isn't)

Something happened to me at forty-five that had a shattering effect on my life . . . I suddenly realized one day that the conductor doesn't make a sound. He depends for his power on his ability to make other people powerful. And when I realized it, it had an overwhelming effect . . . I realized my job was to awaken possibility in other people.

—Benjamin Zander, conductor and musical director
of the Boston Philharmonic Orchestra and
the Boston Philharmonic Youth Orchestra

Five years ago, a colleague and I were running a leadership development program with a global telecommunications company. Over twenty years, I've had the privilege of hearing thousands of leaders and professionals share their personal goals and challenges. This day stands out to me. At the start, we asked each of the thirty-two participants to briefly share their leadership goals and challenges. Each in turn shared their thoughts on the reality, aspirations, and complexity of leadership in today's organizational life. One gentleman from Norway, perhaps a little older than the average participant, shared, "My name is Anders. I'm from Oslo. I've been in this business for eight years and have been in the industry for more than thirty. I'm just a few years away from retirement and I have only one goal for the next few days in this program. I'm only thinking about one thing. I want to leave a good footprint on the lives of those who I work with. That's it. I want to map out exactly what that looks like and how to do it well." I looked around and saw thirty-one smiles around the room. It was not purely his statement that grabbed me; it was the impact it had on everyone around him. Anders had everyone's attention. In that moment, he was the person (we all know them and often wonder, *What is it about them?*) who made us all pause, the one who stood out from the crowd, the one who influenced the way everyone around him thought. Our unspoken, collective challenge was, *When was the last time I thought like that? I want to.*

THE MYTHS OF GRAVITAS

"She has gravitas." "He has gravitas." We use the word *gravitas* as a label for people who are listened to, taken seriously, considered important regardless of their hierarchical position: their opinion matters, their ideas have weight. There are three myths about gravitas, psychological barriers we can face, that we need to debunk in order to build authentic gravitas.

First, we have the Myth of the Gravitas Gift. This is our incorrect instinct that we either have gravitas or we don't; that we are born with it or not; that it is reserved for a few personality types, people of a certain disposition, or even a physical type. Or perhaps it's something reserved for people with decades of experience and gray hair. But for most people, their inner gremlin whispers, *It's not me; I'm not like that.* It's a quiet, immensely personal statement, and we regard it as fact. But not only is it untrue, the myth is dangerously self-defeating. It means that while we might try to be better in meetings, clearer in presentations, and have more impact with our boss, clients, and peers, ultimately deep down many of us believe we just are not one of "those" people with the *gift* of gravitas. If we are not convinced gravitas is something that can be developed, that we *personally* could develop, then we won't engage in the behaviors and disciplines required to develop the skills. After all, what's the point in trying to upskill in something we ultimately can't control?

Second in line is the Myth of Confidence: we believe that for gravitas, we need to have confidence because we *perceive* confidence in those people we consider to have gravitas. But what the research shows is that those people aren't consistently *feeling confident*; they are *choosing to be courageous*. It is courage that drives gravitas, not confidence. Confidence may develop, particularly in response to the successful outworking of courage. But those with gravitas do not wait to feel confident; instead, they choose to be courageous.

Thirdly, there's the Myth of Charisma. We sense that gravitas is reserved for people who would be considered naturally charismatic. Here's the good news: it's not. People with charisma may have authentic gravitas, but gravitas doesn't require charisma (more on this in chapter 2).

THE GRAVITAS JOURNEY

It's time to debunk these unspoken myths in our minds. We look first at the Myth of the Gravitas Gift. The starting point in developing greater gravitas is acknowledging the reality that gravitas is not something a person has or doesn't have. A person is not born with gravitas. Nor is gravitas something you suddenly acquire: "I've got it!" Rather, it's something that builds. We can all increase our degree of gravitas. *You* have the potential for greater gravitas. It's not something predetermined, it's not reserved for a gifted few; it's a choice that we make about what we build into our lives and, as a result, what we give back out. So while we may say someone "has" gravitas—and I use this language throughout the book to keep the discussion succinct—it is not a *fixed* quality. Rather, it refers to people who are regarded widely and consistently by those around them to have a high degree of gravitas. Whether or not you feel like you have it to some degree now, it's something you can choose to build.

My colleagues and I have been asked to coach hundreds of professionals who worry, "I don't have enough gravitas," or whose managers believe, "He/she needs more gravitas." They come to us with a degree of disheartened resignation, because even while these professionals are asking for help, this gravitas myth whispers to them that in reality, not much can be done. But looking at the journeys of professionals we've coached, we have many examples to contradict the myth. Those who previously did not believe they had gravitas now recognize that others tend to consider them someone whose contribution carries weight. Or at a minimum they express (with a palpable sense of relief) that it's "no longer really an issue." Many managers who considered gravitas to be a key development area for a member of their team now assert that the person has more gravitas. So gravitas *can* be developed. It just takes courage and discipline.

OTHERS GRAVITATE TOWARD YOU

Now that we've addressed what gravitas *isn't*, let's have a look at what gravitas is. The *Cambridge English Dictionary* defines gravitas as "seriousness and importance of manner, causing feelings of respect and trust in others."[1] The origin of the word in Latin, *gravis*, means "serious."[2] In this book, we'll explore whether this definition holds true in today's workplace for professionals looking to develop their gravitas.

In my research for this book, I interviewed a wide range of leaders and professionals across various industries from around the world, as well as specialists in, and teachers of, leadership and professional development. I additionally analyzed discussions of gravitas by professionals in coaching sessions over a ten-year period.

I found that people in the workplace considered to have gravitas certainly *are* respected and trusted by others. Colleagues consider their contributions to be important, but they are *not* self-important; that is, they do not demonstrate a belief that they are "more important or have a higher value than other people." They demonstrate "seriousness" in situations that require it, and they give "importance" to the issues that matter, such as those that impact the achievement of collective goals. When it comes to seriousness, others do take them seriously. They are *not*, however, necessarily serious in personality. Some were described as consistently serious, but most were not—rather, while they were all *taken* seriously, some were described as bringing timely "levitas" or regularly using humor to bring lightheartedness to a situation.

There is no personality requirement for gravitas: people described as having gravitas displayed preferences and behaviors across the full spectrum of personality types. In terms of individual attributes, there is no physical, age, or gender requirement for gravitas—it is based on our mind-set, behaviors, and skills that we can choose to develop.

The truth is, gravitas looks different for different people. You can have gravitas and still be you. Professionals show up with gravitas in all kinds of different ways. The way we apply the word *gravitas* around the world does not concern the "manner" or style of a person, but rather is more closely related to one consistent quality: the value they add, and the process by which they do so.

BEING VALUED

We can believe it's just about the way someone speaks or their nonverbal behaviors (body language, tone of voice, and so on), but at the crux of it, people considered to have a high degree of gravitas in the workplace are simply and powerfully bringing substantial value to the situation they're in and the people they're in it with. Their contribution to the conversation is greatly valued. Most of us want to be people who are valued by those we respect, because of the pronounced value we *add*. This is the true foundation of gravitas: being taken seriously *because* you add significant value—in the meeting, to your clients, to your colleagues, and in your work. Not because of your position and not because you're looking to stand out just for the sake of being seen, but because you're consistently and powerfully making a noteworthy contribution to both the people and the situation, and engendering respect and trust because of it. *Lead the room* is a phrase I'll use throughout the book when referring to gravitas. People with a high degree of gravitas were often referred to in interviews as having the ability to "lead the room"—adding value in such a way that they are able to powerfully shape or direct the conversation and decisions for a collective positive outcome, regardless of their title or position.

Psychology professors Brosch and Sander at the University of Geneva note that "value" (the importance, worth, or usefulness of something; principles or standards of behavior; one's judgment of what is important in life) is arguably one of the most central concepts governing human life.[3] Hence the significance of understanding this topic and how we can contribute value to the interactions and the situations in which we find ourselves.

Having a high degree of gravitas at work means you are taken seriously, your contributions are considered important, you are recognized as adding substantial value, and you are trusted and respected.

People gravitate toward you.

What I call "authentic gravitas" comes when we make this contribution intentionally and courageously, in line with our values and our unique strengths. Professionals with a high degree of authentic gravitas make a positive, significant impact on both a situation and the people around them. They are deliberate about it: clear about their goals for impact and influence, and courageous and disciplined in choosing to act on those intentions. They are mindful of collective goals, and intentional about how they show up. As such, they are better able to offer an important contribution, one that is in line with their values and convictions about what matters. They are more likely to be taken seriously and engender feelings of respect and trust in others. They are valued because they add value to the situations they are in and the people they're with.

THE DARK SIDE OF GRAVITAS

Authentic gravitas stands in contrast to what I call "adverse gravitas," the *dark side* of gravitas. It's important to make the distinction, because without it, we may question whether gravitas is something we should actually want. Or, in seeking to increase our gravitas, we can unintentionally slip into behaviors that do not have the impact we intend.

In coaching conversations and research interviews, people made this distinction and clarified their goals around gravitas. For example, "I'd like more gravitas, to be someone others feel is worth listening to and taken seriously, but I don't want to come on too full-on, I don't want to come across like a bully." Or, "I feel like I need more gravitas, to be able to get and hold attention in the room, to be someone others look up to, but I don't want to be like *X*. She makes people feel like rubbish, and you don't feel like you have a choice or a say in anything."

With the dark side of gravitas, the stereotypes play out. A person displaying adverse gravitas may be aggressive, act like a bully, and/or draw on positional power to achieve self-serving goals through manipulation or coercion. They may foster an environment of fear, where others feel they need to walk on eggshells around them.

Adverse gravitas need not incorporate negative intent. It may not comprise manipulation or coercion. The dark side of gravitas can simply involve someone posturing and dominating in such a way that other people or the situation are adversely affected. It happens often when people aren't being mindful about their impact on others. If one person takes up all the space, even without negative intent, they can control the conversation and stop others from contributing. They may fail to give due weight to inquiry and overload on advocacy. As such, they can reduce the potential collective knowledge, understanding, and insight. Sometimes people do this because they want to be seen. When talking in the security of the coaching room with people who demonstrate behavior associated with adverse gravitas, many disclose insecurities and a lack of confidence. The problem is that in their posturing, they have failed to be vulnerable, and those around them interpret their behavior as self-importance rather than self-protection. While others may have sympathy for the latter, they have no patience for the former.

Someone exhibiting adverse gravitas may be unaware of their impact, of when they might be railroading the situation, making others feel less valued or less able to contribute. One of the first executives I was asked to coach was constantly making people around him cry. Jonas was taken seriously, and he was regarded as playing an important role in his organization, but he didn't have a positive impact on the people around him. He added value in content but not in people's experience, thereby reducing others' ability to add value and diminishing the collective quality of that content. He did know that sometimes people on his team or in the wider office would be upset, although he didn't appreciate the full extent of this. But even where he did see it, he didn't know what it was about his manner that was negatively impacting people, nor did he know how to change. He was a strong, dominant, talented professional, but it wasn't his intention to make others feel diminished, so we worked to change his impact from adverse to authentic gravitas. Jonas became more intentional—first by deciding how he *wanted* to impact others. He began adapting his style, proactively seeking feedback, and sending purposeful and sincere messages that he valued others. This wasn't always easy but he was committed. Jonas went on to receive unsolicited feedback from senior peers about the positive changes they saw in his working style and impact.

Whether intentional or unintentional, displays of the dark side give gravitas a bad name. Most of us have encountered people who only display gravitas at a surface level; they can be serious and self-important in manner, acting as though they should be trusted or deserve respect, but have a negative impact on a situation or the people in it. Equally—let's be honest—many of us have displayed elements of the dark side, perhaps unknowingly at the time. When driving a situation forward, it's easy to slip into having an accidental negative impact on others. But if we're clear about what we mean by *gravitas* and what it looks like in practice, we're more likely to add value without detracting from others' ability to do the same. This creates relationships that are rooted in trust and mutual respect. We can start to put into place behaviors that enable us to make a significant, positive impact on the situations we're in and the people we're with. We're giving ourselves a better chance of being taken seriously, making important contributions, and being valued, trusted, and respected.

Who Stands Out (for Good Reasons) and Why

Professionals with authentic gravitas stand out. But *how* do they stand out? What do they do—or not do—that makes them stand out with gravitas?

Throughout this book, we'll look at what underpins authentic gravitas, the research on those foundations, and simple yet powerful techniques for how to develop it. We'll see how, with the right mind-set and behaviors, we can become increasingly valuable at work and have a powerful impact by drawing on intra- and interpersonal power, rather than relying on hierarchical power. We'll discover what we can do before, during, and in all the spaces between encounters, to genuinely be the person who adds substantive value when we are in the room. It's what often comes out when we explore the meaning behind the sentence, "I need more gravitas," going deeper to, "I want to be someone who is legitimately regarded as adding significant value, as myself (i.e., in line with my values and strengths)." This starts with a mind-set shift and then builds by implementing specific skills and techniques to align our intention and impact.

The first step I've identified is debunking the myth that gravitas is fixed and recognizing that it is accessible to you: it is something you can choose to build. You can also help the people you lead to develop it, regardless of your—and their—position in a hierarchy, gender, age, or personality. Once we've moved past that myth, we can engage in two behaviors that underpin authentic gravitas: being intentional and courageous.

CLOSING THE INTEGRITY GAP: FROM INTENTION TO IMPACT

After we recognize that gravitas is something we can work on, the next step is to be clear about what exactly it is we're working on. The goal is to get clarity around your intention for impact and act in alignment with it. I believe the single greatest barrier to a professional's success is failing to have clarity about the impact he or she desires to have on a situation or the people around them. In the busyness of today's working life, it's easy to just run out the door in the morning and rush through the day, never asking yourself the golden question: *What kind of impact do I want to have on the people I encounter today?* In this chapter, we'll look at how to gain clarity around your desired intention and then minimize the gap we all have between our intention and our actual impact. For authentic gravitas, we need to be intentional. It's not just about standing out for the sake of it; it's about choosing how we want to show up and knowing why.

Choosing Your Footprint

When it comes to leadership, clearly choosing what kind of leader you want to be can be the missing step in leading well.[4] The same is true with all our professional hats. What kind of colleague do you want to be? What kind of team member? What kind of adviser? It's the question missing from so many leadership and professional development programs: "What kind of leader/professional do you *want* to be?" In these programs, we facilitate and encourage self-awareness (what kind of leader/professional you are), get participants to map their journeys so far (what has made you the leader/professional you are), share knowledge and ideas (what kind of leader/professional you should be), and help people acquire new skills and adopt new behaviors (this is how you can become that kind of leader/professional).

But we don't focus strongly enough on arguably the most central components to leadership and professional success: intent (the kind of leader/professional you want to be) and impact (the legacy you want to leave). As shorthand, I refer to these two components combined as your "professional footprint."

In my experience, many have thought about their leadership or professional footprint at some point, but few have defined it clearly enough to guide their behavior and evaluate their "success." Even fewer give it regular consideration—letting it guide their daily decisions—or share it with others to get feedback and be held accountable.

I'm not saying we should all have the same leadership and professional success criteria—far from it. To develop authentic gravitas, you need to define your desired *personal* footprint and be intentional in your daily work. You need to give yourself space, time, and permission, and ask for help where you need it, in order to clearly define the culture of leadership and the professional environment you want to build around you. The leaders and professionals who demonstrate authentic gravitas powerfully align their impact with their intention.

Being intentional, however, is not a one-off act of deciding how we want to show up and what impact we want to have. Rather, being intentional in the context of authentic gravitas incorporates regular discipline. People with high levels of authentic gravitas continually reduce the gap between intention and impact by assessing—both from their own observations and others' feedback—how they are living up to those footprint goals, and make the changes necessary to keep building it on a day-to-day basis. The research revealed that the somewhat glamorous notion of gravitas is rooted in the unglamorous reality of self-regulation.

It is this discipline or self-regulation that enables us to have integrity. We all fall short, at times, of what is referred to as "behavioral integrity," or consistency between our words and actions, our stated and enacted values, and our promise-keeping.[5] The reality is that once we clarify and espouse our values and intentions, we set ourselves up to fall short, with our actual impact often not being quite on the mark. But as we stay mindful of the potential gap and maintain the discipline to seek and act upon feedback, we are able to continually reduce that gap and increase our integrity.

Central to creating a positive footprint are:

- Defining the kind of leader/professional you want to be. Write down words you would want others to use if they were asked to describe you.

- Knowing clearly how your personal goals align with, and help achieve, your organizational/team vision and purpose.

- Fostering self-awareness, reflecting on your own behavior, encouraging others to give you feedback, and knowing what naturally energizes you so that you can be someone who brings energy and resilience to the room even amid the pressures and challenges of organizational life.

- Recognizing differences that may arise between your intent and your impact.

- Committing to continually grow and learn in both knowledge and skill.

- Self-regulating. As my London School of Economics colleague Dr. Emma Soane argues, "The strength and the challenge of self-regulation is ensuring that you have coherence between your personality, your behavior, and your professional goals." We need discipline to choose action that aligns our intent with our impact. It requires commitment to prioritize action that aligns our intention and impact—not over but *through* the urgencies, the stresses, the disappointments, the highs and lows of day-to-day life.

My challenge now to every client, whether established or new to their professional journey, is the same question I need to regularly ask myself: *Do you know—and are you mindful of on a daily basis—what footprint you want to make?* The reality is, people with gravitas lead the room. So be intentional about how you want to lead the room—whether you're officially a leader or not—because *deciding* can be the missing step to leading the room well.

"I'm Just Not Like That!": A Question of Authenticity

Deciding on a footprint—this clarity around intention and impact—can make us wary of being inauthentic. When looking to develop gravitas, people often say, "I don't want to pretend to be something I'm not." Building gravitas is certainly *not* about pretending to be someone else.

Authenticity can be thought of as understanding one's real self (such as deep-level and conscious cognitions, emotions, and beliefs) and acting in congruence with that.[6,7] To put it in everyday terms, it's about being aware of what we personally really think, feel, and believe, and acting in a way that reflects our values. Researchers describe this alignment between conscious understanding of oneself and behavior as "authentic living." The quest for authenticity has positive benefits for us personally, with studies suggesting authenticity is one of the strongest predictors of well-being.[8] We can be authentic when we have clarity about our values and beliefs, are transparent with them, and—while nobody ever does this perfectly all the time—be intentional about outworking those on a day-to-day basis. Being authentic does *not* mean being fixed in our habits and the ways of interacting that we've (most likely *un*intentionally) developed over the years.

In this book, we will look at various research-based styles and techniques that my clients have found useful to increase their own gravitas. But this is not about adopting the style of others or pretending to be something we're not. It's about developing our skills to put our own personal best foot forward, thereby minimizing the gap between our intention, our action, and our impact. Our intentions stem from our values and beliefs, so in acting to align intention and impact, we should increase authenticity, even though this usually means trying out new ways of behaving.

Discussing the link between authenticity and gravitas recently with my students at the London School of Economics, I shared with them how I discovered (the hard way) that I have a natural tendency to be stubborn. At the same time, it emerged that the outworking of this in my communication style at work was negatively impacting a close colleague, Sarah. I'll share more on this later, but if being authentic were about being true to my natural style, I would remain stubborn in my future encounters with Sarah. But this is not in line with my values, my beliefs regarding how I should interact professionally, nor my intention: this is not how I want to "show up" with Sarah. The outworking of my stubbornness is not how I want to impact her. Wanting to be authentic was not permission to stick rigidly to my "natural style" or to continue having a negative impact on my colleague. I needed to learn to act in a way that aligned my intention and impact.

A New Natural

One of my clients, Mitan, challenged me on how he could change and be authentic. When I spoke to his senior manager, who had recommended Mitan for coaching, he said Mitan needed "more gravitas, to stand out more in the room and connect with clients more quickly and effectively." Mitan recognized these as areas he was "weaker" in, though he wasn't convinced he should be trying to change. "But I'm just not like that," he pleaded with me. "I don't want to pretend to be someone I'm not. Other people just click and connect with the clients, and I'm just not like that. I can't chat the way they can and I don't get attention the way others do. But my work speaks for itself and I thought everyone was happy with that." While Mitan certainly was valued for the written work he contributed, being able to connect with clients and hold their attention face-to-face was also part of his role. Thankfully, these are skills he could develop. When we discussed behaving differently, he pushed back on the authenticity front. But when we looked at the impact he wanted to have, his intention toward his clients, and his convictions about delivering the best for his company—in every area of his role—he was open to change.

Mitan was skeptical at first that he could change, but we walked through a few techniques he could put into place, and he was prepared, if somewhat apprehensive, to try them. I asked him to just try some new techniques for a few weeks until we met again. For Mitan, this began with acknowledging the Trap of Expertise, building in time for Space in the Middle, being mindful of his Virtual Gravitas, and committing to the Principles of Wisdom (just some of the techniques we'll look at throughout the book). We made some tweaks along the way, but over time, these became second nature to Mitan, and his appraisal feedback and subsequent promotion served as evidence to him that he could be "like that"—if he chose to. Rather than sticking rigidly to his natural style and habits of interacting that had developed over time, he came to agree that it was more important to try to adapt. That way, he'd have a better chance of impacting other people in the way he wanted.

Wanting to be "authentic" is not an excuse to be fixed and say, "I'm just not like that." Yes, one's personality—distinctive characteristics and patterns of thinking, feeling, and behaving—is relatively stable over time. And holding others' attention, being taken seriously, and connecting with and positively impacting those around them may seem to come more naturally to some people than to others. But people who feel (and potentially fear) that it's not as natural for them to do these things can implement practices to have more gravitas and the impact they desire.

Being authentic demands clarity and discipline to sometimes move away from old habits, try new things, and be true to your intention for impact. Throughout the book, you'll find suggested techniques and ideas for shifting your mind-set and behaviors in practice to increase your gravitas. You might not feel that all are appropriate or relevant for your particular context. But if you do choose to try out some new ways of thinking, behaving, and interacting, you might feel awkward or like it's "not you." It might be hard, but don't let negative self-talk or fear of others' judgment (particularly those people who've known you for a long time) let you think you're being inauthentic. It might not feel natural immediately, but if you're clear about how you want to show up, what your goals are for your impact on your situations and other people, you're being true to your intention. You're being more authentic than people who are just running through life without thinking much about their impact and what they want it to be—not clear or mindful of their beliefs and intentions. And while these practices might need a bit of tweaking along the way, if you stick with it, get feedback, and adapt accordingly, you'll find a new "natural," and gravitas—while always a journey—will feel more like you.

CHOOSING COURAGE OVER CONFIDENCE

The next challenge to tackle, when looking to build authentic gravitas, is the Myth of Confidence. People regarded by others as having gravitas are almost universally described as confident. You might feel like confidence is the main ingredient lacking from establishing your own gravitas. So does gravitas require confidence? The surprising answer is no.

Many people with gravitas don't actually have the confidence we imagine them having. They don't all wake up thinking, *I'm awesome. I'm ready.* Numerous clients whom others describe as having gravitas have confided in me that they still have to look at themselves in the mirror each morning and tell themselves, *You've got this. You can do it.* One of my friends who runs multiple large teams, who certainly is valued, trusted, and respected, is consistently making an important and serious contribution, describes how she "team briefs" herself. Others refer to it as their own pep talk. And off they go, showing up in a way where they are widely and consistently taken seriously, valued because of the value they add, trusted, and respected. How do they do it? How do they seemingly *choose* confidence? Here's the reality. They *don't.* They feel the fear and do it anyway. They choose courage. And as they choose to be courageous and act in alignment with their values, they build confidence. Authenticity breeds confidence—not "I'm going to rule the world" confidence, but inner strength that says, "I know who I am, I know what matters to me, and I know how I want to show up." As we'll see throughout the book, this comes with discipline, practice, self-reflection, and humility.

While the virtue of courage has been extolled for a long time, emerging in the management research is now a consensus as to what actually constitutes courage, including these essential components.[9, 10, 11]

1. Intentional action. It involves deliberate consideration and a voluntary willingness to act.

2. A worthy goal. The focus is a positive, important outcome.

3. Perceived risks, threats, obstacles, or challenging opportunities. There may or may not be varying levels of fear, but it does involve significant risk to the person. In a work context, this could be social or psychological risk as one engages in different activities to take up a new, challenging opportunity. It could be speaking up and standing up to

make a positive difference. In the context of servant leadership (in which courage is considered a crucial characteristic), courage is about daring to take risks and trying new approaches to old problems.[12]

Courage and integrity (which we build as we minimize the gap between intention and impact) were found in research to be the two most important virtuous predictors for C-level executive performance.[13] While they are vital for the C-suite, they are accessible to all. Both are choices we get to make.

People who are regarded as having high levels of authentic gravitas may look confident, but actually they are choosing to be courageous. At times, in any given context, they will feel confident, often increasingly so as they become more acquainted with that context and grow in the skills required to add positive, significant value there. They do not, however, feel consistently confident. And with each new venture or opportunity comes a wavering of confidence, but also a continued commitment to be courageous. In line with the essential components, they are (1) intentional; (2) looking to make a significant, positive impact on the situation they are in and the people around them; and (3) in pursuit of a goal that is associated with some risk. For example, they may step forward to take on new opportunities, contribute alternative viewpoints and take a strong position, seek constructive feedback, and try new behaviors when interacting with people at work to better align their intention and impact.

Here's what's great about discovering that it's courage rather than confidence we need for authentic gravitas. As courage by definition involves some perceived risk or challenge, we can see how our feelings of nervousness, anxiety, or even fear are reasonable responses to what we're embarking on. That's true whether it's speaking up to lead a discussion in a room full of new people, putting your hand up for new and unknown projects and challenges, committing to pushing your knowledge base and growing your expertise, engaging in difficult conversations, or trying new behaviors to connect with and influence others. We talk about "confidence," but what we actually need is self-efficacy. As psychologist Albert Bandura noted, confidence refers to strength of belief, but I could, for example, be "confident that I will fail at this endeavor."[14] What we want to feel is the psychological resource of self-efficacy: the expectation that we can perform competently across a broad range of challenging situations that require effort and perseverance.[15] Self-efficacy is fairly stable but can be developed (for example, through successful experiences or role-modeling). Leader self-efficacy involves the confidence to successfully motivate others.[16] Of course, we want this psychological resource! I'm certainly not arguing that confidence is a bad thing. Quite the opposite. It's just that it's not a prerequisite for increasing authentic gravitas. It may be a positive output rather than a necessary input. Interviewees regarded by others as having high levels of gravitas vulnerably revealed that they don't consistently feel this in their quests to continue having a positive impact and adding significant value. They are, however, (1) intentional, (2) working toward a worthy goal, and (3) aware of a real risk that they might not be successful. They are, by definition, choosing to be courageous.

In whichever way you're looking to lead the room, expanding the boundaries of how you add significant value is likely to feel somewhat scary because there's uncertainty around the outcome. We "see" confidence when we look at people who we consider to have gravitas. But that doesn't mean they always feel confident. We don't need to wait to feel confident to have authentic gravitas; we should feel like we're being courageous.

For those who don't think courage comes naturally to them, the good news is, courage can be learned.[17] To sum up, here are four ways to build your gravitas by learning to choose courage and tackling that feeling that you "need more confidence":

1. *Practice* courage. Aristotle suggested that character traits such as courage are made up of habits, which are formed through "repetitious acts."[18] Professor William I. Miller at the University of Michigan suggests that in order to attain courage, one should be courageous: it can only be attained

by doing it.[19] In new or challenging contexts, confidence is something that can build over time. So waiting until we feel "ready" can hold us back. It's often in the doing that people build their courage and subsequently find their confidence. Starting from a market stall, the company Innocent Drinks now produces more than a million smoothies a day. I had the privilege of spending time with the company's cofounder Richard Reed while hosting him at the LSE. Reed had conducted interviews for his book, *If I Could Tell You Just One Thing...* [20] When speaking of his findings, he shared how so many of the interviewees, some of the world's most influential people from all walks of life, disclosed that they didn't always feel confident—not just at the start of their journey, but even now. That doesn't stop them, though. Do not wait to feel confident. Choose to step out and be courageous, and you'll likely find that your confidence grows along the way. Courage precedes confidence.

2. Beware of the self-fulfilling prophesy of *"needing more confidence."*
Recognize that confidence is something that comes and goes—for everyone. Being confident isn't a place or a point in time we suddenly arrive at. It builds over time, but it also wavers. We all take knocks to our confidence. What's important is not to feel bad about yourself for experiencing a lack of confidence. Many clients in search of greater gravitas have disclosed their challenge with confidence, being self-critical for not having it. They believe they should have confidence, that it's part of their role to be confident, and they worry they're not ticking that box. Telling yourself you need more confidence can be a vicious cycle, with that self-talk decreasing your confidence further.

Some people suggest that those who have more confidence automatically seem worthy of gravitas. They deserve to have a more significant impact; they should be engendering greater respect; they should be taken more seriously. This can trigger a downward spiral of wider self-doubt and a sense of helplessness. But as we've already seen, people often project more confidence than they feel—they're simply choosing to courageously act in line with their convictions. And we all take a knock to our confidence at times. Recognizing this means you choose to see your lack of confidence as a current feeling but not as a self-defeating label. The self-label of "no self-confidence" is incredibly unuseful. It may feel real and justified, but it doesn't help you move forward. It's important to rip it off like a Band-Aid and look at what's really going on underneath—what are the circumstances when you feel this, when do you not feel like this, what might be causing it, are there any other words you could use to describe how you're thinking and feeling? Only then can you start to generate solutions for how to build, or get back, your confidence, experiencing an upward spiral effect, with energy-boosting positive emotions and a greater sense of powerfulness. If we acknowledge a lack of confidence as a current feeling rather than a permanent label, we have the opportunity to do something about it; we have more control. And a sense of control itself can build confidence.

3. **Decide that *comfortable isn't the goal*.** We often want to be "more confident" just so we'll feel more comfortable. We don't want to feel nervous. It's natural to want to avoid the negative psychological and physiological effects of nervousness. But "comfortable" can be at odds with your goals. If your goal is to increase your contribution, you're continually going to be stepping out of your comfort zone. That feeling of unease is perhaps not a sign that you're "not good enough" or "not cutting it," but rather that you've chosen to be courageous and venture into new territories. That you've put your hand up for responsibilities and opportunities that stretch you. In this book, we will discuss ways to manage nerves and negative self-talk, but to start, consider reframing the labels you've given to the psychophysiological response to challenging situations. "I'm nervous" becomes "This is the stretch that comes with a growing opportunity." "I don't want to" becomes a reminder: "I choose to." For some professionals, feeling too comfortable for too long can actually be a sign that they're not moving forward and making the potential impact that they could. Professionals with high levels of authentic gravitas have clear convictions about what matters. They have convictions about their

desired footprint, and they seek to align their impact with their intention. Researchers conducted two studies with over one hundred full-time workers and 475 managers at the executive level. They found that behavioral integrity (the perceived patterns of alignment between one's words and deeds) had a direct effect on behavioral courage.[21] Choose conviction before comfort, and it will fuel your courage.

4. Make *plans* to grow your confidence with courage. Instead of that defeating self-talk of "I'm not confident," ask yourself, *What would give me more confidence?* Is it being more informed about your industry? Make specific plans to grow your knowledge. Is it having more experience like others around you? Be intentional with how you can broaden and expand your expertise. Is it nervousness about public speaking? We'll address this in greater detail later in the book, but you could look into courses or for small-step opportunities to expand your skills and expertise. And if you're not sure how to grow your confidence, think about the situations in which you feel least confident and why you feel that way. They'll guide you toward possible actions to grow your confidence. Don't focus on not having enough confidence; focus on what you can courageously and practically do to build it.

People with gravitas appear to others to have confidence. But that does not mean they consistently feel confident across all aspects of their professional life. Some even experience imposter syndrome. Despite being high-achievers, they experience intense feelings of intellectual phoniness and doubt their own abilities, which they believe to be over-estimated by others.[22]

There are many people who are highly regarded by others but who must daily choose—and need—to encourage themselves with their own personal pep talk: *It's okay. You've got this. You can do it.* You don't need to wait to feel confident to increase your gravitas. Clarify your convictions—what matters and why—and be intentional about how you want to show up and the impact you want to have. Make choices toward operating out of your strengths (we'll look more at this later). Don't worry as much about confidence, and instead choose the courage to step into new opportunities, take on new responsibilities, speak up, learn new things, and try new ways of interacting. As you do, you'll likely see your confidence grow on the journey with you, because confidence is often an outcome of, not a prerequisite for, positive impact.

DOUBTING YOUR OWN CREDIBILITY: "I'M TOO *X*. I'M NOT *Y* ENOUGH."

We can incorrectly believe that we don't *deserve* authentic gravitas. That not being "that person" is justified. Most people are all too familiar with their own perceived inadequacies, failings, and lack. Whether it's a quiet whisper or a loud, resounding sound, negative self-talk is powerful (we'll look at this in detail in chapter 6). The credibility comments we say to ourselves are usually, "I'm too [insert your own]" or "I'm not [insert your own] enough." Here we look at some common self-perceived credibility barriers and suggestions for how to reframe or tackle them.

When Your Knowledge Isn't Sufficient: "I Need to Be an Expert"

Here's the thing about authentic gravitas: it is not just what you know, but also *how* you use that knowledge, combined with your interest to know and understand more, that counts. My research highlighted that people regarded as having a great deal of gravitas had the ability to offer clarity and insight, particularly in challenging or complex issues. But some of these people were *not* the most knowledgeable in the situation. They were, however, able to identify the crux of an issue by seeking and facilitating clarity, getting others to open up and explain a situation, and fueling greater shared understanding. They offered insights that were not only important but could also be understood and utilized by others because the people offering the insights were able to adapt their message delivery to their audience.

People can have a great deal of knowledge on a topic without having gravitas. They may be trusted and taken seriously and their ideas considered important, but they may not be respected. An interviewee shared their experience of a professional whose expertise was trusted but who was not personally respected. He was regarded as highly specialized in his field, but others felt he regularly failed to understand, or give due consideration to, the client's point of view. This manager came across as fixed in his ideas and opinions and close-minded, and did not create an environment where others (colleagues or clients) felt heard or able to contribute. Knowledge is never a permission slip to be dogmatic.

Another person may have a strong foundation of knowledge but not be trusted. A coaching client of mine offered the example of a woman on a manufacturing management team whom colleagues regarded as experienced and knowledgeable, but who did not trust her underlying motives, often feeling she had a hidden agenda. Trust is about more than just a perception of another as being competent, or even having good intentions. Trust is the willingness of a person to be vulnerable to someone else, based on positive expectations about their motivation and behavior.[23] If I trust you, I am prepared to be vulnerable with you. Knowledge aids, but is not sufficient for, authentic gravitas. If we are to truly build trust, a recognized sign of gravitas ("respected and trusted"), we create an environment where others feel willing to be vulnerable and courageous themselves.

People with a high degree of gravitas may seem confident in part because they appear aware of the potential value of their own contribution. But rather than being self-important, considering themselves above others, they in fact place value on others as well, creating conditions for them to engage and contribute. They are not threatened by intellectual competition or challenge, instead focusing on getting to the best outcome regardless of its source. As one interviewee described an executive,

"He always makes the best insights of anyone in the room and everyone listens to him. But he manages to do this without making anyone else feel stupid. Somehow I always leave feeling good about myself!" While people with authentic gravitas act out of courage, not necessarily confidence, they do instill confidence in others. And while many have a strong knowledge of the topic or situation at hand, more important, they remain curious and committed to increasing their knowledge, and to facilitating an environment where the potential of collective knowledge is valued above individual expertise.

When It's All Brand-New: "I'm Not Experienced Enough"

Knowledge certainly affects the extent to which someone is taken seriously. It can foster trust and respect. But as described in the situations above, it certainly is not a free pass to being trusted and respected. So is it a requirement at all? Often in my coaching experience, clients feel they are too young, inexperienced, or unknowledgeable to have gravitas. Equally, when professionals change fields or are promoted into more senior roles, they may be concerned about not having gravitas in their new "space."

One client I have worked with for many years, Erin, had concerns when asked to join a senior board looking at business growth across the United States. Erin is a senior executive at one of the most influential American firms in her field. She is widely respected within her industry, and her clients and colleagues regard her as having a high degree of gravitas. She's not, however, known outside her particular field, and her expertise is specialized. She described to me how other board members are "famous." Erin listed their honors and contributions to wider business in the United States and in markets around the world. She felt she wasn't enough. Her concern was that she would lack gravitas in this context, not making a noteworthy contribution and failing the person who'd recommended her for the position, whom she highly valued.

Here I saw firsthand how someone who has gravitas in one context still has to be intentional and courageous to have authentic gravitas in an expanding role when faced with new opportunities. I encouraged Erin to recognize that both her sponsor and her future board colleagues knew her background and expertise. She had not positioned herself, nor had others positioned her, beyond the reality of her knowledge base. Similarly, when a young graduate is invited for an interview, the prospective employer has seen a strong but honest CV and has found that the candidate already has enough of whatever it is they are looking for in terms of knowledge and expertise to be successful in the role. The decision-making is usually then about fit, style, commitment, and how the candidate outworks their expertise. But the invitation to the table suggests their foundation of knowledge is sufficient. Whatever Erin needed to bring to the table, she had. She didn't need to pretend to be someone else, nor did anyone expect her to be. Erin's sponsor did not simply value her knowledge of her particular industry. That was useful, but only to a small degree, given the context of wider business across the United States. It was not the reason for his recommendation. Erin's sponsor shared with me that what he valued was Erin's ability to connect well with other professionals and create an environment of trust and openness, combined with her ability to analyze and offer insights. None of those contributions require a body of knowledge about a certain topic. They do require interest, openness, and a commitment to learning. Gravitas in this context would not lie in posturing; it would emerge through Erin's authenticity, as vulnerable as that might make her feel.

After her first meeting with the board, Erin told me with a relieved smile how well it had gone. To put it in the language of gravitas, she felt her insights were taken seriously and that her peers would trust and respect her. It is possible for people who are just starting out on their professional journey, who have left one field for another, or who have been propelled into a more influential position, just like Erin, to have gravitas. So while knowledge serves as a useful foundation, it is possible to have gravitas without being the most knowledgeable person in the room or without having the most experience. You can lead the room even when you're the newest person in it. And while you can develop gravitas in your new position, position doesn't determine your gravitas.

When You Don't Have the Position: "I'm Not Senior Enough"

I sat in a meeting with twelve corporate executives, each responsible for the "people side" of their various companies, all global leaders in their respective fields, confidentially sharing their challenges and opportunities. It was an honor, as a guest speaker, to be invited into this closed-door conversation for three days. While I would never disclose their conversation, I can share one observation. People gravitated toward one man in particular. When Tom spoke, or even moved to suggest he was about to speak, the others paused and were attentive—with their silence and their body language. Yet they were all peers. He was not more senior in his organization, which was not more influential in its field, than any of the others represented that day. I watched them watch him, and wondered, *What was it that made him stand out?*

People who are regarded as having a high degree of gravitas take ownership and responsibility for moving an issue forward, regardless of their place in the hierarchy. Authentic gravitas does not require positional power or hierarchical authority. People in positions of power often do have high levels of authentic gravitas, but it is not a prerequisite. It is likely to influence your position in an organization, but your position doesn't determine your ability to have a high degree of gravitas.

Tom didn't have seniority over the people around him at the table. What he did have was humility and curiosity. Halfway through the first morning, Tom, who had built a successful career over more than twenty years, quietly shared, "We just haven't been here before. Our business is in a world that hasn't existed before—the potential is new and the challenges are new. And what I know is that I need to be different. I need to be better. I need to learn more from the people around me, both here in this room and at home in the field. Together, I'm certain we can work out a way forward in these uncharted waters." It takes courage to recognize that there is more to know than what we know now, and it takes discipline to act on this despite the realities of our daily pressures. Professionals who are recognized for adding the greatest value are not complacent or arrogant. They don't wait for a position to take ownership of driving value, and they don't posture in a position to pretend they know it all. They demonstrate curiosity and humility, fueled by a belief that the potential of a project or business is greater than their existing skills and understanding can take them.

THREE COMMITMENTS

My research revealed three key commitments that professionals with gravitas make:

1. A commitment to COURAGE: courage over confidence

2. A commitment to CONNECTION: connection over charisma

3. A commitment to CURIOSITY: curiosity over certainty

Throughout this book, we'll look at what it means to make these commitments. We've seen how people with authentic gravitas choose courage rather than feel confident. In the following chapters we'll explore how to choose connection rather than worrying about being the most charismatic person in the room, and being prepared to be vulnerable enough to build mutual trust and genuine connection. We'll also explore what it means to choose curiosity, having the humility to continually seek to learn and grow, understand and explore. This begins with looking at where we invest our energy.

Not Trying to Stand Out

We can spend countless hours secretly trying to determine how to stand out from the crowd. Despite our declarations of teamwork and collaboration, we can quickly find ourselves spending immeasurable time and energy differentiating ourselves *from* the people around us. Instead of focusing on how to stand *out* from the crowd, gravitas comes when we're able to focus *on* the people in the crowd—those around us. Instead of trying to separate ourselves and stand apart, we connect and stand behind (supporting), stand beside (collaborating), and stand ahead with a guiding hand (leading). While someone displaying adverse gravitas can position him- or herself as a standalone superhero, authentic gravitas comes in moving toward people, not away from them. So ironically, the priority is to stop thinking about how to stand out. The truth is, the people who (positively) stand out are those who aren't trying to. A focus on standing out can be self-defeating and unhelpful.

True gravitas has never been about seeking to stand out for the sake of it. Someone with gravitas has the skill to weave through the intricacies and complexities of their daily work, and draw out the factors that really make a difference in a situation. They draw out potential in others that enables those people to contribute more and have a positive impact. People with authentic gravitas do not only seek to be great themselves; they seek to inspire greatness in others and add great value to the situation. They stand out in the crowd because they can add value to and for the crowd. They can change the atmosphere if it needs to be changed and, even in situations of extreme pressure, bring ease and instill confidence in others.

THE TRUTH ABOUT GRAVITAS

To sum up, here are the surprising truths about authentic gravitas:

- It's more about courage than it is about confidence. Courage precedes confidence.

- It's about leading—taking ownership and responsibility for a situation to help others achieve collective goals; it's not about waiting for a position of leadership or a title.

- It's more about a commitment to developing the skills for connection than it is about natural style. It's not something you're born with and there's no fixed personal characteristic requirement for gravitas.

- It's not about being stereotypically serious and self-important. It's about being taken seriously and considered important—being valued—because you're making a valuable contribution.

- It's as much about inquiry as it is about advocacy. It's not being the loudest voice in the room that counts. It's about clearly and persuasively explaining your thinking, offering insights, and not shying away from sharing your point of view. It's about having conviction without being dogmatic. Equally, your understanding of the situation and others' motivations and perspectives matters. Curiosity counts. The people who stand out in the crowd are those who move toward the crowd, not those who focus on standing apart from it.

- It's about integrity and credibility grounded in a commitment to learning and increasing knowledge, and how you use that knowledge; knowledge itself is not enough. Inspiring people live inspired.

- Anyone can authentically have gravitas. You can be "like that" and still be you. Because being authentic isn't about staying the same, true to "natural," unintentional habits. It's about adapting and growing to increasingly act in ways that align clear intention with actual impact. Authenticity requires agility.

- Rather than being an invincible superhero, gravitas demands vulnerability, discipline, and humility. It requires vulnerability to get feedback about ways in which your impact may not line up with your intention, discipline to keep trying out and sticking with new behaviors to achieve the impact you're after, and humility to accept that two or more heads really are better than one. People with authentic gravitas are collaborators, not independent heroes.

The reality is, we all have a gap between our intention, our action, and our actual impact. To have gravitas, be clear about your convictions (what really matters in a given situation), be clear about your intention (how you want to show up and impact that situation and the people in it), be disciplined in checking that your impact is lining up with your intention (through your own observations and seeking feedback), and be committed to continually adapting your style.

We want to add great value, but habits and busyness can get in the way. Did we add the most value today that we could? Perhaps not, but the truth is, a few small changes could lead to a big difference in our impact, and our answer going forward could consistently be "yes." What separates those who have authentic gravitas from those who don't are typically just a few small differences found within their thinking and actions over the course of a day . . . every day. To build a life of authentic gravitas we simply need to prioritize it, not over but *through* the urgencies, the stresses, the disappointments, the highs and lows of day-to-day life. We can all increase the extent to which we make a positive, meaningful impact on others. It starts with being intentional in our mind-set—choosing who we want to be (what kind of leader, colleague, employee, friend, etc.) and how we want to show up. If we choose to increase our skills and commit to doing so, we can all engage in the courageous behaviors of authentic gravitas.

PRACTICES FOR BUILDING THE FOUNDATIONS OF AUTHENTIC GRAVITAS

- On the point of authenticity, spend a few minutes to articulate the following: *When do I most feel like me? What really matters to me?*

- On being intentional, ask yourself, *What footprint do I want to leave every day? How would I want other people to describe me?*

- On being courageous, challenge yourself, *What upcoming opportunity is going to require me to choose courage?*

- On gravitas, think about, *What would help me start building new patterns of thinking or behavior that will take me on my journey of increasing my authentic gravitas?*

TWO

CONNECTION OVER CHARISMA

Where Intention Meets Impact

"I had a conversation with Sal and she said this one line that just changed everything for me." As I heard Xavier describe what had happened, I wondered how many times I had heard a friend refer to a conversation with Sal in that way. I, too, had experienced a few "one liners" from Sal that had dramatically shifted my thinking and subsequently made a big difference in my career. In the various contexts in which I've seen her, across more than a decade, I've been witness to the widespread respect and trust she engenders. She consistently adds significant value. *How does she do it?* I wondered. *Where do these "one liners" she's become known for stem from?* "Old soul" and "wise owl" were descriptions that came to mind. But more than that, I knew her ability to connect is rooted in her commitment to making people feel comfortable—comfortable enough that they want to be open and vulnerable. It's in the way she constructs conversations, what she says and what she doesn't say. It's in her humility and curiosity, and in her ability to focus on that one conversation. Even if it's just a short chat, she seems to learn, reflect, add value, and simultaneously reframe and challenge in the best possible way. (I bet you want to be friends with Sal, too!) Then I realized, there's one word that sums her up that I can see all these other qualities stemming from: *intentional*. She's intentional with how she connects. Sure, Sal absolutely has a gap between her intention and impact at times—that's true for all of us. But she's mindful of it, and that just leads her to be more intentional and disciplined about reducing the gap. The challenge is that most of the time we don't realize when there's a disconnect between our intent and actual impact. And this gap doesn't only occur in our speeches and presentations; it's equally in one-off encounters and in ongoing relationships. It's (annoyingly) sometimes in our big "wow" moments, and it's in our everyday life. The key is to be mindful of it.

If we do become conscious of this gap, it tends to be after the fact, when the other person has told us how they felt, or we observe a change in their manner around us, or we are told by a third party. Our first instinct (let's be honest) can be defensive, assuming that the other person is at fault. It's their problem, their bad attitude, their insecurity, their inability . . . it's their lack. We feel that they have "misinterpreted" us. To have authentic gravitas, we must own the misinterpretation and clarify our intention. There is a continual gap between our own intentions and others' experience of those intentions outworked. The key is to anticipate that it will be there. Being aware of the gap means we pay greater attention to cues that a gap has formed and is leading to unintended outcomes, so we can quickly close it. Better still, being conscious of the potential gap can mean it never actualizes, as we are more intentional with how we communicate and act, and check the interpretation of our messages to ensure what is received is what we intended to send. The simplest, and perhaps most powerful, way to be intentional is to ask yourself one golden question. This can greatly increase your authentic gravitas:

> *How do I want them (the people I encounter) to*
> *think, feel, and act as a result of this encounter with me?*

You don't have to have the answers now. You just need to be consistently mindful of this question, to metaphorically keep it in your pocket, ready to pull out when the moment arises. Ask yourself this simple question before going into a meeting, whether it's one-on-one or with a group, face-to-face or virtual. If you're preparing for a presentation, don't succumb to the temptation to open your laptop to a new (or, worse still, an old, ready-to-be-revisited) slide deck. Sit down with a blank piece of paper and ask yourself how you want your audience to think, feel, and act as a result of this encounter with you. Your content, structure, and style will flow out of, and be guided by, your answer (more on this in chapters 3 and 4). Equally, though, if you're having a more informal or spontaneous conversation—for example, if you just got asked to meet someone who has popped into the office, or you're catching up with a colleague—ask yourself this question in the few minutes (or even seconds) you have beforehand. It will shape the way you engage with them, the questions you open with, and even your body language, particularly your facial expressions. You will be more likely to minimize the intention-impact gap by clarifying your intention through this simple question before the encounter.

GENEROSITY OF SPIRIT

The question is easier to answer in the moment if you've already determined your broader goals for how you want to show up. What are your values, convictions, and decisions about the ways in which you want to approach a situation and interact with other people, and what kind of culture or environment do you want to create around you? Once you've decided that, it's easier to act in alignment between this intention and desired impact on a daily basis.

Here's an example of how that looks in action at work. Gail Kelly, former CEO of the Westpac Group, one of Australia's biggest banks, spoke openly and honestly about her personal leadership legacy goals when she joined us at the LSE. She described one of these goals as "generosity of spirit." There are two key elements to generosity of spirit, according to Kelly. The first is believing in the power of people to make a difference (leadership intent). The second is creating an environment that empowers them to flourish and be the best they can be to make that difference (leadership impact).

Kelly also thinks about leadership tactics, but these act in service to the greater leadership goals she's defined. She describes leaders who have this generosity of spirit as having humility, listening to others, and demonstrating empathy. These are qualities I experienced firsthand when we had dinner together after her talk. She noted that leaders with generosity of spirit are not selfish, intolerant, judgmental, or quick to shoot the messenger or find scapegoats, and they don't sit on the fence to see which way something works out before they decide if they're going to support it. They deliver feedback honestly and in a timely manner, rather than waiting six or twelve months for a performance review. Poor performance is dealt with quickly. And perhaps most important, good managers choose their assumptions. As Kelly puts it, "I choose to assume that you (my colleague) want the best for me personally and for others. I am generous in my assumptions of your underlying motivations and your intent toward me. Hard as it may be at times, I will assume good intent."

This approach seemed to work for Westpac—at the time, in their internal engagement surveys, 97 percent of Westpac Group employees reported that they could see how their work is linked to the purpose of the company. Kelly herself is recognized as one of the most powerful women in finance, sitting on the Global Board of Advisors to the US Council on Foreign Relations and being the first female member of the Group of 30. In 2010, *Forbes* named her the eighth most powerful woman in the world, just after Indra Nooyi and Lady Gaga.[1] The day after I met her, I mentioned it to a friend from Australia over lunch, who surprised me with his personal experience. "Oh yeah, Gail," he said casually, as if talking about his next-door neighbor. "She arranged for our charity to be given office space in Westpac's building—it made a huge difference for us."

I'm certainly not arguing that generosity of spirit is the one-stop shop for everyone's leadership and professional success. It works for Gail Kelly because it's a footprint she has personally chosen and defined. She built it into her leadership team and tied it directly to results she wanted to see in the business.[2]

If you're clear on your goal, you're able to reduce the gap between intention and impact. Sure, you need feedback, courage, and discipline to address the gap, but clarity of purpose is an important first step. Just remember to ask yourself this simple question:

How do I want them (the people I encounter) to think, feel, and act as a result of this encounter with me?

Feelings Influence Decisions

I find that the hardest part of this question is feelings. What we want other people to do—how we want them to act—can be fairly clear. What we want them to think often flows out of this. But how do we want them to feel? This is not as easy to articulate. Yet feelings guide decision-making at work more than we realize. Here's an example of a client and his journey to take others' emotions into account when setting goals for his overall impact.

Drew, the managing partner of a firm in London, was excellent on strategy but needed some help with his influencing and leadership skills. When I suggested this question during a coaching session, he looked me in the eye and—laughing but showing embarrassed sincerity—declared, "Rebecca, I've never used the word *feeling* at work before!"

"Drew," I encouraged him, "it's time to start."

Drew is not alone in his skepticism around the role of emotions at work. Jennifer Lerner from the Harvard Kennedy School of Government and her colleagues, in a study covering thirty-five years of research on emotion and decision-making, note that Western thought is largely dominated by a negative view of the role of emotion in reason.[3] However, their research reveals how emotions constitute potent, pervasive, and predictable drivers of decision-making. Furthermore, that scientific evidence suggests that integral emotions (i.e., emotions arising from the judgment or choice at hand) can serve as a beneficial guide. Other research suggests that being in tune with feelings is linked with improved performance. In a study of 101 stock traders published in the *Academy of Management Journal*, the authors made the surprising discovery that higher decision-making performance was achieved by people who experienced more intense feelings. Those who were better able to identify and distinguish among their current feelings achieved higher decision-making performance through their enhanced ability to control the possible biases induced by those feelings.[4] Neuroscientists argue that a view of "cold" rational thinking fighting it out against a "hot," irrational, emotional system is an inadequate conceptualization, noting that studies suggest that the amygdala (most commonly associated with emotion) may also play an important role in complex decision-making.[5] Whether we like it or not, our decisions are likely to be influenced by our emotions, so it's better for us to learn about our emotional responses than to "intellectualize" them away.

Emotions guide the decisions we make and influence the way we behave. The same is true for those around you: emotions play a key role in *their* decision-making. Rather than negating the role of emotions at work, people with authentic gravitas recognize emotions' key role in decision-making and performance. They're not afraid of conversations around how someone really feels. Emotions can shape the way a colleague or client thinks and potentially how they act upon your input. When we set meeting objectives, we typically decide beforehand what we want people to do differently afterward—what we want out of the meeting. We may have considered what we want them to think. But rarely are we mindful of how we want them to feel—about what we're saying, about the situation, about our relationship. Choose not only what you ideally want people to do, how you'd like to shape their thinking, but also how you want them to *feel*. Powerful connections form when we value how others feel as a result of an encounter with us.

THE MYTH OF CHARISMA

In the first chapter, we looked at the Myth of the Gravitas Gift (page 3) and the Myth of Confidence (page 15). The third psychological barrier we can face in fostering authentic gravitas is the Myth of Charisma. Charisma can be defined as a compelling attractiveness or charm that can inspire devotion in others; at times described even as a *special power* that some people have naturally that makes them able to influence other people and attract their attention and admiration.[6] The Myth of Charisma is the false notion that people with gravitas are the most charismatic. And with that often comes the self-defeating internal whisper, *I'm not charismatic enough.* But in my interviews with business leaders, the vast majority did not use the word *charisma* to describe people with gravitas, other than to negate the myth—highlighting that people with gravitas may or may not be charismatic. Charismatic people can have authentic gravitas, but people with gravitas don't necessarily have charisma.

While it's not determined by charisma, people with gravitas are consistently noticed for their ability to *connect.* This goes beyond having an *intention* to connect, but also the ability that develops from a commitment to curiosity. I say "commitment" because while many people value curiosity in theory, this doesn't necessarily translate into their daily practices and behaviors unless they commit to it.

Curiosity Means Embracing the Unknown

In order to have authentic gravitas, we need to acknowledge, own, and act upon the fact that we don't know everything about the people with whom we interact and their situations. Not that many people would presume to think they know everything, but too often we don't actively engage with this unknown. We step intentionally and courageously into new and unfamiliar areas in our own lives and careers, but frequently we don't effectively explore what we don't know about other people—what's really happening with their career, project, team, or business, beyond a surface level. But to have a significant, positive impact on others and on a situation, it seems obvious that we will be better positioned if we have a genuine interest in, and understanding of, those people and what's happening. So why don't we proactively seek to understand others as much as we could? Let's take a look at three things that can hold us back from practical curiosity.

1. "I Knew It!"—Confirmation Bias

Celine had met with Piers on at least eight occasions over the last three years, usually when the various departments of the large cosmetics company they worked for were thrown together on a big campaign. This time, it had been only a little over two months since she had seen him last in France, where she was based. As her train to London pulled out of the station in Paris, Celine flicked through her notes, smiling as she remembered their last encounter and how smoothly it had gone. Piers had appreciated her input. She was hopeful that he would again be impressed with the ideas she and her team had pulled together, this time for a new cosmetics line. She knew his position on the market challenges, having seen some evidence of this in the industry press and their company's in-house magazine since their last meeting, and had taken this into account when directing her team on the product design.

Once at their company's London office, Celine made her way to the meeting room that Piers's assistant had booked for them. He arrived, and after sharing brief pleasantries, she launched into her ideas. A few comments he made along the way reinforced to her that she was on the right track, so she was both surprised and disappointed when she later received an email explaining that he didn't feel it "clicked" and that her positioning "wasn't quite right." Piers wanted her to come up with more options. Worse still, he also suggested getting an external team to look at the brief, "just so we have some options." Where had she gone wrong?

Celine's knowledge, or rather, her perception of her knowledge about Piers's position on the market competition *could* have helped her. Instead, it hindered her. The danger with prior knowledge about a person or a position is that we can succumb to confirmation bias. In social psychology, confirmation bias is recognized as a robust tendency for a person to look for, select, interpret, favor, and recall information in such a way that confirms their preexisting beliefs and underweighs disconfirming evidence.[7] Researchers at the University of Missouri examined confirmation bias in a study of 142 tax professionals.[8] Participants tended to focus on information in line with their earlier recommendations to a client, even when the recommendation conflicted with the client's subsequent position. Another study, using data from an experiment in South Korea, examined how information from virtual communities, such as stock message boards, influenced investors' trading decisions and investment performance.[9] The study looked at 502 investor responses and found that in processing information from the message boards, investors exhibited confirmation bias. Investors used these boards to seek information that confirmed their prior beliefs. Furthermore, those investors who exhibited stronger confirmation bias demonstrated greater overconfidence. They had higher expectations about how they would perform and traded more frequently, but actually obtained lower returns on their investments.

We are drawn toward information that confirms what we already know. In a world where we are bombarded with new information daily, confirmation bias can serve as an automanagement technique to help us get through all the novel information and make decisions. We have to choose to recognize the potential for confirmation bias and, while drawing on our prior knowledge and understanding, be intentional about asking questions to explore changes in others' thinking and circumstances. We need to choose to attend to cues that disconfirm our existing beliefs about others, their situation, the market, the organization, etc. Such changes may be broader than our particular topic of engagement, but these could be influencing the decision-making of that person. Celine didn't connect with Piers as well as she might have because she wasn't considering what might have changed in his thinking since their last meeting.

So the first reason we don't act on the unknown is that we fail to recognize it. We can hold a subconscious assumption that we do know what's going on with the person we're dealing with, that their thoughts and feelings are static. We know where things were before, it seems as if all is on the same track, and surely in response to our quick, "How are you?" they would say if things had changed. We have a past reference point and, unless a red flag appears, keep using that as the basis for our interactions. Sometimes after a fleeting, "How are things going?" people will open up and proactively share new information. But often, they don't. Not necessarily because they don't want to or can't (although both could be the case), but usually because they fail to recognize the new information themselves. In Piers's case, his changing views about the market situation resulted from an industry conference he had attended a month before his meeting with Celine and was old news to him. He didn't particularly remember previously sharing his take on things with Celine, so he didn't think to share his modified views now. Others also often don't share their changes in perspective because they seem outside the scope of the immediate discussion.

2. A Life of 30-Minute Windows

Another reason we don't engage in enough discovery is that we simply lack the time. Or rather, we find it, understandably, difficult to prioritize. Often we barely have enough time to get through the agenda points for the meeting at hand. Discussing wider topics is a luxury few of us afford ourselves in a demanding working day. Exploring changes in people's thinking and situations is time-consuming and hard to prioritize when we're all very busy. We can have a niggling feeling that we should be taking more time to explore what's going on with them, but find it hard to carve out a window in our day for it. Most people are aware that "connection conversations" need to happen at the right time and place. It's not as though we're about to yell from our desk to theirs across the busy open-plan office, "So, what's really going on with you? How are you feeling about how the company's changes will affect you?" Unless a major red flag appears, we often just push the niggling to the back of our minds. While we need to get through our to-do list for the day (more on managing this in chapter 5), it can be at the expense of connecting, and as a result, we might miss a window for significant, timely impact.

We also may just miss the opportunity because of the culture and structures within which we work. One head of human resources for a large multinational company told me that she was considering implementing a half-hour-meeting rule across the whole organization—globally. It sounded to me like a surefire way to kill off much potential for powerful connections and collaboration. I understood the driver: too many meetings, taking too long, with the wrong people in them, or dominated by two people having a lengthy conversation that really should be taken off-line. But surely the answer is to equip people to have good meetings, not to regulate their behavior with a stick. We can all easily succumb to meeting habits that hold us back from genuine connection. I've noticed an increasingly common tendency among professionals across industries and geographies to automatically schedule half-hour meetings. In the rush of daily working life, we may plow through meetings and tick off agenda points at a rapid rate, but this can come at the cost of connection and collaboration. Sometimes half an hour is all that's needed—sometimes *less*. But if we consistently cap meetings at a half hour, we'll likely be missing some opportunities that may bring greater benefit than just getting through the sheer volume of work.

3. The Trap of Expertise

The third, and perhaps most dangerous, reason we don't consistently and effectively explore areas of the unknown is our familiarity and comfort with our own expertise. We are "safe" inside conversations within the realm of what we know.

Mehira has spent years developing her expertise as a financial consultant. She is carving out a space and name for herself at her firm, and has recently been promoted to lead a small team. She is hoping to soon be the primary consultant on large client accounts. But one thing is holding her back: her expertise. Not her lack of it, but rather putting all her confidence in it. Mehira is excellent at what she does. She's confident talking with clients about her knowledge areas—discussing challenges, debating options, and giving them advice. But she doesn't ask questions about the clients' wider business. She's not particularly conscious of it, but she stays within her circle of expertise out of fear and uncertainty of what lies outside of that circle. She's not entirely sure what to ask. Even if she did ask sensible questions, what if the client gave answers that she didn't fully understand? Worse still, what if they asked her questions she didn't know the answers to? Mehira prides herself on her expertise and ability to help her clients. She values the trust they have in her knowledge and skills. If she steps outside her circle of expertise, she may trip over her own feet and lose some of that trust and value in her clients' minds. So while she offers a polite, "How are things going?" she doesn't drive the conversation to broader issues. Perhaps the most challenging obstacle to connecting to the degree that we could is when we succumb to the trap of our own expertise.

Space in the Middle

Mehira is not alone. Most of us cover "corridor conversation"—polite small talk—as we walk through the reception area, from the elevator to the meeting room. Then, once we enter the room and make sure everyone is settled and comfortable, we go—*bang!*—straight into the meeting agenda, which usually addresses key, specific points. We wrap up at the end and go back into closing small talk. We miss out on what I call the "space in the middle," where we find out what is actually driving the other person's thinking and decision-making. It's where we understand the real challenges they're facing and where unexplored mutual opportunities lie. This space lies between the two ends of our conversation spectrum—small talk at one end and specific agenda points at the other.

But rather than spend time in the space in the middle, we jump from one end of the spectrum to the other out of habit and possibly because, like Mehira, we feel comfortable and confident in that space.

Yet connection for authentic gravitas demands courage and vulnerability. We have to be bold in asking open questions about the goals, challenges, and wider contexts of the people we're with. It requires us to follow through on conversational cues down a route to different business areas outside of our comfort zone, rather than plow on with our planned conversation. Being vulnerable doesn't just mean we are prepared to share our deepest challenges and fears with others. We also need courage to intentionally facilitate a line of questioning that will open up the possibility that we don't look like the expert; that we may even look uninformed. But it's our only route to a deeper understanding of the other and therefore to the possibility of real connection. We have to courageously believe that genuine interest wins out over posturing.

My least favorite topic to teach in executive education programs is "Asking Questions." It seems so obvious, but for the three reasons I outlined above, we don't always live up to our questioning potential. And the people who do—who ask great questions, in the right way, at the right time—have greater potential for gravitas.

Even the most senior executives admit that it's easy to slip into only using directed or narrow questions. They find it useful to spend a few minutes thinking through powerful open questions. Here are some examples of questions that could help increase understanding and build connection.

- What are you most excited about right now?

- What's your biggest concern?

- What matters most to you at the moment?

- If there was one thing you could change today, what would it be?

- What is your gut instinct telling you about this situation?

- How do you feel about what's happening?

- What is the main thing stopping you from making progress?

- What are the forces at play in this issue?

I'm not suggesting you have to use my list of questions. Often my Aussie way of framing things isn't quite right for my British clients, so they rephrase my suggestions, and you should tailor your questions to sound like you. There's an endless list of questions you can ask. Mehira came up with her own list of questions with which she felt comfortable enough (although for her, she still required boldness to ask them). Her list (and her courage to use it) was a turning point in having more "space in the middle" conversations and fostering greater connections with clients. How and what we ask are linked to our ability to build authentic gravitas. So, too, of course, is the way we respond to questions.

Silent Messages of Value

Do you ever get the feeling that you're just annoying? (I assume I'm not the only one who feels this way at times.) You might ask someone a question and they respond with a curt tone. You're left wondering if you've said or done something wrong. I think we all know that feeling. Sometimes we also unintentionally send those messages to others, detracting from our ability to have a significant, positive impact on people around us and our wider context. The danger is that if someone does this regularly, particularly if they are in a position of leadership, others typically have one of two responses. They can feel anxious and walk on eggshells in that person's company—which may create a sense of power, but certainly does not build the relational ease that comes with authentic gravitas. In fact, it can have the effect of adverse gravitas by shutting others down. Alternatively, others may avoid dealing with that person at all and try to go around them, so they end up out of the loop and increasingly relationally detached. People who have authentic gravitas don't rush through interactions. They create a sense of ease around them. Not because they're not busy, but because they've learned to quickly still themselves amid the busyness of a day, even just for a moment, to show that they value others in the way they interact with them.

Researchers from Carnegie Mellon University conducted a study looking at how people's brains reacted in response to a male walking toward them silently with a happy or angry facial expression.[10] They found that several brain regions, including the amygdala (known to be involved in the viewing and interpretation of emotional expressions), showed greater fMRI activation in response to the angry man compared to the happy man. The researchers note that as humans, we have a need to assess one another's intentions during every social situation, and that facial expressions provide us with cues to help us in these assessments of others' intentions, through associations with emotion, the likelihood of affiliation, and personality.

We read the facial expressions of others and from that interpret their emotions and their *intention* toward us. Of course, cultural differences play a role in our interpretations. Recent studies, for example, highlight variations in the extent to which we attend to nonverbal cues, and the ways in which we integrate information from a variety of senses (face and voice).[11, 12] But across all cultures, we read facial expressions and body language and then make assumptions based on our interpretations. We can interpret value—the extent to which another person values us. Equally, we all have the ability to *send* silent messages of value to others. Without any words, we can say, "*I value you. In my mind, you have value.*" This creates an environment where that person is more likely to feel they can be vulnerable. Having gravitas means others trust us, and trust requires a willingness to be vulnerable. We are able to send these messages regardless of our place in the hierarchy. This doesn't mean we always agree with the other person—far from it. But we can show value and constructively disagree. We can also do this through the reality of busy days.

People with authentic gravitas are typically efficient and of course have moments of intense time pressure, but still have an ease with others that sends the message, "I have time for you." The question, then, is how to send the unspoken message that you have time for someone when the truth is you feel like you don't.

When a colleague would walk into Michael's office and ask, "Do you have a second?" his automatic response would be yes. Thinking he was doing the right thing with an open-door policy and a positive response, this telecommunications executive was surprised to learn from feedback that he often came across as unapproachable. People never felt certain of his regard for them. Michael would say yes, even when he didn't really have a minute. And of course when they're asking, "Do you have a second?" or "Do you have a minute?" people never really mean a second or a minute. They mean three minutes, or ten minutes, or "time for a decent chat about something important to me." He would often glance at his screen while the other person was speaking, or would be curt in his response, wanting to get back to his work. What was his impact on others? It certainly wasn't one of positive, significant difference.

Japanese researchers conducted a study of over two hundred employees at a brewing company in the Kansai region of Japan. They assessed the impact on subordinates of their supervisors' active listening (listening and responding to another person in a way that improves mutual understanding, empathy, congruence, and unconditional positive regard).[13] The researchers found that people whose supervisors demonstrated more active listening reported a more favorable psychological stress reaction than those who worked under supervisors with lower active listening. Of the many potential unintentional impacts, these findings suggest that active listening by a supervisor (or lack of it) has an effect on employees' psychological stress. For Michael, his inability to be fully attentive to other people gave them the impression of self-importance rather than authentic gravitas.

Michael needed to realize one thing: it is better to say no than to give halfhearted attention. People feel more valued when you say no than when you throw out a fake yes, as long as the no is followed up with scheduling an actual time when you can talk. Here are some of the ways Michael now responds when the many people around him ask for his time:

- "Yes, I have about three minutes now, or we can have a longer conversation later today at two p.m."

- "I've got a tight deadline but I certainly do want to discuss this. I'm free in the afternoon—when suits you?"

- "Yes, I've got ten minutes—will that work?"

- "I'm just in the middle of something, so later would be better, but if it's urgent or it's holding you up, then let's chat now."

And when he does meet, he is focused 100 percent on the person who asked to speak with him. He's present. It sounds simple, but we all slip into saying yes when we really should have said no or been explicit with the boundaries of our yes. This one change had a huge impact on Michael's authentic gravitas, and subsequent feedback suggests he is now not only respected but also trusted.

When Others Gravitate toward You

One reason for Michael to be mindful of the messages he sends is that value is often reciprocated. Think of someone you know personally and most value in your professional life. This is likely to be someone who makes you feel valued and respected. We either move toward or away from people. When we sense that people don't value us, we can experience a subconscious "threat" response and move away from them. In a study published in the journal *Neuron*, Japanese researchers described their fMRI experiments relating to monetary and social rewards.[14] They found that acquiring a good reputation robustly activated areas of the brain associated with rewards, overlapping with areas known to be activated by monetary rewards. How others perceive our attitude toward them can have a direct and powerful impact on them. If they don't think that we value them, they can experience this psychologically as a threat, leading them to move away from us, psychologically or practically. But professionals with gravitas lead in a way that means others psychologically and practically gravitate *toward* them.

The Messages in What We Don't Say

One study of over seven hundred people looked at workplace incivility (rude, discourteous behavior, with an ambiguous intent to harm), noting that it can impact physical health and employee burnout and satisfaction. The study offered an example that resonates with the stories of workplace challenges that many professionals have disclosed to me in the quiet of the coaching room:

"A coworker passes you in the hallway and you say 'hello.' The coworker does not respond. You might perceive this as incivility, assuming the coworker was intentionally rude. Another person, however, exposed to the exact same situation, might not consider this to be incivility, assuming that the coworker did not hear the 'hello,' or was otherwise having a stressful day."[15]

This scenario highlights one difference between authentic gravitas and what I refer to as surface gravitas. Someone regarded as having surface gravitas may be seemingly self-important, too busy for the "small stuff," and indifferent. Surface gravitas may be a form of adverse gravitas if the impact of this posturing on others or a situation is negative. The colleague who appears to be ignoring you in the hallway could be perceived as having surface gravitas. On the other hand, people who have authentic gravitas are intentional about having a positive impact on others and are careful not to ignore them (whatever the reasons why). They engage and connect both in the serious moments and the fleeting encounters. Michael described to me one day, with tears in his eyes, how on receiving challenging feedback about ignoring people at work, he made a decision to walk more slowly around the office, acknowledging and greeting all who passed and sometimes stopping at desks for quick chats to see how people were getting on. He described the impact of this decision as one of the most important in his professional journey. For many, it may seem strange to even have to think about this courtesy. But for Michael, and numerous others I've met, neglecting this practice can simply become an unintentional norm in their jam-packed day. For others, it may be a reaction to frustration or disappointment over performance with a particular person. But it's more effective for everyone involved to have what may be a difficult conversation, rather than sending nonverbal messages which are likely to be misinterpreted or, at a minimum, perpetuate a lack of relational clarity. Michael was aware, to some degree, of what he was doing, but failed to see the negative impact he had on those people he was essentially ignoring.

Michael's impact was magnified by his position in the organization. The researchers in the study on workplace incivility found that rudeness from supervisors was perceived as more uncivil than similar behavior from coworkers or customers. For people in positions of leadership, their behavior can trigger stronger responses—positive or negative—in those who are more junior.

It is up to us to be intentional about the messages we send regarding how much we value others. We can't control exactly how our messages are perceived, but we can choose to take ownership of the messages we send. If we actively seek feedback to check how our messages are received, and if we adapt our behavior accordingly, we can minimize the intention-impact gap in how we're perceived. When we send silent, unintentional messages that we don't value others, it can decrease their perception of *our* value—we lose their trust and their willingness to be vulnerable, which decreases our authentic gravitas. Conversely, when we are intentional, we can send silent messages that we value others, creating ease in our interactions (that is, making others more at ease around us) and building our authentic gravitas.

Creating Conditions for Others to Perform

Another reason for Michael to care about the messages he sends others is that they can impact the other person's performance, particularly if Michael (even unintentionally) makes him or her feel excluded or isolated. Researchers at the University of Chicago noted that perceived social isolation may contribute to a range of performance factors, such as poorer overall cognitive performance and poorer executive functioning.[16] Executive functioning includes verbal reasoning, problem-solving, planning, sequencing, sustaining attention and resisting interference, utilizing feedback, multitasking, cognitive flexibility, and the ability to deal with novelty.[17] When I asked professionals to describe others whom they considered to have gravitas, they didn't just describe that person's performance, but also how that person made them feel empowered or inspired to better contribute to a team, situation, or project. People with authentic gravitas not only add significant value, but also create conditions for those around them to do the same. Silent messages of value and inclusion not only benefit another's perception of you, but their perception of the extent to which they belong and can contribute at work. In Michael's case, others not only report that they now know where they stand with him, but they also feel emboldened in their interactions with him. They are able to be vulnerable and courageous. They don't feel uncertain looking at someone with surface gravitas from a distance; they feel energized by someone who equips them to add significant value. Authentic gravitas fosters authentic gravitas.

BETTER IN "REAL LIFE"

Whether others believe we have authentic gravitas is shaped substantially by our informal conversations and nonverbal messaging—how we interact on a daily basis, how we create "space in the middle," and how we send others silent messages of value. Gravitas is also shaped, however, by our ability to connect in the "big" moments—for example, when we're giving a speech or when we're responsible for presenting in a meeting.

When I first met James, I was surprised. He was a senior executive at a large energy company and had oversight of the whole "people side" of the business. Each year, James gave a presentation to the board, and his annual meeting was coming up. He was looking for a leadership communications coach, so a mutual acquaintance recommended me. When we met, I found James to be charming, articulate, and engaging. I was surprised he had asked for coaching on communication. As I followed him out of the marble reception area, up the long escalators, and eventually into the boardroom, I wondered what we would talk about. I could not imagine anything I could say that would help him. I couldn't imagine he needed help. After he briefly outlined the context, I took a seat, role-playing a board member, while James, standing at the front of the room, launched into his planned presentation. Suddenly, I knew why I was there. James became one of the most boring speakers I had ever heard. Verbally and nonverbally, he was cold and stoic. I struggled to keep focused on what he was saying. There was no engagement, no impact. He seemed to have lost his gravitas somewhere between the escalator and the meeting room. I called a time-out and cheekily asked him if he knew where James from reception had gone and if I could please have him back instead.

What was happening here? Why did James present as a polar opposite of his natural self? James disclosed that this was his fourth annual board presentation. For the previous three consecutive years, this day had been his worst professional day of the year. The board members had, in each previous encounter, criticized him and picked holes in his summary and plans for his area. He had felt attacked and not good enough. His subconscious response was self-preservation from what he perceived as another likely attack. The less emotion he showed, the less engaging he was, the more secure he felt. He minimized the emotion in his voice in an attempt to maintain control. Surely if he just coldly shared the facts, he subconsciously whispered to himself, he would be relatively safe this time around. In the coming chapters, we'll take a look at some of the techniques and behaviors for managing this challenge of feeling better in "real life" and come back around to see what worked for James.

It is possible to intentionally build skills to ensure your best "real self" is coming across in your most pressure-filled moments. Authentic gravitas is possible when we shift our focus from what we are going to say to the impact we want to have. It's as much about what we do and how we think

before the interaction, how we think *about* an interaction, as it is about
what we actually do in the room. The former shapes the latter, so once
we've decided on our intention—how we want to impact the people we
encounter—the next step is to practically plan for those encounters.

The intention-impact gap—between the way we intend to impact
those around us, and the impact we actually have—regularly plays out
in our presentations and meetings. Annoyingly, often the more important the meeting, the bigger the gap becomes. We can spend countless
hours writing and rehearsing our content for delivery. The more important the meeting, the more time we spend on the content. But gravitas
is as much related to our mind-set and preparation as it is to our actual
content and delivery.

The strategies outlined in the following two chapters for how to effectively impact those you encounter are based on powerful research evidence and client applications. The methods can be learned and applied
quickly for those big, pressure-filled moments—even five to ten minutes
of *different* preparation on each point can lead to powerful results.

PRACTICES FOR CONNECTION

Here are some practical takeaways and questions to consider as you
strengthen your ability to connect:

- Be intentional about how you want to show up. Think of your work
  this week—what meetings you have, which colleagues you're likely
  to spend time with. How do you want those people to think, feel,
  and act as a result of an encounter with you? (Don't skip over the
  feeling part!) You might want to start with a general answer as you
  clarify your broader personal intentions for impact, before answer-
  ing the question for specific individuals you're likely to spend time
  with this week.

- With the people you encounter, ask yourself, *How are they feeling
  about the situation/project/proposal? How might this be shaping the
  way they are making decisions?* If you don't know, ask.

- Thinking about your current interactions and what you're working on, challenge yourself with these questions: *Is there any area where I could be succumbing to confirmation bias? What questions could I ask to explore further?*

- Review the meetings you have coming up this week and look at how they're scheduled. We can't control all meetings, but we can influence the structure of some. For those you can shape, ask, *Are there any meetings where I might need to build in more time for meaningful conversations and discovery?*

- Consider the encounters you have had recently where you felt the most pressure. Ask yourself, *Are there any situations where I could be succumbing to the Trap of Expertise? Am I making time (and if I need it, choosing to have the courage) to ask "space in the middle" questions?*

- Challenge yourself with these questions: *What are the silent messages I am sending to people, particularly when I'm busy or feeling under pressure?* Reflect on your body language (especially your facial expressions and eye contact) and vocal tone. If you're up for the challenge, ask others for feedback: "When I'm busy, how do I come across? What messages would you say I send people?" Choose what messages you want to send, and how you'll frame your responses when people ask for your time—especially when you don't have it!

THREE

THE IMPACT MODEL

"Leading the Room" with Clarity and Curiosity

People sometimes think gravitas is all about style—the tips and tricks that make someone stand out. But to have authentic gravitas, we must first gain clarity around our desired IMPACT: Insight, Motivation, Perception, Advocate, Content, and—only *after* these other points—Technique. I've used my IMPACT model with hundreds of mid- to senior-level professionals looking to have more authentic gravitas. It's a framework for how to prepare for meetings, presentations, and speeches—whether it's an important encounter with just one person, a presentation in front of a group of twelve, or a speech to a large audience. Going through this process tends to not only make the preparation process more effective, but also more efficient. By spending a few minutes on some key topics *before* you start writing, even before you start *thinking* about what you're going to say, you end up better equipped to have a more powerful, positive impact in the meeting. You have more authentic gravitas. So just for a few minutes, close the slide deck, put away the laptop, and stop thinking about what you're going to say, while we take a look at a few things that will increase your likelihood of having the impact you want to have.

Think of an important meeting or presentation you have coming up, or one you're likely to have in the near future. Focusing on a specific, real context can help ground the concepts and make this section very practical. Use this context to apply the IMPACT model throughout chapters 3 and 4.

In this chapter, we'll look at the first five parts of the IMPACT model. The first three—insight, motivation, and perception—concern the *imp*rint we want to make. The second three—advocate, content, and technique—are focused on what *act*ions we need to take to achieve our goals for impact. Using this framework forces us to push against our natural tendency to think about what we're going to say and instead start with a focus on the people we are going to encounter.

INSIGHT

Before we start thinking about what we're going to say, we need to have clarity around two things.

1. What do I believe about this topic (the situation/opportunity/ project, etc.)? Take a position. We can manage the perceived risk of failing in a meeting or presentation by hedging our bets. Hester was well-regarded by her peers, but there was one thing holding the senior management team at her firm back from offering her the position of partner—her advice, or rather, the lack of it. She could outline all the pros and cons to clients, talk through the intricacies of the benefits and the dangers of one approach and then another . . . and then another still. It's one thing to give clients clear options so they can make informed decisions—ultimately, the final decision-making does rest with them. But clients wanted to know what she thought was best. She knew their situation and their goals, and she understood the technicalities of the issue better than they did (hence why she was there). Yet Hester was afraid of giving clear advice.

Having gravitas isn't about being a bossy "bull in a china shop" where your opinion is the only way (that may come across as surface gravitas, but it certainly isn't authentic gravitas). But it is about *clarity*—knowing what we think and why, and not being afraid to share it. What's the worst that can happen? The most influential person disagrees? So what? Often there is no "right answer" in business, and conflict is not a bad thing (more on this in chapter 9). So long as it's clear that the decision-maker is the decision-maker, and yours is just an opinion, if it's invited, give it![1] Hester could only move forward in her career once she was prepared to offer her point of view among a room of senior professionals. For her, this required courage. Clarity of opinion and informed advice are more in demand than we think. They are greatly desired in the professional world, and by playing it safe, we can do ourselves and those around us a disservice. So before you start thinking about what you're going to say, be clear about what it is you *think*.

2. What insight do I want others to have? The second issue we need clarity on is what insight we want our audience to take away from our interaction. Here we can apply the golden question regarding intention:

How do I want them (the people I'm about to meet) to think,
feel, and act as a result of this encounter with me?

We need to be clear about what impact we want to have on others. We focus so much on the content—what we're going to say. Often we start writing this before we can articulate (even to ourselves) what it is we want to achieve. What's the goal of your message? Rarely is the goal simply to inform: "To give people an update on how the new project is going." It's more likely: "To get people excited about where the new project is going by showing them the progress we've made, and gain their buy-in on the changes." Imagine the difference in the two scripts. Consider what you would write if you went into it with the first line of thinking, which is basically an update, compared to what you would say if you went in with the second objective in mind, which has a clear goal for impact. Think about these questions in the context of your upcoming meeting. Consider what insight you want others to have as a result of this encounter with you. Write it down (seriously, pause your reading here and spend a couple of minutes writing it out). You may want to run this by your boss or a trusted colleague before moving on, but essentially this action of clarifying your insights should take only a few minutes. These few minutes might be the most important ones you spend preparing for this meeting or presentation.

So you've mapped out the insights—what you believe and what you want others to take away. Now it's time to get curious.

MOTIVATION

As a young Visiting Fellow at Harvard, I was surprised and delighted when Professor Paul R. Lawrence, renowned sociologist and one of the most important figures in organizational behavior, agreed to have coffee with me to discuss resistance to change. He had written about it many years beforehand, and it was of great interest to me as a topic in my doctoral research. I will never forget the words of this then elderly man, sitting on the bench as we drank coffee: "Do you know what I'm thinking about now, Rebecca?" he offered without any prompting. I could not imagine. He had lived a long and impactful life. "Social capital. I'm thinking about the value of the relationships between people." I had not seen this coming. I found it extraordinary and incredibly generous that he would take time to meet with me. But what struck me was his curiosity. I aspired to be as fascinated by the world and as intellectually curious as he was. Of her late father, Anne T. Lawrence commented, "Dad was intensely curious. He loved tackling a new topic and learning as much as he could about it . . . Among his very last words to me were these: 'There is nothing as powerful as an idea whose time has come.'"[2]

In his book *Driven: How Human Nature Shapes Our Choices*

Lawrence and his colleague Nitin Nohria outlined four drives behind all we do as human beings: to acquire, to bond, to learn, and to defend. On the drive to learn, they noted, "Humans have an innate drive to satisfy their curiosity, to know, to comprehend, to believe, to appreciate, to develop understandings or representations of their environment and of themselves through a reflective process: the drive to learn."[3] We are wired to be *curious*. I think that sometimes in the busyness of our day, it's easy to forget that. According to Lawrence and Nohria, we can neglect our drive to learn, as well as our other drives. We'll look at practical steps to ensure we don't neglect this drive in chapter 5, but here we'll consider how to apply this framework to our understanding of others.

Coming back to your pending presentation or meeting, before you start mapping out any of the content, it's time to get curious about your audience. This goes far beyond just thinking about who they are and what they do—it requires considering what is truly driving them.

In two major studies, Nohria and his colleagues looked at what actions managers can take to satisfy these drives and thereby increase their employees' overall motivation.[4] They found that an organization's ability to meet the four drives explains, on average, a huge 60 percent of the differences in employees' motivation scores. Fulfilling the drive to bond, for example, has the greatest effect on employee commitment. Fulfilling the drive to comprehend is most closely linked to employee engagement. For your own audience, consider which of the four drives may *not* be being met in their current context. Given your upcoming meeting, and the reason behind it, which of the four drives could you potentially meet for your colleagues? Which drive is currently the most important to them? Why will they be in the room listening to you in the first place? And what outcomes do you want to generate?

Going through these questions is what researchers looking at executive influence refer to as "target assessment."[5] This is the assessment we make of the people we're trying to target our influence toward. It means considering factors such as their role, resources, personality, influence on others, potential to resist our ideas, and prior success in influencing that person or group of people. I always think "target assessment" sounds particularly cold! But it's actually the opposite—it's about giving greater consideration to the people you're going to encounter. We spend so much time thinking about what we're going to say and what we want to happen, and worrying about what might not go our way, that we can forget to give enough attention to the motivations of the people in the room.

For the meeting or presentation you have in mind, consider the people you will encounter and do this target assessment. It can take just a few minutes to think through how their drives may shape what you say and how you say it. Delivering a slick, funny, inspiring message can be a display of charisma. That's not a bad thing. In fact, many of us would be very happy to get a tick in the charisma box. But the more we are able to understand the people around us, the more likely we are to have a significant, positive, and lasting impact. And in doing so, we increase our authentic gravitas.

Below is a list of suggested questions for target assessment. Obviously, there will be a range of answers to each question if you have an audience of more than one! The list is not designed to be comprehensive; you may think of other questions to ask about your particular audience. It's also not designed to be cumbersome—you don't need to respond to all the questions in full, and it's likely you won't know some of the answers. The idea is that by going through the IMPACT process, doing target assessment, and considering your audience's motivation, you shift your thinking at this stage away from yourself and your message, to give greater consideration to your audience. What you end up saying as a result of this process will naturally be more targeted and effective.

- Who will be in the room?

- What are their roles?

- What are their style preferences for interacting?

- How much experience do they have in this field?

- What level of knowledge do they have about my topic?

- Why are these people in the room—why will they be listening to me?

- Who is/are the most influential person/people in the room?

- What do they want to achieve from this encounter?

- What do they most value when it comes to this area?

- What are their greatest challenges right now?

- What resources do they have available to them?

- Who has successfully influenced them in the past, and why?

- What have they resisted in the past, and why?

"Am I Too Nosy?"

The reality is, to have genuine insight into the values and motivations of others, we need discussion. As humans, we have a tendency to believe we can see others' values and motivations from what we see them do and hear them say. But we can't simply infer someone's values from observing their behavior. Consider the environment. Researchers from Michigan State University show, for example, that someone who claims environmental protection is a value they hold may not consistently act in an environmentally friendly way.[6] A person's behaviors are often influenced by factors outside of their control—in the case of environmental protection, for example, not having access to quality public transportation means a person who may otherwise avoid driving to work because of the environmental implications may use their car. Psychologists argue that the link between core values and behavior is sometimes relatively weak.[7] So the behaviors we observe in others can be an indication, but not a sufficient guide, to infer their values. This is important, because while values and behavior may not always be a perfect match, values do guide people's decision-making. But we can only see behavior. We can't be of value to others if we don't understand what value looks like for them.

What happens if we go through our questions and realize we can't answer many of them, which suggests that we don't really know what is motivating the people we're meeting? That's okay. At least we're mindful of what we don't know! And now we can ask. If you can't answer a fair number of these questions, including the trickier ones in the second half of the list, it's probably time (before you start writing your content) to seek out someone who can. This could be a colleague who has worked with these people more closely, the conference or meeting organizer, or an influential member of the audience. It might feel like a hassle, but the few minutes spent on this conversation could again make a huge difference to the level of authentic gravitas you have with this group. These questions also tend to be well-received. Wanting to better understand your audience is rarely considered nosy or annoying, but rather thoughtful and considerate. You might be able to take an informed guess, but if you don't know with some certainty what's motivating your audience, *ask*.

While we may discover a need to have conversations before our meeting, so far we've only spent five or six minutes thinking through the answers to these questions. It might feel like a *lot* of work when you're reading through it here, but if we were face-to-face, doing this together, we could make good progress after spending only a few minutes on insight and a few minutes on motivation. Next we need to consider perception before we start writing any content for our presentation.

PERCEPTION

The way you see the world is different from the way I see it. It's different from the way anyone else sees it. Research shows how both personality and context can shape our perceptions.[8] The personality of the person we're with can impact their perception of our words and actions. (We'll take a closer look at differences in our preferences and social styles in chapter 7.) And different experiences shape our perceptions. Our position and role, relative to theirs, can also impact how another person perceives what we say and do.

The way the people we're speaking to see work, projects, new opportunities, and strategies is often different from our way of seeing those things. But we can be so focused on wanting to make a good impression, to make our encounter a success, that we think solely about our content and fail to give sufficient consideration to the differences in the way our audience may see things. If we don't challenge ourselves, our subconscious assumption is that others see things the way we do.

For the meeting or presentation you have in mind, consider two simple things:

1. What is your audience's perception of the topic you are discussing?

2. What is their perception of you?

The first is easier to address. And as with motivation, if we don't know the answer, we can ask. Being proactive and finding out or confirming in advance their perception of the issue at hand is likely to influence where you focus your content and the extent of your impact. But it can make us uncomfortable to consider what people think of us.

People close to us typically have a good understanding of what we're like. Our close friends, family, and coworkers often know our personality and how we are likely to behave. The American Psychological Association's *Journal of Personality and Social Psychology* published a study showing that close contacts are just as likely to accurately predict our daily behavior as we ourselves are.[9] We feel relatively comfortable considering what our close family and friends think of us—where we have a high degree of trust and psychological safety. What they think is likely to be similar to how we think of ourselves. But outside our inner circle, other people's perceptions of us become more unknown.

The sense of uncertainty we feel around what others may think of us, unless that person is a close family member, friend, or trusted longtime colleague, can be unpleasant. We implicitly understand that their perceptions are likely to be different from our sense of self and/or how we would like to be perceived. As a result, we tend to do one of two things: we can simply try not to think about it (because—let's be honest—unless we're confronted with some feedback, nobody forces us to think about what others think). On the flip side, we can spend a lot of time worrying about what others think of us. This self-imposed obsession can consume much of our thinking. The reality is, neither ignoring nor obsessing is particularly useful. We need a healthy middle ground of caring about the impact we're having on others and being proactive about getting constructive feedback.

For the context you have in mind, ask yourself the question, *What is their perception of me?* Write down a few words that you think that person might use to describe you. Now think about how you would *like* to be perceived by them. To build authentic gravitas, we not only have to be intentional with what we say, but also clear about how we would like others to experience us. Someone's perception of you is not something that just happens to you—you are able to shape that perception more than you likely think you are.

If you think they perceive you to be serious but not fun, then you get to choose to adopt a lighter approach in the meeting . . . if you *want* to be regarded as fun. If you think they perceive you to be nice but not an expert, then you get to choose to structure your talk in a way that highlights more of your expertise and experience . . . if you *want* to be considered an expert. If there's a gap between how you would like to be regarded and how you regard yourself in terms of your level of expertise, then it might be time to focus on self-development (more on this in chapter 5). But if you feel there's a gap because you don't have the confidence you'd like to have, remember that confidence is not the immediate goal here. You most likely lack confidence because you are stepping out into new territory—a new position, new opportunities, new challenges, new contexts, etc. You're moving forward, and that never feels comfortable. If you were completely comfortable and confident, that might suggest you weren't taking big enough steps into your professional potential. Stop beating yourself up for not feeling confident, and instead choose to be courageous and do it anyway.

Here's the key—it's about being intentional with how you want to be regarded by others. In chapter 1, we looked at the importance of deciding what kind of leader/professional you want to be, in order to have authentic gravitas. For the meeting or presentation, ask specifically about this context: *How do I want them to perceive me?* You get to decide, and it's likely you can shape it more than you think. You probably won't be able to create a perfect match, but you can reduce the gap only if you've first clarified your intention.

Gravitas on the Spot

I've had the opportunity to serve as a faculty member on professional development programs for many years. Having just finished a design meeting, I was walking around the offices of one leadership consultancy and heading to the kitchen to grab some water, when I heard my name. "Rebecca!" Shona called out to me. She came over and explained that two executives from a potential client company had arrived for a meeting. Shona asked if, now that I was here, I could "pop in" to meet the prospective clients as a means of demonstrating to them what the faculty were like. Of course, I agreed to go in. The executives were from a leading company that was doing inspiring work in its field. This was a very important encounter to me, not just because of the potential client relationship but also because of my relationship with Shona and her firm. But I wasn't expecting the meeting, so I wasn't prepared. Normally, before a prospective client meeting, I would have done a huge amount of research. But I had no opportunity here. Shona had just jumped out of her meeting when she saw me walking past, so we had to go straight back in, meaning she didn't even have time to brief me on the basics of the potential program and client goals. As I headed into the meeting room, I had just a few seconds to gather my thoughts.

What happens when you don't have time to prepare? Annoyingly, many of the career-defining encounters we have are spur of the moment. We can't plan for them; we didn't even know they were just around the corner. Sometimes we find ourselves in an encounter and only in the middle of it realize just how important it is. This could be a great opportunity, meeting someone influential in your field whom you weren't expecting to meet. It could also be a serious conversation about your work performance that you didn't see coming. How can we have authentic gravitas in this situation?

Given what we know about insight, motivation, and perception, here are two simple steps to be prepared for the unexpected:

1. **Stop worrying about what you're going to say.** Instead, focus on the impression you want to leave with them. Ask yourself the key questions: *How do I want them to think, feel, and act differently as a result of listening to me? What insight do I want them to have?* As I walked into the office and asked myself these questions, two words came to my mind: *impactful* and *tailored*. I wanted them to leave with a belief that my colleagues and I delivered programs that were impactful for participants, so I needed to be clear and give some strong comparative examples of where we had made a positive impact on other clients' programs. The other fact I wanted them to take away is that we tailor our work—it's not a one-size-fits-all approach, but rather, we take great care to ensure the interventions and experiences we design are specific to each client's needs and goals. So I needed to ask questions to ascertain their needs and goals, preferences, and past experiences, and to share our bespoke approach.

When you find yourself in the middle of an opportunity, it can be useful just to think of one or two words you would like to frame others' experience of you. Intelligent and experienced? Passionate and determined? Thoughtful and knowledgeable? Calm and influential? Right now, imagine you are heading into an unexpected, important meeting; think of words you would want others to use to describe you. One of my clients, Maya, decided to adopt just one word for all the ad-hoc meetings she regularly has:

strategic. A strong, passionate communicator in marketing, she realized the one shift she needed to make when talking with internal senior managers was to highlight how she was thinking strategically and driving things forward in her work. Now every time she finds herself in an unexpected meeting, she just thinks "*strategic*" to guide her conversation in a way that better aligns her intention and her actual impact.

2. Choose to be *interested* rather than worrying about being *interesting*. Don't focus too much on how you're going to wow your audience with your smarts. Instead, put your energy into understanding them. Decide to be interested in them and their situation (e.g., their needs, challenges, changing environment, opportunities, aspirations, and goals—whether personal or organizational). Being interested is a choice. Sure, we are naturally more interested in certain things, and those things vary for each of us. But when it comes to other people and their situations, we can choose to be interested and engage with great questions. Focus on being interested instead of worrying about coming across as interesting. You'll end up being able to contribute ideas and thoughts that *are* interesting, because your contribution will be tailored to your new understanding of others' motivation and perception.

ADVOCATE

I've done one experiment more than one hundred times over a ten-year period. I ask for two volunteers from the audience and then ask them to role-play a business meeting. They are instructed that they are managers in a Norwegian energy company and I'm a consultant visiting from the UK. I bombard one volunteer with information—facts about the "project," my opinion of our working relationship, what value my company adds to their business, etc.—while the other volunteer waits in a separate room. There are between ten and twelve pieces of information. For each piece of information I communicate, I put a blank Post-it note on their arms, shoulders, or torso. As soon as I've shared my points, I immediately bring in the other person and ask the person with whom I just spoke to tell their colleague (who wasn't present) what I said. They can never remember everything. Not one person, in over one hundred trials, across seniority and experience levels, ages, genders, roles, industries, and geographies, has been able to remember them all. The most anyone has remembered is three. These are not the three that are the most important, but the maximum is three. Many cannot remember one single thing I told them. Not one. Their peers, who have been watching, laugh. It's funny to watch. A little humiliating, perhaps, for the person covered in Post-its who hasn't been able to recall any significant part of this conversation (although typically, they are laughing, too, and any embarrassment is assuaged when I reveal that everyone has trouble remembering). But as funny as this is, the reality is that we do this regularly with clients, customers, colleagues, leaders, and stakeholders. In our attempts to persuade people of our point of view, we often bombard them with information. Our slide decks are packed with data and ideas, our proposals with a long list of reasons why this is the best option. And people just don't remember. Sure, they can refer back to the notes or handouts we gave them, but what do you notice about people who have gravitas? You remember what they say.

We previously looked at the importance of having an opinion and being able to clearly and boldly articulate it. At this stage in our preparation (again, before you've started writing your content and thinking about what you're going to say), clarify what you would like to advocate by asking yourself one question:

If nothing else, what would I like them to remember?

Pass It On

Consider the fact that you might want them to pass your message on. There are likely other stakeholders and decision-makers who won't be present to hear you. Considering the people who will hear you, what would you like them to pass on to someone who wasn't in the room? What would you ideally want them to remember years later about their encounter with you? Write down three messages. It's important to note that these "sticky messages" are *not* agenda points—they are messages. So rather than, "I'm going to talk to you about the reporting process, the team, and IT," you may position your advocacy points as, "I'd like to share with you changes we propose, including a more structured reporting process, an increased number of senior staff on your client team, and more tailored IT solutions."

In the experiment, we then do a second take. I convey three messages, and only three, on Post-its, and then ask my role-player to pass those messages on to their colleague. This time, they can do it. You may only need one or two messages, but I wouldn't recommend offering more than three sticky messages in one go.

The key here is not just that people can only remember a limited amount of information; it's about being intentional with what message you want to convey. If nothing else, what would you want your audience to remember? Of course, you will have more to say than just these three bullet points. But having clarity about what you want your audience to remember will guide the way you structure your content and will make it more memorable. This process will enable you to have a greater impact on your audience and add more value to the discussion. Be intentional about what you want them to take away and clearly define your key messages right at the outset of your meeting preparation. While you may still give people the same amount of data, your focus will be on memorable messages that you intend for them to take away, rather than overloading them with information or leaving what they actually remember and pass on to chance.

Finally, we're going to start to think about content (I heard you breathe that sigh of relief!). What is it you're going to say? Now you can open your laptop.

CONTENT

In total, working through insight, motivation, perception, and advocate requires about fifteen to twenty minutes' preparation. On top of that, you may have discovered that you would benefit from having a few conversations with key people to increase your understanding of your audience. But this additional prep time saves you in the long run. By following the IMPACT framework for planning your meeting or writing your presentation, you save time as your content tends to flow more naturally as you have clarity around your message goals.

"You Had Me at Hello"

I can't guide you on what to say. It's your area of expertise. But I can highlight a few areas that matter and are often overlooked. The first is which part to script. When preparing for an important meeting or presentation, most of us naturally script the main content in the middle, although the main content is actually the part we know best. The middle is our expertise—it's where we get into the flow and probably the reason why we've been given the opportunity to share. I clearly remember the day I met Barry, a smart engineering consultant specializing in the automotive industry and doing well in his career. In his late thirties, Barry was on track to become a partner in a few years, if all went well. He was asked by the managing partner of his firm to present for ten minutes at a conference for 350 clients and potential clients. He was scheduled to take the stage right after two of the most senior partners in his firm— experienced speakers who were known and influential in his industry. No pressure. Barry had two audiences—the clients *and* his bosses. When we met, he described to me what was important. It wasn't that he wanted to be the star of the show. He didn't need to be particularly funny or charming. He just wanted to put his best self forward. He's good at his job and has genuine expertise on his topic. He told me what he wanted was more gravitas.

Barry walked me through the main content of his talk. We made some slight changes—some parts were too long, some were too confusing with industry-specific jargon, and some sentences needed to be rephrased to be punchier. But overall, it was good—because he knows his stuff. Then I asked him to stand up so we could do a practice run. His opening was not a moment that would induce Dorothy Boyd's famous line to Jerry Maguire: "You had me at hello." Sadly, Barry lost me somewhere between "hello" and reciting his title.

There are two times when your audience is most likely listening: the beginning and the end. They're listening at the beginning to decide whether they're going to keep listening or start thinking about their next meeting or whether they're going to the gym after work. There are so many easy distractions lurking, just waiting for a window to take over people's thoughts. People will naturally tune back in (if they have tuned out to any degree) at the end, once we suggest it's coming by saying, "So to wrap up . . . ," or "In conclusion," etc. This happens because we know that when a speaker is wrapping up, we're likely going to have to do something next. It might be our turn to speak, someone might ask a question, or we might need to get up and move. Increasing our attention to what someone is saying when we know they're coming to a close is an intuitive response. Hopefully, we have their attention throughout, but we are most likely to have our audience's full attention at the beginning and the end, yet we script the *middle* of important talks and often wing the portions people will probably attend to the most.

When I pointed this out to Barry, he said, "Yes, I can see that. So I guess the start is the most important." Not necessarily. Yes, it shapes the perception your audience has of you. At the start, they make a subconscious decision about the amount of mental effort they will put in to following you. But in your final words, you get to decide their lasting impression of you. The point is that you get to decide. We need to be intentional with our beginning and our end. And by that I don't just mean the introduction and conclusion. Do script those. Write, test, and rework the three introductory and three concluding sentences. But the introduction is not the first thing you say, nor is the conclusion the last. We also need to script our opening and our close—the very first and very last words we say. Here's an example.

Barry originally planned to say, as soon as he was introduced by his colleague Angela, "Thanks, Angela, my talk today is about technical challenges in the automotive industry." And then he planned to launch into the introductory points of his talk.

We changed his opening to, "Thank you, Angela. [*pause*] Good morning, all. It's great to have you with us today. It's a critical time in our industry. We're currently facing uncertain market conditions, unexpected legislative changes, and rapid technological developments. Navigating this environment seems more challenging than ever. I'd like to share with you . . ."

He needed to make the thank-you to Angela a real thank-you. Cursorily slipping it into the opening sentence with the subject of his talk did not seem sincere. He also needed to genuinely greet the audience. It was powerful for him to welcome them, even though others had spoken and done so before him, showing both the audience and his colleagues that, in his mind, he had ownership of the event as much as anyone. What he didn't need to do was recite the title. The audience could read! And in the few seconds he spent walking to the podium after Angela introduced him and his first slide went up, they would have read it. What he needed to do was connect. But he subconsciously wanted to rush through the beginning because once he got into his area of expertise, he'd be psychologically safe. For those who are comfortable presenting front and center, this may seem silly. But for those who are not yet comfortable speaking in public—which can be even the most experienced professionals among us—it takes courage to own the introduction. Whether it's in a large auditorium or a small client meeting room, choose to make space for the introduction, and to engage and hold the room at the outset—verbally and nonverbally—before rushing into the details of your meeting.

A Verbal Wet-Fish Handshake

This might seem like a lot of thinking about a little thing. But the thirty minutes we spent reworking Barry's opening and closing had a more powerful impact on his gravitas than the rest of the time we spent looking at the middle of his content (because he's good at his work and knows that content). And it's not just relevant for large audiences and formal presentations—it's true for small-to-medium-size meetings, too. Giving thought to what we're going to say first is powerful. We know that our handshake needs to be firm but not too tight. But we can offer the verbal equivalent of a wet-fish handshake if we haven't thought through our beginning—even the most articulate professionals can just stumble into a conversation. Yes, they're likely to pick it up with powerful points as they get into their message, talking about their areas of expertise where they feel confident, but they can't take back that first impression. We can have powerful, strong body language and a great handshake, but we need our words and body language to *align* to have the best first impression (more on this in the next chapter).

Owning the Flow

Even when we're really prepared for the formal part of a meeting, we can shoot ourselves in the foot in the informal encounters by tripping over small talk. Some of the brightest, most impressive professionals I've met are extremely confident talking about their area of expertise, but when it comes to the opening chitchat, they stumble. It's not silly, and if this is you, you're not alone. I've written lists on areas of small talk with many coaching clients. Obviously, we can't script these sentences the same way we can for a presentation. We need to respond, not just project, but we can preempt the need for small talk and have a couple of questions or comments up our sleeve. Again, it's not about pretending to be someone else. Being authentic is about being true to the impact that you want to have on others. "I'm just not really a talker" is a lazy excuse. Yes, it might take more effort and courage for you than for someone who is naturally more "chatty," but you do get to choose. I know many professionals who don't feel natural or particularly comfortable generating small talk, asking questions, commenting, and facilitating conversation—but you would never know it. People who have authentic gravitas take ownership of the conversation, of the interpersonal "flow." It's the difference between a conversation that has a sense of ease and one that's stilted and a little awkward. It's not the responsibility of the supposedly natural talkers of the world to make sure there's flow in every encounter. If you want to have gravitas—to create a positive encounter for and a powerful impact on the people you're with—then, regardless of your personality and preferences, you have the responsibility and the opportunity to facilitate the conversation.

Time to Get Personal

When it comes to content, we can be cold or we can be prepared to be personal. I say "be prepared" because it can be more comfortable to keep our content neutral. Being formal and impersonal can feel safer. But the goal with authentic gravitas is impact with connection. Being personal doesn't mean being less of an expert.

Here's an example from Christine, an energy consultant, pitching to an existing client in a small group meeting to renew their contract. Her original opening was, "Hello. This presentation I'm giving is on our consultancy and how we work with you. I'll be speaking for forty-five minutes, which should take us nicely up to lunch, and then after lunch I believe we have some time for discussion. I'll be speaking about how we currently work with you and how we could work together going forward."

It was a nice enough introduction, but we made some slight changes. Primarily, we needed to make it more about her audience and less about

Christine. Listening to someone tell you what they are going to say and how long they are going to talk is not particularly engaging. And this was her opening—her "they're definitely listening" moment. Someone telling you what he or she is going to do *for* you is more likely to get your attention:

> *Good morning. Thank you for the opportunity to be with you today. My goal is to understand how we can better serve you, to strengthen our relationship and ensure we add great value to your company both now and in the long run. As you requested, I've brought a presentation to share some ideas about how we might be able to do this. At the end, you should feel fully equipped to make a decision about how you'd like to go forward. This should take around forty-five minutes, which will take us nicely into lunch. Please ask any questions along the way; I'm more than happy to discuss anything throughout that is important to you. I'll be here over lunch as well and am looking forward to spending that time together.*

Throughout the presentation, Christine was planning on making fairly objective points—for example, "The energy regulator says that organizations in this sector must . . ." Even the smallest changes to personalize throughout a presentation can increase the engagement of your audience and thereby the extent of your connection and impact: "The energy regulator has determined that you, and other organizations like yours operating in this sector, must . . ." Making these small changes throughout can result in your audience experiencing your presentation as being about them and for them, compared to an information dump. You are telling them what is relevant to them, rather than simply telling them everything you know. We are bombarded by information all day, every day, but we take note of what is personal.

The Science and Art of Storytelling

We can make our messages personal to our audience, but for true connection, we need to share what is personal to us. We can feel particularly vulnerable in doing so, but people remember stories more than information. Many people feel uncomfortable sharing stories or think they have none to offer, but if you've been working for more than ten minutes in your life, you likely have some stories that will increase your connection and add value.

The key is to make sure you add them at this stage of your planning. Stories are supplements to your message—they should support and reinforce a point or your overall goals. So let's return to the beginning of our preparation. How do we want the people in our audience to think, feel, and act as a result of this encounter with us? If nothing else, what do we want them to remember? This guides our decisions around storytelling. The story doesn't have to be yours—it can be an organizational story, or it can be someone else's story (if you have their permission to share it). But if you choose not to share one of your own stories, question your motives behind that decision. Being vulnerable and sharing things that are personal can increase trust and connection for authentic gravitas. Brené Brown's groundbreaking research shows the power of vulnerability both for us personally and in terms of our impact on those we encounter at work, our teams and organizations.[10]

You may be concerned about the audience's perception of you personally, but you can manage this. If it's a negative story highlighting a flaw, use it to show that you're human, but proactively learning and growing. If it's a positive story and you're concerned you'll come across as boastful, just be careful of phrasing and use the word *we* instead of *I* wherever possible and accurate. You then highlight the strengths of all the people you were working with, not just your own.

Few people feel naturally comfortable sharing stories as part of a talk or presentation. But becoming a storyteller is something we can learn and practice. The art of storytelling includes brainstorming ideas and connections to creatively get across your main point. The key to success is to treat it like a science experiment—test it, consider the results (determine impact by seeking feedback), make some changes, test it again and look at the results, etc. We often seek feedback on our technical points—the "what" of our message. We rarely seek feedback on the "how"—how we're getting our points across, including our stories. It can be an uncomfortable experience to share our stories in a role-play context. Let's face it—it feels silly. In executive education programs, I have the interesting responsibility of getting participants to role-play. Not because it makes them happy, but because we know it can be a useful method of gaining feedback to fuel development. Most people hate the idea of it. But time after time, they find that role-playing the meeting or presentation with a group of colleagues is invaluable. It's not invaluable to practice; it's invaluable to get feedback: "Make the story shorter, punchier." "Explain this part in more detail—I couldn't really follow what was happening." "What happened after that? I felt like I was left hanging." Whatever feedback you receive, there's a strong chance it will make your storytelling even more powerful and, as such, your personal connection stronger.

Scripting your beginning and your end, owning the flow, and making your content personal will increase your connection and your authentic gravitas as you close the intention-impact gap.

THE DANCE OF GRAVITAS: BALANCING CLARITY AND CURIOSITY

Authentic gravitas comes when we balance clarity and curiosity. We need clarity around our intention, as well as a commitment to curiosity—not only about the issues at hand, but also about the people we're engaging with and about our intention-impact gap. As we continually move between clarity and curiosity, one shapes the other. Our discoveries from being curious shape our thinking, intentions, and messages, and the clarity around our messages and goals for impact shape the questions we ask.

The IMPACT model serves as a guide for planning important meetings and presentations. It's not designed to increase the amount of time you need to spend preparing, but rather to make sure your preparation process is structured in a way that's efficient and helps you balance clarity and curiosity. Once we have the foundations of insight, motivation, perception, advocate, and content, it's time to consider which techniques are best to apply.

PRACTICES TO "LEAD THE ROOM"

Below is a summary of the key points we've looked at in chapter 3. This is for you to use later—a quick checklist to easily refer back to when you're preparing for an important meeting or presentation.

- Insight: What do you believe about this situation/possibility? Before you start thinking about what you're going to say, think about what you really *think*. Articulate your viewpoint in one or two sentences. What insight do you want the people you're about to encounter to take away?

- Motivation: Which of the four drives (acquire, bond, comprehend, and defend) could you help the people you're encountering meet? Which drive is most important to them right now? Do your target assessment. If you end up with a lot of questions to which you're not sure of the answers, consider whom you could ask to better your understanding of your audience's motivation.

- Perception: Consider your audience's current perception of the topic. Also consider their perception of you. What do you want it to be? Write it down.

- Advocate: Decide on your sticky messages (maximum of three). Ask yourself, *If nothing else, what would I want them to remember?*

- Content: "You had me at hello." Remember the two times your audience is most likely listening: your beginning and your end. Script both (prioritize these over scripting your content in the middle word for word). Make it personal to your audience and be prepared to be personal yourself by sharing your stories (you can start by jotting them down in one list and getting feedback on them, too, not just on your content and technical points).

- Try following the process structure outlined above, even though it's tempting to just start writing! Setting yourself up to have a powerful, positive impact in your meeting requires a pre-meeting commitment to both clarity and curiosity.

Finally, prepare for unexpected encounters by deciding to stop worrying about what you're going to say, and instead choose one or two words to describe the imprint you would like to leave them with. Choose to be *interested* rather than worrying about being *interesting*.

FOUR

TECHNIQUE

"What Is It About Them?"

The final component of the IMPACT model for authentic gravitas is technique. This is the part that we traditionally associate with gravitas—how we come across nonverbally. But it is only effective in building authentic gravitas if we've followed the previous steps of the IMPACT model to influence with our words as well as our voice and body language. It is the icing on the cake—not the cake itself. In this chapter, we look at how we can unintentionally trip ourselves up, and which techniques can help build authentic gravitas.

The differences between verbal and nonverbal communication are often misinterpreted. Nonverbal communication is distinct in that it is not linguistic, referring to *how* a message is sent (for example, tone, accent, pitch), while verbal communication focuses on the *content* of a message.[1] We give a lot of energy and attention to what we're saying (the content), but often less to how we deliver it. Both, however, communicate meaning. Fascinating research by Harvard Business School professor and social psychologist, Amy Cuddy, shows the ways people can meaningfully increase their presence through small, yet powerful changes.[2] Nonverbal communication not only sends a message to others, but, as revealed in extensive research, also impacts our own psychological processes. It's important that we are as intentional with the meaning and messages we send nonverbally as we are with our verbal communication.

Researchers highlight the numerous ways that nonverbal behavior can interact with our verbal messages. It can *repeat* our verbal discourse (such as a nod to demonstrate agreement), it can *substitute* for it (for example, eye rolling), it can *accent* it (like a slap on the back after a joke), or it can *contradict* it (for example, wiping away tears while saying that you are fine).[3] All uses of nonverbal behavior can support, reinforce, or add to our verbal messages. What we need to be careful of is that our nonverbal communication doesn't *unintentionally* contradict and undermine our verbal messages. When faced with an incongruence between verbal and nonverbal messages, we tend to believe the nonverbal—because it seems less conscious, these subconscious messages are interpreted as a better reflection of that person's true self or meaning; the nonverbal communication is perceived as "authentic."

What matters is alignment. We need congruence between our verbal and nonverbal messages. So once we've established our core messages, we can be intentional in aligning our "what" with our "how."

POWERFUL VS. POWERLESS LANGUAGE

What is it about those people everyone stops and listens to? Yes, it's the quality of their contributions over time that leads people to trust that their input will be positive and meaningful—worth listening to—as soon as they start talking. That's true when there's a history with that person. People lean on past experiences with them. But what about when there's no history? Perhaps they hold a particularly prominent position in their organization or industry, or they have a title that cries out, "Listen to me!" But we know that people can have authentic gravitas regardless of their place in the hierarchy. Is it something about the substance of their speech or their nonverbal presence? It's both. Their communication—both verbal and nonverbal—is powerful.

We do things, often unconsciously and certainly unintentionally, that undermine the power of our communication—regardless of what we're saying, we can shoot ourselves in the foot with the *way* we're speaking. Researchers conducted experiments to study what they called "powerful" and "powerless" language.[4] They identified certain linguistic markers that occur in powerless language, such as:

- Hedges (e.g., "I guess" / "Sort of")

- Intensifiers (e.g., "I really did")

- Using overly polite or overly formal language

- Tag questions (e.g., "That's right, isn't it?")

- Hesitating (e.g., "You know . . ." / "I mean . . ." / "Umm . . .")

While most of us don't necessarily think about speaking in a "powerful" way in our day-to-day lives, it's important to recognize the potential impact of power*less* language. It can create the perception that you're unsure about what you're saying. This, in turn, can make the audience doubt you, and they may be more likely to come up with counterarguments attacking your position. To demonstrate to others that you have confidence in the content of your *message* (even if you don't feel particularly confident about your *self*), and reduce the likelihood of people arguing against your points, try to cut out powerless markers.

Have you ever caught yourself analyzing a speaker instead of his or her message? We all have those moments when we realize we've thought long and hard about the speaker as an individual—what they're wearing, what they do for a living, where they might live, all kinds of personal things about them—and haven't paid much attention to what they were talking *about*. How can we avoid this happening to us and have people focus on our message rather than analyzing us personally? Researchers also found that powerless language actually diverts attention to the speaker and increases the audience's thoughts about the speaker. So by avoiding these powerless markers in your speaking, you'll be better able to get your audience focusing on your message more than on yourself.

The research results imply that your audience is not explicitly aware of the language characteristics that affect their attitude toward you, but those characteristics are making an impact nonetheless. Language appears to act as a cue—the recipients' perception of you (whether one-on-one, in a small meeting, or in a large presentation) actually shapes their thoughts about your message or argument, regardless of its merits. This means that someone with expert knowledge and an excellent argument might still fail to be persuasive if they use powerless language when conveying their argument. Subsequent studies suggest that if the distracting influence of powerless language is great enough, it can lead to little or no thinking at all about the argument or content of your message.[5] It's easy to spend so much time thinking about the content of our message, but the way we speak may be just as important as what we're saying.

IT DOESN'T HAVE TO BE NATURAL TO BE AUTHENTIC

Powerless language tends to detract attention from the idea or argument you're making. It can render persuasive components of your message ineffective. People of all personality types and interpersonal styles could use powerless linguistic markers. Equally, powerful language (defined by the researchers as an *absence* of powerless markers) is not reserved for people who are talkative, nor those who are taciturn. Once again, we can't fall back on using personality or natural style as an excuse. We need to eliminate the self-whisper—*I'm just not like that*—because this isn't about what we are or aren't. It's about communication choices, feedback, discovery, and intentionally creating new habits that communicate the messages you intend.

Along with these powerless verbal cues, there are numerous ways we can unknowingly decrease our gravitas through unintentional messages we send with the way we speak, our vocal tone, and our body language.

A Race to the End

Cynthia was a self-described fast-talker. She had an energy and excitement in her manner that often endeared her to people. But it was a problem when she was in meetings and presentations. Not because talking fast is the "wrong" thing to do, but because her audience couldn't give their full attention to what she was saying; they were too busy expending their mental energy on simply deciphering her words. This might sound extreme, but many people tend to increase their talking speed in important meetings or presentations. It's challenging to remember to slow down while you're talking, as you just want to be able to focus on what you're saying and how the audience is responding. If you script your talk, one useful adjustment can be to shorten your sentences. Then you're more likely to be able to maintain vocal energy right to the end of your sentences—instead of trailing off which happens when we simply run out of breath, but which dangerously has the unintended consequence of taking away from the strength of our message. You're also naturally more likely to breathe, as you'll have more full stops. Allison Shapira, a former opera singer who now teaches communication at the Harvard Kennedy School of Government, recommends that people practice breathing at every punctuation mark.[6] Doing this outside the meeting room, on a plane, in your office, or when you're reading at home or reading to your kids can start to shift your natural habits and increase the likelihood of your slowing down when your are in a higher-pressure situation.

Of course, there are some people who need to speed up their speech! The speakers who make the most positive impact are certainly not necessarily the slowest. So is there one right pace? No. It's about accepting that your natural pace may not always be the best one for getting your message across or for creating the atmosphere and level of engagement you intend. It's about the power of fit.

Message "Fit"

Researchers from Michigan State and Columbia Universities looked at the role of nonverbal cues on persuasion. They found that messages were more effective when the nonverbal cues of the speaker "fit" the motivational orientation of the message *recipient*.[7] Participants who experienced "fit" had more positive attitudes toward the topic and greater intentions to behave in ways that were recommended than people who received messages that weren't in line with their motivational orientation. What does "fit" look like? For audience members who were "promotion-focused" (who represented goals as hopes and aspirations), "fit" meant viewing messages that were delivered in an "eager" nonverbal style (conveyed by animated, broad opening movements; hand gestures openly projecting outward; forward-leaning body positions; fast body movement and fast speech). "Prevention-focused" audience members (those who represented goals as duties and obligations) experienced "fit" when they viewed messages delivered in a "vigilant" nonverbal style (conveyed by gestures showing precision; slowed speech; slightly backward-leaning body positions; slower body movement). This is just one example of how adapting for your audience is important not only with verbal communication but nonverbal communication as well. In another example, researchers in Canada studying cultural diversity compared nonverbal messages in negotiation and looked at cross-cultural differences.[8] They found that Canadian negotiators communicated a positive perception of their counterpart and their active involvement in the negotiation through faster speech and expressiveness in their voice. Chinese negotiators, however, communicated self-control by remaining calm and suppressing emotion in their vocal tone. These findings highlight the importance of how we communicate, not just what we say. Audience analysis is not just the reference point for deciding on the content of our speech; it's also the starting point for choosing *how* we will deliver that content.

To highlight how powerful this concept can be, let me share one of my worst professional moments with you. I was asked to be a keynote speaker to the four hundred partners of a transatlantic law firm. Still fairly early on in my career, I was simultaneously excited and extremely nervous to have this surprising privilege. Beforehand, I had numerous meetings with the conference organizer, who communicated to me, with great certainty, insights into what the partners were looking for and what they "needed to hear." After working on my speech for weeks beforehand, I rehearsed in front of my team and was assured it was a great talk. The focus of my talk was leadership—a topic I'm passionate about and a field I had, at that stage, been working in for a few years. So, with nervous energy running through my body, I walked with a fair amount of message confidence onto the stage. What followed was forty-five minutes of torture. It felt as if the words were coming out of my mouth and falling straight onto the floor with a giant *thud*. Sharing my genuine energy and enthusiasm for leadership, to surreptitiously encourage these lawyers to be leaders (as per the goal I had been tasked with), was met with flat, silent disengagement. I told myself that perhaps I was reading too much into their response—or lack thereof. It was only afterward that my worst fears were confirmed. As a speaker, you can often gauge your level of success by how many people come up and ask questions following your talk. As I walked through the crowd to get coffee, not one person asked me a question. Not one. The managing partner naturally approached and thanked me, but I knew he was being gracious. I'd had so many meetings beforehand; I had prepped extensively and thought my content was exactly the right fit. What had gone wrong?

The speakers presenting right before me were from one of the large strategy consultancies. I had been briefed on their talk and understood that they were speaking about the future of the legal industry and giving the partners the results of some research they had undertaken. Fine. That all sounded fine. Except it wasn't. In the session before mine, the consultants had shared with the partners how the legal industry was changing globally. How if they didn't drastically and rapidly change their culture and way of doing business, they would not only fall from their place as one of the leading firms in their field, but, in just five to ten years, might not exist at all. That was the message they gave the *partners*—the owners of the firm. Then, immediately afterward, with only a brief "thank you" and a short introduction between us, this energetic young Australian woman got up, and with a massive smile might as well have said, "Yeah, leadership, woo-hoo!" Don't get me wrong—the words I said were appropriate. The content of my message was spot on. But because I had been too focused on my upcoming talk to really take in the gravity of the message before mine (even though I had been in the room), I failed to give consideration to the new state of the audience. They were in shock, extremely concerned about the data that had just been presented to them. "Be worried," they had been told in so many words. "Get ready to change in ways you can't even imagine right now." It was as though they had just seen a severe weather warning, and oblivious of the looming tornado, I then suggested we go have a picnic. I needed to adopt a vigilant nonverbal style. I could have said the same words in a different style, more appropriate to the mood the audience was now in, and had the powerful impact I had intended.

Although my example may seem extreme, it's important to recognize that in the busyness between meetings, if we're not doing discovery well, not paying attention to the verbal and nonverbal cues of the people we're with, not making time for "space in the middle," not rerouting our agenda at the first sign of any red flag, our vocal tone and/or body language can have an impact far from the positive one we intended.

Is There a Gravitas Voice?

There's speculation that former British prime minister Margaret Thatcher took voice lessons, with videos and studies of her supposed "before" and "after" voice. Why would she do this? There is much research to suggest that success in business and politics is associated with a deeper voice. One study of 792 male public-company CEOs, conducted by researchers from Duke University and the University of California at San Diego, found that CEOs with deeper voices managed larger companies, made more money, and that they had longer tenures.[9] It appears the possible preference for lower voices when it comes to leadership holds beyond the boardroom and men. Studies led by Casey Klofstad at the University of Miami suggest that both men and women select male and female leaders with lower voices.[10] However, Klofstad found an exception to the lower-voice preference: when facing female opponents, candidates with higher voices, particularly male candidates, were more successful.[11] So while success and leadership are often associated with a lower voice, the correlation is not universal. There is no one-pitch-fits-all approach we need to land on. Style, like the content of our speech, requires being intentional and versatile. And while there is a physiological basis for the pitch of our own unique voice, each of us has a range at our disposal. Perhaps it's useful to revisit the eager and vigilant nonverbal styles. The higher end of our own natural range may be more appropriate to apply when choosing the eager communication style, for a positive audience, and the lower end of our range might be more appropriate for the vigilant style, when working with people in challenging situations. You do not have the right or the wrong voice for authentic gravitas. You have the choice to be intentional in using the full range of your voice, adapting it for the situation and goal at hand, to minimize the gap between your intention and impact.

Although you should adapt your tone depending on your circumstances, one thing that never needs to be part of your repertoire is distracting body language. One interviewee, an executive at a global branding company, highlighted the need for feedback to develop gravitas: "Can it be learned? Yes. But probably only if someone calls you out on it—how you engage, how you show up, particularly when it comes to body language." Let's take a look at some of the most common unintentional distracting body language habits and what to do about them.

The Waltz

My husband and I practiced our first dance over and over again in the weeks leading up to our wedding. I would like to say that our first dance as a married couple at our reception was perfect. I try to remember it that way, but there's a little part of me that thinks we probably looked quite silly. But we had fun and my husband kindly reminds me that's what matters.

Moving around the dance floor, whether we are natural movers-and-shakers or the awkward people bopping around, is part of the fun of a celebration. But meeting rooms are not the forum for any kind of dancer. I often catch clients doing a subconscious "waltz." Shifting from one foot to the other, taking little steps side to side, or swinging from their back leg to their front leg and front leg to back . . . over and over again. These slight movements suggest nervousness—they are the body language equivalent of the powerless language we looked at earlier. That's not to say you can't move. There's just one rule: move . . . or don't. By that I mean stand still and hold your ground, with your body centered and your weight spread evenly, or take intentional steps around the space you have, moving toward different people in your audience. Don't float around. Not because it's "wrong," but because it's distracting. It takes attention away from your message and thereby reduces your likelihood of impacting your audience in the way you intend. This can seem like a trivial point, but when facilitating peer practice presentation sessions with professionals at all organizational levels, there is always at least one "dancer," and the feedback is universally, "It was distracting." Typically, the person doing it was in no way aware that they were shifting their weight or taking little steps.

Move. Or don't. It's your choice. If space allows, a mix of the two is usually best: move part of the time and don't during other parts. But no floating. Save the waltz for the dance floor.

Don't Add. Subtract.

Jean-Luc had come from France to join us in Switzerland for a leadership program organized by his global media company. He was friendly, articulate, and interested. My team and I were spending three days with Jean-Luc and his peers from across Europe to train them on increasing their influence and gravitas. One part of the program required participants to take turns practicing presenting and chairing meetings. When Jean-Luc spoke, he was funny and thought-provoking. Many of his peers in this proactive group raised their hands at the end, wanting to offer him constructive feedback. "It was good, but you did this with your hand the whole time," one colleague said as he circled his wrist over and over again to mimic Jean-Luc's gesture. "Yes, that's what I was going to say," said another. Sure enough, all the feedback was about Jean-Luc's circling hand.

Many people ask, "What should I do with my hands?" The question for most people isn't about what to *start* doing, but what to *stop* doing. As you manage to reduce nervousness (more on this to come), your hands will naturally start to reflect your words. What you need to *stop* doing is making distracting gestures, which you might not even be aware you're making. You don't realize the impact it's having. You may have prepared an interesting and engaging message, but if you don't take away your distracting hand gestures, your audience will not be able to focus on the message as well and you won't have as great an impact. Worry less about what to do with your hands and more about what *not* to do with them.

Hiding in Plain Sight

Suzanne was ready. She had all the findings of the latest industry report graphed and documented beautifully in her slide deck. She'd been practicing her talk and was hoping to make a strong impression on her company's management team. This was an important opportunity for her, and although she felt somewhat nervous, she was confident her slides were just what they were after. Her boss even looked over them and said he thought they were "spot on." As she got up from her chair when it was her turn to share, Suzanne picked up the clicker and smiled at the audience. As she started her opening, she turned away from the management team seated at the large oval table in front of her and glanced at the screen, as if to show them where to look so they could go through the deck together. And that was the moment. The action in that moment meant she stood—and stayed—facing sideways, the left side of her body toward the management team and her right side toward the screen. She was essentially facing the window. Sure, she looked at the audience sometimes, but she looked at the slides just as much. She was confident about the slides, more confident than she was about herself. But her subconscious desire that her audience look at the slides instead of her led to a silent but clear instruction: "Focus on the slides, not me."

But your slides are not the message. You have the message—your slides are just there to support you. That's why in the IMPACT model, you don't design your slides until the end, once you've already decided on your key messages and content. Standing in a way that naturally focuses your attention on your slides rather than on the audience sends a message that you are just the delivery person chosen to read the slides and pass on the slides' great messages.

It sounds silly, but many professionals fail to deliver with gravitas because they unknowingly "hide" behind the slides. The same can be true of a flip chart. Have you ever seen someone so close to it, facing it rather than you? Or someone looking down at a report being discussed far more than necessary? It can be our way of self-protecting. Perhaps they no longer need to self-protect, but the slides, flip chart, or report made them more comfortable when they first started their careers, and they established unintentional habits that still make it look like they believe the audience should value the visuals more than their own personal contribution.

Face Freeze

Rishad's senior partner handed the meeting over to him. The clients had promised to make their final decision within a week of this meeting.

Usually engaging and approachable, Rishad was conscious of saying all the right things, but wasn't conscious of the fact that his face appeared stiff. He barely changed his expression throughout the meeting. His face seemed frozen. Rishad was unknowingly engaging in another form of self-protection common in important meetings: reducing the use of his facial muscles and keeping still. In psychology, we refer to it as restricted affect—a reduction in the extent to which outer emotional expressions match how we feel on the inside. This is different from apathy (a lack of emotion). It can be partnered with a monotonous tone. Rarely is it intentional. The restricted affect (or "face freeze") can occur naturally as a self-preservation mechanism when we experience pressure.

Months later, Rishad asked for coaching because he was about to present at an industry conference. This was an important moment in his career. After discovering his goals and needs, I invited a friend of mine to join us. She is an Olivier Award–winning West End and Broadway musical theater star. We were grateful to have her input. We rented out a West End theater in London so Rishad could practice presenting in a large space to re-create the upcoming conference experience. When Rishad started speaking, my friend spotted his face freeze right away. She offered advice that he would have laughed at had it come from me. "Put your hands into fists," said this enchanting, celebrated performer, "and roll your knuckles in circles around and around in your cheeks. It loosens your face and you become more conscious of your facial muscles, enabling you to feel the tension in them and make the choice to relax them." The three of us stood in that empty theater, rolling our fists around our cheeks, and to Rishad's and my surprise, we could feel the difference. Now, you obviously can't do this while sitting in the front row of an auditorium waiting to be invited up, or in a meeting room waiting for a customer to join you! But you can do this in a bathroom stall before you go to your meeting or presentation. It enables you to be intentional with what I believe to be the most important part of body language—your facial expression. And with that you can choose to align your nonverbal communication with your verbal communication and minimize your intention-impact gap.

Positive Vibes

We can hide with our eyes as well. In a large auditorium, we naturally look to the front of the room. But hiding with our eyes happens in small meetings, too. Time and time again in meeting role-plays, I'll see a speaker give substantially more attention to one or two people at the table than the others. Directing their eyes at a select few sends the message, "I value you more." The ones who don't get eye contact later reveal, to the speaker's surprise, "I felt like you cared more about what he/she thought than what I thought." It could be that the speaker is paying more attention to the decision-makers or key influencers in the room, whether consciously or subconsciously. While that might seem like a sensible decision (and you certainly don't want to ignore those people), leaders often make judgments about someone not just based on how that person treats them personally, but on the level of respect he or she shows to their colleagues and the more junior members of the team, too.

Another reason we might look at some people and not others is positive validation. In a presentation, we look mainly at the people in the front row, not merely because they're closer (and we can often see them more clearly than those in the back), but also because the people at the front are likely to be more positive or engaged than the ones who came in late or chose to sit way back. I've seen countless times that those audience members who are given more eye contact are those who are smiling or conveying positive affect in their facial expression. Naturally focusing on those who send positive vibes is not surprising. We seek positive affirmation—not just because we want to feel good about ourselves, but because we want to have authentic gravitas and make a positive, meaningful impact on the people around us. We want to add value. And when others give us positive affirmation—not just verbally but also nonverbally, with engaged body language and focused eye contact—we receive a signal that we are achieving our goal. And *that* feels good.

The problem is that we inadvertently make others feel bad or annoyed. Don't they deserve our attention? Likely unaware of their negative or neutral nonverbal messages, we can make the experience less positive and impactful for them.

GRACE FOR *THEIR* GAP

We need to be gracious and remember that others have an intention-impact gap, too. We have to intentionally create alignment between the messages we want to send and the messages we actually send through our body language and facial expression. But often people don't give thought to this. They may be positive and interested, but their face is simply not showing it. People talk about reading the body language of the audience, and yes—if you see a big yawn or people looking away, it is certainly time to shake things up if you're the speaker! But if they just look serious, sometimes it might be worthwhile to ignore their silent signals. My husband is a pilot and recently took on a new role. The day before he went for an important line check (a flight assessment) he was warned by a colleague, "The instructor you have looks very serious, but actually he's a really nice guy." I was so thankful his colleague shared this. Had he not, under pressure my husband would have been more likely to interpret a serious disposition as concern regarding his performance, which in turn could have had a negative impact on his actual performance. Going in with a belief that the instructor was well-regarded by colleagues and friendly—regardless of his facial messages—my husband was better able to be his natural best self.

So don't hide from people who don't give you positive nonverbal affirmation. Choose to give everyone equal energy and attention. While our responsibility is to intentionally minimize our own intention-impact gap, we need to have grace for others—remembering that they have a gap, too.

The easiest way to do this in a large audience is to look at a back corner of the room and slowly use your eyes to follow an "S" pattern down through the crowd to the front row. After a minute, go back up to the opposite corner and wind down again, following an inverted "S." In a small meeting, be mindful from the outset of your decision to give everyone eye contact. And whether sitting or standing, center yourself from the beginning so your eyes naturally fall to the middle of the room, making it easy to follow through on your intention of attending to all.

Out of the Shadows

Many people don't like to be the center of attention, but *hiding*—whether it's with our body language, eyes, or face freeze—is dangerous. There are two unintended consequences. The first is that people remember the messages of the slides and the content of the speech—but not the messenger. The second is that if they do notice behavior used as a defense mechanism, they may interpret it as you being uncertain about your message. They may then begin to question whether they should trust your message. With unintentional powerless language (verbal and nonverbal), we can undermine all the good work we've done in developing impactful messages.

SILENT GRAVITAS: THE MESSAGES WE SEND WITHOUT SAYING A WORD

People can hide in plain sight. In meetings, most notably, people hide in their chairs. Whenever Rose is in a meeting with senior colleagues or clients, she positions herself in the corner of her chair. She's ever so slightly hunched over, her arms are tucked tightly in at her sides, and her hands are typically together on her lap. This is a habit she unintentionally developed over time. Without realizing it, she is trying to hide in plain sight. Although it might feel bold and unnerving, you need to "come to the table." Center yourself in your chair, pull it in close, and move your upper body inward toward the table. Choose to be present in your body language. Not everyone with gravitas is leaning in at the table. Some of the most powerful contributors in meetings will lean back, look away, or even walk around while they're talking, certain they have others' attention. If you're comfortable with this, it's appropriate for the context, and others remain focused on your contribution, these behaviors can be impactful. But that's only while you're talking. You may not be one of the most senior people at the table. Without much to contribute, it can be difficult to come across with gravitas. Can you add value without saying a lot? Yes. For starters, you can choose to "come to the table" and sit centered, facing your audience—courageously demonstrating participation rather than sending the silent message, "*I shouldn't be here.*" If you make this choice rather than giving in to the common desire to hide, then without even saying much, you can have a more positive, lasting impact on those around you.

So come to the table. You can choose to relax while you're talking and have others' attention, but gravitas isn't just for those moments when you have the floor. You send messages when you're silent and listening as much as when you're speaking. The students in my class are sending a message to me as they're listening, and to the guest speakers who come in. How those guests, typically very influential in their fields, choose to respond to a particular student who decides to approach them at the end of class, will be partially shaped by the messages they've received from that student during their talk. I see participants in leadership programs shape their peers' perceptions of them. When listening, they do so by the messages they send through their eye contact, their facial expressions and facial responsiveness, their quiet energy or lack of it. The people who have silent gravitas are those who are conscious that they send messages when they're listening as much as when they're speaking. The ones who are not aware of, or in that moment not conscious of, the messages they send as a listener rarely have silent gravitas. This could influence who gets invited to be part of an important business project. It could guide a decision someone is making about your career opportunities. Your silent messages can shape your future, so be as intentional about the message you want to send others when you're *not* speaking as when you *are* speaking.

Here are four practical ways you can ensure your actions lead to your desired impact:

1. Commit to your beginning and your end. In previous chapters, we've seen the difference this makes. These two windows are also times when we are most likely to use powerless language, verbal and nonverbal. Imagine that Alice has just handed over to John in a meeting. John looks half-heartedly toward her and then flicks his eyes toward the audience before looking down at the paper in front of him. "Yes, right, thanks, Alice. So, well, if we have a look at, um, the second half of the report . . ." The audience's subconscious first impression? Powerlessness. Alternatively, he could look to Alice, smile, and thank her. Then pause, focus and keep his eyes on the people in front of him, and with a calm smile, say, "Ladies and gentlemen, if you'll please turn to the second half of the report, we'll begin there. I'm going to share with you . . ." Or, "Thanks, Alice," followed by a funny opener. The point is to speak with clarity right from the outset, avoiding powerless linguistic and nonverbal markers. The audience's subconscious first impression then? Powerful. What matters is not that you come across as powerful, but that as a result, the audience is more likely to focus and give greater consideration to your message. This will increase your likelihood of making a significant, positive contribution—"You had me at hello."

2. Self-evaluate. Once you're mindful of these verbal and nonverbal markers, you'll pick them up yourself. As horrible as it can feel, record yourself or ask someone else to help you do it while you're practicing or even in the moment if possible, and do actually watch it! Look out for specific things you can intentionally begin to change.

3. Seek feedback. We may not be aware of regularly using some of these powerless verbal or nonverbal markers. Our use of them might be habitual. Ask for feedback after every time you speak, and encourage real and specific input. A dear friend and mentor of mine, Flip Flippen, asks his team for feedback every time he speaks. He insists on it. Once a new, young member of his team, David, went with him to a keynote, and on the return drive had only flattering comments to make about the speech. Flip pulled the car over and said that he would call a driver to take David back to the office. The young man was obviously surprised, and Flip said,

"David, I don't want to spend three hours in the car with someone who can't make me better. So speak up or catch a ride!" Of course, David quickly got the idea and had some suggestions as to how Flip could improve. Flip wanted to show David how serious he was about this—that asking for feedback wasn't a trick to get positive reinforcement but a fierce commitment to getting better, and that the people he wanted around him were those who would help him improve. It's no surprise that he is one of the most impactful speakers I know. We should never graduate from seeking feedback, regardless of our position or how long we've been in our industry. When seeking feedback, be specific—for example, "After my talk, I'd appreciate your feedback not only on my content but also on my style." Ask questions about your content, takeaway message, and style. For example, "Did I hesitate or use filler words often?" Rarely is feedback tough enough. When facilitating feedback, I find most colleagues are happy to offer one another positive feedback and make one or two small suggestions for change (which means I often end up playing the bad guy and giving the tough feedback!). So if you do value others' opinions, you will most likely need to push for honesty and ask them to be specific about what you could do differently.

4. **Choose small changes.** Some of what I've outlined in this chapter might not be relevant to you. But the smallest changes can lead to big differences as you create alignment between your verbal and nonverbal messages. And some points may be useful in equipping you to help others by giving them feedback. Be committed to the development of others' authentic gravitas, and be prepared to give constructive feedback even when it would be easier to just stay silent.

We all have areas where we need to grow and improve. There's a difference between natural and authentic. Being authentic is not about simply embracing the natural style that we have (most likely inadvertently) developed over time. It is about committing to our *intention* for impact.

Virtual Gravitas

"Rebecca"—Lincoln pulled me aside during a lunch break at an executive education program—"Can we chat?" He had just stepped into a new role in California, and the majority of his new team was based overseas. We had been working through some of the principles of authentic gravitas that morning, and Lincoln was concerned about his ability to have the same positive impact he was used to having now that he was leading teams virtually.

Let's wrap up our discussion of the IMPACT model by taking a look at virtual gravitas, because, let's face it, for much of our work today, we may not be physically present with our colleagues and clients. One study comparing electronic and face-to-face communication for 230 people highlighted some of the challenges of virtual working. Compared to face-to-face interaction, virtual communication fluency was reduced by around 90 percent! The study also found that electronic communication increased encoding effort for information givers, and increased communication ambiguity and cognitive effort for both parties.[12]

How can we build connection and communicate with impact when we're facing the challenges of not actually being in the same room? While it can require more effort and add complexity, the principles stay the same. If anything, they are more important. We certainly would consider the impact we want to have on an audience before an important presentation. But we can be less intentional when it comes to a smaller meeting. And even less so as we jump onto a conference call or fling out an email. Certainly, we may give great consideration to important communications, but we tend to consider the content of what we say/write more than how we want to impact those we encounter. Following the IMPACT model provides a useful guide to ensuring that we minimize the gap between intention and impact. What are your insight goals? How do you want them (the people you engage with via video chat/call/email/text) to think, feel, and potentially act differently as a result of this encounter with you? What is motivating them? What is their perception of this situation and of you right now? If nothing else, what would you want them to remember and pass on? How should you open and close? What stories would be relevant and support your message? And finally, think about your technique.

On a conference call, building in time for the "space in the middle" is difficult. We are even more likely to stick to our agenda, swapping quickly from niceties and small talk (usually once everyone is on the call, or after a couple of minutes, if there are just two people) straight into the agenda items. And rarely are broader business questions and a discussion about shifting industry environments, structural changes, altered priorities, or professional/personal developments on that agenda. But the discovery process doesn't become less important just because we have structures and virtual working habits that reduce our likelihood of engaging with it. Those who are able to build authentic gravitas are the ones who push against the virtual norms and intentionally create windows to engage in discovery.

Many people work with others regularly but almost exclusively remotely. We have clients, suppliers, and colleagues in other parts of the world. We have to be especially intentional about building genuine connection when it's more difficult, as is the case in the virtual world. It doesn't just happen in the office over months and years of making coffee in the same place. The risk of creating a large gap between intention and impact is greater with virtual working relationships. We more frequently misinterpret tone when we can't see others' facial expressions. And we misinterpret words on an email without a tone to color them. My advice to Lincoln was, whenever possible—if in any way possible—to *start* his relationship with someone who would be primarily a virtual connection face-to-face. We remember faces and we remember tone. When I hear someone I know speaking on the phone, I picture their face as they speak. When I read an email from someone I've met, I subconsciously add his or her tone to the words I read. Even one encounter at the beginning can reduce misinterpretation in virtual connection and increase the likelihood of having the intended impact. Of course, there are situations where it's just not possible to meet face-to-face at the start of a relationship. Use virtual technology to experience facial expressions and tone as much as possible, before shifting into more of a written (email) relationship (if possible, limit email to routine communication, and keep the calls and visual exchanges for any areas requiring explanation or exploration, or where there's a chance there may be sensitivities).

As technology continues to rapidly advance, it will likely decrease our misinterpretation gap, affording us more and better-quality virtual interactions where we can clearly experience not only tone but also body language, particularly facial expressions. Most of us already have access to high-quality applications that allow this. But I've met executives across many different fields, even—surprisingly—technology companies, who do not regularly utilize these resources in leading their virtual teams and working with remote clients and suppliers. It's up to us to prioritize these tools and to build in windows for discovery and connection, the way we would more naturally when meeting face-to-face.

Authentic IMPACT: Confidence in Your Message and the Courage to Change

As we come to a close on how we connect for authentic gravitas, let's return to James, the senior executive who wasn't himself in his annual presentations at the board meeting, who we met at the end of chapter 2. All the gravitas in his daily working life disappeared when he went into that room each year (and even when we role-played being in the boardroom). His style was stoic and his content was lackluster, devoid of any personalization. After James disclosed how he felt about the board meeting, I suggested we take a break and walk around his office. As we wandered through various sections where his team worked, I asked him what these people were doing. "Oh, they're working on some important new structures. They will really help with our regional expansions!" he replied. "This team is looking at how we drive engagement. It could impact the whole of our global business," he asserted. James went on and on. He was passionate. There was energy in his communication—both verbal and nonverbal. James kept talking throughout our walk, explaining projects and plans for the year ahead. When we finally circled back to the board-room, I directed him, "Now, just say that." The rehearsal was now completely different. James had his gravitas back. He was right to be passionate and excited about the work of his team and the impact they would have on the wider business in the years ahead. He stopped focusing on the potential of this being a terrible day for him and instead chose to concentrate on communicating the good work his team was doing. He was connecting with me (and later with his board members) in an authentic way. Because he was being real, he was confident in his message, even if he still didn't feel confident personally. He had to choose courage to deliver the message to his audience because it felt dangerous, in this career-defining talk, to openly share his personal convictions and goals for his team. And he needed to embrace a few new styles, breaking some old unintentional habits. But by being courageous enough to change and confident in his message, James found his authentic gravitas. It sounds too good to be true, but James honestly told me later that it went from being his worst professional day of the year (every year) to his best.

Whether it's in small internal meetings or large presentations, be intentional about the type of impact you want to make on those around you and be disciplined in making adjustments to your behavioral habits to minimize the gap between intention and impact. How you impact other people and how they regard you are not things that happen *to* you; they're a choice you get to make. Ensuring you increasingly make that positive, significant impact you're after requires a commitment to self-leadership, which we now turn to in chapter 5.

PRACTICES TO DEVELOP YOUR TECHNIQUE

Quickly review these seven points before future meetings or presentations. They are designed to serve as a reminder of the technique principles to align your intention and impact:

- Be intentional about your nonverbal messages as well as your verbal communication (how you're communicating, not just what you're saying).

- Seek specific feedback, for example, around any powerless markers and distracting gestures.

- Consider the motivational state of your audience (e.g., promotion- or prevention-focused) and choose nonverbal behaviors that "fit"— including the full range of your voice, pace, and hand gestures.

- Be still, or don't. Or do both. Just avoid the meeting room or presentation floor "waltz."

- Watch out for "face freeze" and practice muscle-loosening exercises (like the one on page 95), if necessary.

- Whether in your seat or standing up, start your presentation with your body centered, and be aware of giving everyone equal eye contact, regardless of the (likely unintentional) messages they are sending you.

- Follow the principles of IMPACT when working virtually. Build in time for exploration and "space in the middle," and utilize the virtual technologies available to you.

FIVE

INSPIRING PEOPLE LIVE INSPIRED

The Promise and Practicalities of Self-Leadership

I would like to emphasize to both young and old the importance of creativity, of struggling for honesty, and of accepting there will be failures along the way in any career. To me, the most important things in life are to struggle to improve, to struggle to be honest, and to struggle to re-evaluate one's prejudices.

—Dr. Graham Farquhar, biophysicist and Senior Australian of the Year 2018

Authentic gravitas is built upon a foundation of trust and integrity. If we consider someone to have authentic gravitas, we not only trust their intention (that their professed intention is their actual intention), but we also trust their abilities (they will deliver, to the very best of their abilities, what they say they will deliver), and we trust their commitment to improvement—to developing both themselves and their sphere of influence and responsibility. So ability—or at least a commitment to growing our ability—does matter when it comes to gravitas. Going beyond the loud voice and grand gestures of surface gravitas to add meaningful, significant value, we need to not only attend to what we say and how we say it, but also to our abilities that give integrity to what we say. A commitment to growing our skills and abilities underpins a capacity to authentically "lead the room." Gravitas requires a commitment to ongoing self-leadership.

While we might think that increasing our gravitas is all about how we relate to others, it's not. *Some of it is just about me.* I have to focus on myself to positively impact others and the situation I'm in. I need to lead myself to bring integrity to the contributions I make. Self-leadership is the influence a person uses to control their own behavior and thoughts, including behavioral and cognitive strategies intended to increase their personal effectiveness and performance.[1] In this chapter, we'll look at various behavioral and cognitive strategies for self-leadership to increase authentic gravitas.

Once I lead myself well, I have the potential to effectively "lead the room." And people with gravitas lead—influencing and facilitating others toward achieving collective goals.[2] This is not because of their place in the hierarchy (although they may be in positions of authority), but because of their personal power and influence that transcend hierarchy (more on this in chapter 7). When we look at "leading" here, we are not speaking to the formal position of leadership or management within an organization. Rather, this is a consideration of the extent to which professionals lead themselves and are able to influence and facilitate others toward achieving collective goals. They take responsibility and are able to contribute in a positive, significant way to lead the conversation, lead the project, and lead through challenges, regardless of position. We can only add true value to others by first, and continually, challenging and changing ourselves.

Two studies on "Leading Yourself and Leading Others," one of 447 professionals with leadership experience and another of 35 leaders and 151 followers, found that the notion of effectively leading others is associated with first effectively leading oneself.[3] If we are to lead the room, we need to lead ourselves. The findings were consistent regardless of the participants' sex, age, and even leadership experience. It doesn't matter if you've been a leader for decades or you're new to leading the room. Self-leadership matters. Self-leadership can be thought of as the process by which we influence ourselves.[4] It includes behavioral, motivational, and cognitive dimensions.

The researchers found that self-leadership was positively associated with active styles of leading (transactional and transformational leadership) and negatively associated with passive styles of leadership (laissez-faire leadership). Transactional leadership refers to exchange processes between leaders and followers. Transformational leaders also look to further develop their followers. A transformational leader establishes high standards and goals; gives meaning, purpose, and direction to followers and their work; leads followers with enthusiasm, inspiration, charisma, motivations, and emotions; and creates an atmosphere of intrinsic motivation. Laissez-faire leadership, however, indicates a lack of active leadership and thus is regarded as a passive and ineffective leadership style in which leading followers is avoided or practically nonexistent.[5] People who engage more in self-leadership are more likely to lead others in positive, active ways. Your self-leadership influences the way in which other people regard you as a leader.

Self-leadership can impact not just how you're seen, but also what you get done. German and Swiss researchers, in a study of forty teams with a total of 310 members, found that self-leadership is positively related to our individual performance.[6] A recent Norwegian study found that self-leadership influences work effort and creativity, and Austrian researchers identified a positive link between self-leadership and "expressivity": those people higher in self-leadership were stronger in terms of their ability to express themselves and thereby influence others.[7, 8] Self-leadership enables us to bring integrity to our intentions for making a significant contribution through our abilities, ideas, and outcomes.

It's easy to spend all our time reacting to others' requests (whether a boss's, team's, client's, or peer's), but in constantly giving *out*, we can end up giving *less*. In the same way that we're able to be better leaders, colleagues, employees, friends, partners, and parents when we're physically healthy, we're able to give more to others and therefore have more authentic gravitas when we're mentally healthy with good habits. In this chapter, we'll look at how those with authentic gravitas lead themselves—proactively driving their own personal growth and development—and how to do this effectively and sustainably. They are intentional, choose courageous behaviors, and are disciplined in following through on the choices they've made, evaluating the impact of their new actions, and continually adjusting to align their outcome with their intentions.

A ROUTINE OF EXCEPTIONS

As much as we may be trying to excel, we often get to the end of the day feeling anything but excellent. Without realizing it, we can get stuck in a Routine of Exceptions ("It's because today . . . "), and day after day, year after year, we fail to personally change to accomplish our ambitions and meet our potential.

It's often the small, daily choices that, over the years, shape who we are and whether we are able to make a positive, meaningful, and lasting impact on others. The somewhat glamorous notion of gravitas is realized in the unglamorous reality of self-discipline. People who are disciplined and effective at self-leadership engage in self-regulation—they proactively direct their thoughts, feelings, and actions to achieve established goals.[9] But it's more than merely setting goals. Interdisciplinary research across educational, psychological, social, and organizational studies reveals the complexity of effective self-regulation. Factors that come into play include our affect, cognition, behavior, context, and the reality of multiple, and at times competing, goals. We can succumb to a self-generated myth that to have gravitas we "need to do more." Over the course of twenty years of teaching leaders, I've seen how easy it is to focus on our output—how we lead, influence, produce, manage, and drive change. But to be better leaders, we equally need to focus on our *input*—nurturing our own abilities, whether that's by staying up to date on industry news or taking courses to improve our skill set. Only then can we continue to see greater value in our output.

The people others describe as having authentic gravitas have new ideas and a fresh approach, actively driving change. To be such a person, here are six factors to build into your life:

- Space for "Thought Leadership"

- Clarity Around Your Game Plan

- Being Curious through the Busyness

- Commuting Well

- Being a Target of Influence

- Choosing Wisdom

"IT'S JUST ME AND THE ROAD": THE PRECIOUS, LOST ART OF THINKING

As professionals advance into roles with greater responsibility, they increasingly have so many demands on their time that it's easy to slip into the habit of not doing one of the main things they were recruited or promoted to do: think. Caught up in tasks, emails, endless meetings, supervision, and conference calls (all of which are important), it's easy to lose sight of thinking, the precursor to all these. We give more in time, data, and content, but we can end up giving less in quality and impact—less than we have the potential to give. This is not just less for our business and our field, but less for the people around us. We need to develop sustainable thought leadership practices.

We all need to purposefully carve out headspace, wherever that is. But it's not enough—it must be the prequel to action and change. I do need time and space to focus on myself because authentic gravitas doesn't start with my interaction with others, it starts long before those encounters, with just me. There are two forms of headspace we need to intentionally build in: free-flow thinking and thought leadership windows.

The Top of the Red Bus

For me, it can be hard to find space to think in London. But respite from the busyness can come in the most random places. Years ago, after traveling from my home in southwest London into the center of town one day, I realized I had made a major breakthrough in my doctoral research. I had also come up with some good ideas for my work with a colleague. I had just let my mind wander on the bus and now my brain was buzzing. Had I eaten something different for breakfast? Slept particularly well? The difference, I noted, was having freedom to simply think—upstairs, in the front window seat of a red double-decker bus. Since then, many a time I have gone for a bus ride—up top, at the front—just to have some headspace. I ride around London whenever I get the chance, *thinking*. As I look down at the buildings, parks, and people we're passing by, my mind tends to wander between random thoughts about what I'm seeing and ideas or reflections about colleagues, things I've read, goals I'm working on, challenges I'm facing. To me, the red bus now strangely symbolizes being intentional and resolute about the importance of carving out headspace.

I recognize this red bus experience to be free-flow thinking, and there is much evidence of its powerful effects. One study led by David Creswell at Carnegie Mellon University highlighted the role of unconscious thinking in decision-making.[10] He and the research team looked at how the brain operates when faced with a challenge—in this case an imaginary car purchase with multiple factors to take into consideration. They found that better decisions were made by people who were distracted by other tasks. These people had time to engage in unconscious thought, and they outperformed people who were asked to make an immediate choice as well as those who had some time to consciously think about their decision. A friend, fellow psychologist, and mentor challenged me when I felt I wasn't making much progress in my thinking about work. When I explained to him how I felt stuck, like I was just running around getting stuff done but not really significantly moving things forward, I thought he'd suggest I was overloaded and needed to drop some activities. That's often people's response. But (thankfully) he rarely follows the norm. He advised me to decide on one thing I want to move forward and then park it in the back of my brain while I'm doing other stuff—when I'm dropping my kids off at school, shopping, out with friends, traveling. He said to just have one thing I'm *not* thinking about that gets a special parking space in the back of my mind. Sure enough, once I followed his advice, I made some major breakthroughs, and once again felt I was adding significant value above and beyond the daily "stuff."

Your Personal Thought Leadership Window

We need to think strategically (or strategically *not* think, so to speak) through the busyness. But we also need time to step away from the busyness and think in a more focused way—regularly. This might sound great but in reality it's hard to step away from the to-do list, whether it's written neatly in one place or a flurry of thoughts churning around in our head. It's hard to stand still, even if we know that we should. Israeli researchers conducted a study of 286 soccer penalty kicks in top leagues and championships worldwide.[11] The results, published in the *Journal of Economic Psychology*, suggest that given the probability distribution of kick direction, the optimal strategy for goalkeepers is to stay in the goal's center. The researchers noted, however, that goalkeepers almost always jump right or left, highlighting that the goalie will feel worse if the other team scores after inaction (staying in the center) than if the other team scores after action (jumping). They argue that this action/omission bias has implications far beyond soccer. It's not only on the field that jumping is the norm. We need to fight our learned professional habits of constantly moving and sometimes just *be still*. This is another form of headspace we need to proactively build in to be able to give our best.

An activity I advocate to all clients involves scheduling a regular personal "thought leadership window." First, you commit to spending at least one and a half to two hours at the start of the month on personal strategic thinking—a window of time for you to just think. Then, at the start of each week through the rest of the month, you put aside forty-five minutes to an hour. These windows are time to think about your larger goals (your personal career goals and/or your goals for the area of business you're responsible for) and how they're progressing; to reevaluate your strategy for achieving them and what you currently spend most of your time on, and reprioritize if necessary, shifting or refocusing the direction of where and how you spend your energy. It's different from thinking about what tasks you need to get done on a daily basis. It's time for thinking strategically about the areas you are responsible for and the people you have the opportunity to influence. This sounds like professional common sense. It sounds too easy. But in the quiet confidence shared during thousands of executive coaching hours, less than 5 percent of my clients were doing this before we met. Not all keep it up perfectly, but the majority have adopted this as part of their professional routine and have experienced firsthand the positive difference it makes in their ability to contribute in a noteworthy way when they are with others. People around them have offered unsolicited feedback about the difference they see in them, unaware that they have had any professional coaching or development. They are not just thinking clearly and being more strategic, they know they are better than their former professional self. And with that, they add substantively more value. Some people feel that it's something they would like to do with their team. Strategic thinking time with the team is vital, but as we all play a unique role, it doesn't replace the need for our own personal thought leadership window.

In the movie *What Women Want*, Mel Gibson's and Helen Hunt's characters pitch a Nike advertisement showing a woman running. When brainstorming the idea, Darcy Maguire (Hunt) imagines this woman's experience: *"She's running, it's early, it's quiet, just the sound of her feet on the asphalt . . . She likes to run alone; no pressure, no stress. This is the one place she can be herself . . . She can think any way she wants. No game playing; no rules."* As a working mom of three busy little kids, I can certainly relate. When I'm running, I often turn the first corner, exhale, smile, and think, *It's just me and the road*, and off I go. But that's only once I'm back in the habit. Over the years, I've often gotten out of the habit of running. And when I start up again, I'm certainly not smiling. If I'm honest, I'm just thinking, *Keep going, don't die; keep going, don't die . . .* I hate running when I first start again after some time away from it. But if I can just get through the first few weeks of making it a priority, in a fairly short time I love it. I'm able to run a distance I'm happy with and enjoy it. Not to mention that it's the one window in my day when nobody is asking anything of me. I'm in love again with my running window and annoyed if I can't have it. It's just me and the road.

Creating a personal thought leadership window habit is like starting to run again. At first it can seem impossible and a pain. There is so much to get done; work is already busy enough—carving out peaceful, personal time just to think seems like a luxury you don't have time for. But actually, it's a necessity you can't afford not to have. So if you can see the potential benefit, choose it and put it in your calendar (not ten minutes here and there, but substantial time at least once a month).

Carving out this time for thinking offers you a regular window to check in and, if necessary, realign yourself with your goals for how you show up. To be intentional, reflect on what kind of professional or leader you want to be, and assess if your intention is aligning with your impact. Of course, we can consider this at any time, but it's difficult to remember to do it in the busyness of daily working life. Top of your agenda for this meeting with yourself can be checking if you're showing up in the way that you wanted to. The ideal is to have a substantial monthly window, as well as the shorter weekly one, but even if you can't make this work as regularly as you'd like, it's always worthwhile. And just like Nick Marshall (Gibson) notes, *"You can call on the road whenever you feel like it. Whether it's been a day, or even a couple of hours since your last date, the only thing the road cares about is that you pay it a visit once in a while."*

YOUR GRAVITAS GAME PLAN

Through regular thought leadership windows, we can set ourselves up well to achieve our broader goals, but how do we maintain gravitas through the day-to-day pressures? Let's take a look at how one client, Juan, made choices to increase the value of his contributions through his challenging career on a daily basis.

The Pregame

Juan is a smart, high performer in a corporate real estate team. He feels well equipped to keep up with the demanding role and his busy schedule. In working with leaders across many departments of the global corporation, Juan prides himself on building strong working relationships, meeting deadlines, and setting high expectations for himself. His energy and can-do attitude make him well-regarded by the business's leaders. Yet one thing is holding him back from consistently showing up with authentic gravitas: his pregame. Juan rushes from one meeting to the next. Perhaps overrelying on his ability to connect with the business's leaders, he bursts into internal meetings with a smile, puts the last meeting behind him, and gives his colleagues his full attention. But through coaching conversations, Juan came to realize he wasn't giving his best. While he would prepare extensively for external meetings with clients and suppliers, he failed to give the same consideration to his internal colleagues, even the most senior. He saw internal meetings as more relaxed and informal, which they were, but he recognized this didn't mean they were less important. Juan realized on reflection that his colleagues represented perhaps the most important professional relationships he had.

We introduced a ten-minute pregame into his meeting routine. Juan decided to carve out ten minutes before any planned meeting in the office where an important project or topic would be discussed. He wouldn't use this time to prepare notes or reports (these would already be done). He certainly wouldn't use it to get on top of emails between meetings. He would use it to think about what he thought of the topic at hand. He would shift his mental attention to the upcoming issues and clarify his thinking. This enabled him to go into meetings with a grounded, clear opinion. His colleagues may not agree with his opinion, and he was certainly open to being convinced of alternatives. But from the moment Juan committed to his pregame, he noticed a tangible difference in his ability to contribute ideas and thought leadership to the meeting. He shifted from being just a positive, on-the-spot contributor to someone who added greater value. How he behaved before the meeting shaped his contribution during the meeting.

The Reactive Rule

Good for Juan, you may be thinking. *But how can I keep adding all these windows for myself to just think when I'm already so busy?* First, you must accept how reactive your day is. It's a lovely idea to be completely in charge of your time and to set your own agenda, but even the most senior professionals don't have full control of their time. Often they have the least control because many other people need them. Whether it's face-to-face, on a call, via email or some social platform—clients, customers, stakeholders, and colleagues regularly need us to do things for them. They need us to communicate decisions, to offer input, to deliver. We spend a significant part of our day simply responding to others. If leading with authentic gravitas requires us to create new windows, then in order to fit these windows in, we need to adhere to the Reactive Rule.

Consider your week. What percentage of your day is spent reacting? What percentage is beyond the scope of your own control? I find it typically varies from anywhere between 30 to 80 percent. It's likely to change daily, but try to identify an average to use as a reference point. Then, when thinking about your week or your day, accept that you only have the remaining percentage to plan around. Often we plan 100 percent of our working hours, as if we live in a bubble with complete control of our day. It's easy to unintentionally succumb to this desire to plan all our time. When we max out our day with all the tasks we want to get done and don't make room for unexpected demands on our time, the reactive realities kick in. We finish the day much later than planned, or feel frustrated that we couldn't accomplish what we set out to do. And when we're already feeling behind, it's nearly impossible to make time for "luxuries" like personal, strategic, or pre-meeting thinking time. If, on average, 40 percent of your time is spent reacting to others' requests or demands, then at the start of the day, plan only 60 percent of your work time. You may be in the office for ten hours, say, from eight a.m. to six p.m. Now only plan to achieve six hours' worth of work and leave the rest open. When requests come up, you've made space for them.

But again . . . you've just reduced the number of hours you have in the day! Following the Reactive Rule only helps to create space when you can first get some time up your sleeve.

Our Professional Tendency to Move the Goalposts In

Juan and I not only introduced Pregame Thinking Time and the Reactive Rule into his workday, but also looked at the way he was responding to requests. "Yes, sure, I can get that to you by Thursday," was his instinctive response if Thursday was the very fastest he could envision achieving the request. This was true for his interactions not only with his managers, but also with clients, suppliers, and people who reported to him. In our fast-paced professional life, we feel pressured to give our best as quickly as we possibly can. It's probably something that we learned relatively early in our careers as a way to differentiate ourselves from our peers and fast-track our success. And then this habit remains unchecked as we progress, so we retain a natural professional tendency to move the goalposts in. But in doing so, we can create deadlines for ourselves that are earlier than required. Often we declare we will deliver sooner than the other person needs us to. And so our new timeline, which may have pleasantly surprised our counterpart, is set as the new goalpost.

Recently, I was on a call with an American friend and colleague in my field. We were discussing a new venture together. When I suggested it would be useful for me to see a list of his goals for the project, he quickly offered to have something to me by the end of the week. But knowing how much he has going on, and that we were only looking to have a plan in place by the time he visits London in a few months, I pushed back. "Darryl," I replied, "any time in the next six weeks is fine.

It will help me to prepare for our meeting in London when you're here. But I don't need it before then. I know you've got a lot going on."

"Yes, of course"—I could hear his smile over the phone—"that's great." It's easy to just say, "Okay, thanks," to offered time frames, regardless of whether I need them that quickly or not. I've had to learn to push back when people are trying to get things to me quickly if I don't need them quickly.

For Juan, he now suggests wider goalposts when he receives requests. His natural instinct may be to say, "Yes, in three days?" He now pushes it to "Yes, in four (or five) days—is that okay?" If his first thought is, "Sure, in three weeks," then he now offers, "Sure, in four (or five) weeks—does that work for you?" Be confident that people *will* tell you if they need it sooner! But Juan finds nine times out of ten, his counterpart says, "Yes, great, thanks." He has gained days and sometimes weeks by not giving in to his learned professional tendency to offer to deliver as soon as physically possible. And in doing so, he is now able to be realistic about reactive time, and to build in pregame thinking and thought leadership windows. And when the answer is, "Actually, I really need it sooner (e.g., tomorrow, or next week)," Juan is able to confidently say yes and deliver, because he's built more time into his schedule overall. Always make sure the goalpost you suggest works for the other person. With these habits in place, you have more flexibility to deliver quickly when it's needed. This is particularly important in matrix organizations, where you have multiple people from various areas of the business asking things of you, or where you manage multiple client/customer accounts simultaneously.

In moving the goalposts out when possible and appropriate, Juan is able to live within the reality of the Reactive Rule and have meaningful pregame times. This enables him to not only get clarity around his thinking and goals regarding the issue at hand, but also means he can build in space for free-flow thinking and personal thought leadership windows. The goal is not to reduce the amount Juan gets done in a day, but rather to position him to give strategic, high quality contributions on a long-term, sustainable basis. This means creating space for him to be broadly curious—questioning and brainstorming novel ways to approach the complex realities around him.

CURIOSITY THROUGH THE BUSYNESS

Part of building authentic gravitas is a commitment to *choosing* curiosity, an interest in continually learning and understanding. People who do this effectively and sustainably make this happen not outside of but rather *through* the busyness, with simple habits to ensure they keep growing despite the continual immediate pressures. Arrogance is based on a belief (whether we're aware of that belief or not) that we know "enough"—even thinking more highly of our current knowledge and abilities than the *potential* of activities we're engaged in.

Researchers from Boston College, Georgia Institute of Technology, and Arizona State University looked at the role of curiosity in how well people adapted in a new organization.[12] They note the importance of understanding this "newcomer experience"; many of us will have multiple new roles and join new organizations throughout our careers. I would also argue that we can regularly experience being a newcomer each time we build a new key client, customer, or stakeholder relationship and look to understand and fit into their ways of working, as well as when we move to a new team within the same organization. How do we have authentic gravitas when we're in a new role or environment? Choosing curiosity is key.

In the study, the researchers found that *broad* curiosity (wider interest, not just wanting to have specific pieces of data or job-related questions answered) was related to positive framing (when people try to change how they understand a situation, intentionally choosing a positive lens for the way in which they see it). People with a desire to explore and look for a diverse array of data (this broad curiosity) were more likely to try to change their understanding of a new situation. That, in turn, was positively associated with "taking charge" (when an individual ventures to change the status quo where, for example, procedures or policies are inefficient). This is as an extra-role behavior—meaning it's not dependent on hierarchy or position. People who lead the room, making improvements and adding value, are curious. The researchers note that this "taking charge" behavior is an especially important part of the newcomer experience because newcomers can innovate as they come to understand the organization. Newcomers are able to offer a fresh perspective and aren't as entrenched in the established ways of doing things. Are we able to lead positively, adding significant value, regardless of position, even when we're new? Yes. To do so, we can't afford to underestimate the importance of choosing a curious mind-set, and we can't allow ourselves to be too busy to act on our curiosity.

Being curious isn't just reflected in asking questions and exploring ideas in a meeting. It's also seen in our attitude to, and action toward, continuous learning. On a regular basis, are we hungry for, and equipping ourselves with, the right kind of brain food?

When Nobody Is Watching

In his bestselling book *The 7 Habits of Highly Effective People*, Stephen Covey directs us to a simple yet powerful framework for thinking about ways we can spend our time on a 2x2 matrix.[13] He encourages us to differentiate between what is urgent and important, what is urgent and not important, what is not urgent and important, and what is not urgent and not important. Of course, we naturally attend to what is both urgent and important. But after that, we typically fall into attending to what is urgent but not necessarily important. And often the career-defining and professionally differentiating activities are *not* urgent. Taking a course, writing in an industry magazine, keeping up to date with developments in the field, and starting a new initiative are just some examples of activities that in the medium- to long-term could significantly impact your credibility and your ability to contribute, to lead the room, and to lead in your organization and in your field. Usually, these are the things that nobody else is asking you to do or checking on.

People who have authentic gravitas lead themselves and prioritize such things that are not urgent. It's difficult when there's so much to do that *is* urgent, regardless of its importance. Look to create meaningful windows in your schedule to make progress in those (most likely niggling) things that are not urgent but could be important for your professional development. At the top of the list of important but not urgent tasks is what we are reading and who we are listening to. In the confidence of the coaching room, clients often disclose the reality of their busy schedules and one consistent challenge: staying on top of industry developments and learning new skills when nobody is watching.

LIFE AS A COMMUTER: PROSPECTION, REFLECTION, AND BRAIN FOOD

In a coaching session with Emma, a recently appointed junior partner at a London firm, she revealed to me that her goal was to become a senior partner within the next four to five years. With less than 20 percent of the junior partners ever making the transition to senior partner, I knew this was an ambitious goal and time frame. She had asked to see me because she felt she needed more gravitas. "How's your thinking life?" I asked. Emma was surprised, having come in with the expectation that we would be talking about tips and tricks for (surface) gravitas. "Not great," she replied. "I feel like I spend all my time in meetings or reading." "What are you reading?" I was interested to know. Emma looked down. "Well, emails mostly," she answered, quickly rolling her eyes. "I'm reading emails. Oh, and client reports . . . that either I or other people have written." And after a long pause, "I'm way too busy in my day-to-day. I never have time to think about anything else other than what I have to get done and the meetings I'm in. And at the end of the day and on weekends, I'm exhausted and trying to keep a semblance of a social life."

I asked Emma what she felt she should be reading. She aspired to regularly read the news, various industry magazines, commentaries on wider business and societal issues, and leadership and professional development books. The reality is that most of us know what would be great "brain food" for us, but can't seem to find time to build it in to our daily life. When I asked Emma to give me the names of three to five people in her firm whom she considered to have gravitas, she readily offered a few. "Do you think they're reading some or all of those things fairly regularly?" "Yes, I'm sure they do," she conceded. "And are you busier than them?" I said with a friendly grimace, both of us knowing what the answer would be. "No, no. Okay, let's do this."

Emma made a decision to leave home just fifteen minutes earlier each day, giving her time to get coffee on the way to the train station and briefly sit and read the newspaper. She felt this was enough time to skim the front pages and take a deep dive into one or two articles in the business pages that were particularly relevant for not just her own work, but the wider work of her firm. She had to be disciplined to not just use this extra time for her usual work—fifteen minutes' more work would be wonderful. She continually felt she needed all the time she could get! But Emma could see the value of setting aside time to read the news and was disciplined about doing this each morning before work. Of course, on the odd day, Emma wouldn't be able to get up fifteen minutes earlier, or she'd have to go in to work sooner, but this was the exception, not the rule.

Then we looked at her actual commute. She was on the train for half an hour heading into London each morning, then switched to the subway ("the Tube"), where she would spend another fifteen minutes before reaching her offices. She also had the reverse forty-five-minute journey on the way home. Usually during her commute, Emma would be on email, responding to the multiple requests that had come in since she'd last checked, or flicking through social media. Occasionally she would read a novel, which she found relaxing. What was the best way she could use these 7.5 hours per week?

Interesting studies in the UK and US, discussed in a Harvard Business School working paper, looked at the effects of lengthy commutes and the different ways people use their time.[14] The authors note that globally, the average commute is thirty-eight minutes, and that with longer commute times, there can be negative effects on employees' well-being and greater levels of stress, linked to decreased job satisfaction and increased emotional exhaustion. Looking at the commute to work, they found that engaging in future-oriented "work-related prospection" (the tendency to *think about the work day ahead and make plans about work tasks and goals*) positively influences job satisfaction. They found that people who were higher in "trait self-control" (the ability to alter or override dominant response tendencies and regulate their behavior, thoughts, and emotions to consistently stay on track with their goals) were less likely to experience the negative effects of lengthy commutes because they engaged in this work-related prospection. Importantly, the researchers noted that although some people with higher levels of trait self-control might be more predisposed to use their commute this way, others may be able to learn to engage in this type of thought during their commute and reap its benefits. *As* commuters, we get to choose how we use our commute time, and being intentional and disciplined will make a difference. The research suggests that thinking about our working day ahead and making plans and goals is a beneficial way to spend this time. How we get to work influences how we show up at work.

So what does this mean for Emma? She decided she would use her commuting time in two ways. First, she would read industry-relevant magazines that would energize and inform her thinking. Then, for the remainder of her journey, she would focus on the day ahead—planning not just what she had to get done, but also reflecting on her wider goals and those of her team. She would think about the meetings she had planned for the day, who she would encounter, and how she wanted to show up. She could do that whether she managed to get a coveted seat on the train so she could open her notebook, or if she was standing. In the latter case, as soon as she arrived at work, she'd quickly jot down some bullet points to capture her thoughts. On occasion, Emma had to drive to another office about an hour and a half away. On these days, she would engage in prospection while eating breakfast, thinking about the day ahead and her wider goals, and would use the car time well by listening to audiobooks on professional development that she had on her list.

And That's a Wrap: Ending as You Mean to Go On

What about at the end of Emma's day? Researchers from HEC Paris, Harvard University, and the University of North Carolina conducted studies looking at the role of reflection in learning.[15] Their research suggests that once a person has acquired a certain amount of experience with a task, the benefit of getting more experience is less than the benefit of reflection—deliberately articulating and codifying (organizing into categories) their experience accumulated in the past. And the effects aren't a one-off, but appear to endure over time. Individuals who spent fifteen minutes at the end of the day reflecting on lessons learned performed 23 percent better after ten days than those who didn't reflect. Looking at this "deliberate learning" (as opposed to "experiential learning"), the researchers questioned whether this reflection that fuels learning is common wisdom or if it's contrary to most people's intuition. When given the choice between deliberate and experiential learning, the overwhelming majority chose to gain more experience rather than use the time for reflection, expecting it would enable them to perform better in the future. Except it didn't. Participants scored higher in the following round of the experiment when they decided to reflect upon the experiences they'd already had, instead of collecting more experience.

Emma decided that she would make an effort to finish work earlier and build in reflection time, instead of working as late as possible and then being too tired to think about anything. Rather than succumb to the call of social media on her commute home, Emma would use the time to reflect on the day gone by. She would then consciously switch from work-related thinking to reading more broadly on general business, economic, and social issues. On Fridays, if she'd been disciplined throughout the week you'd find Emma on the way home still reading, except it would be *Vogue* or *Grazia*! It's like the diet where one day a week you get to eat whatever you want, so long as you've eaten healthily the rest of the week.

I asked Emma to think about the difference between what she'd be like as a professional in four or five years if she built these simple practices into her life, compared to if she didn't. Her look said it all. Emma believed these practices would significantly increase her ability to contribute powerful insights. And we hadn't even begun to look at the time she actually spent at work. Work-related prospection, reflection, and "brain food" are not urgent needs, and rarely is anyone asking you to do them, but they are important. Emma was surprised to learn that the seemingly intangible, inaccessible quality of gravitas could be strengthened by being intentional and disciplined in just a few small, practical ways.

INSPIRING GREATNESS: LESSONS FROM THE BASEBALL HALL OF FAME

By committing to growing continuously, we are better positioned to lead the room—to be an *agent* of influence. However, we are even better positioned to lead the room when we are also committed to being a *target* of influence. To do this requires being intentional, courageous, and disciplined.

Research looking at inductees into the Baseball Hall of Fame, published in the *Academy of Management Journal*, highlights the importance of being a target of influence. Induction into the Hall of Fame is the highest honor an MLB player can receive. The researchers looked specifically at first-ballot inductees (those athletes selected in their first year of eligibility). They wanted to know who contributed to these inductees' success and how. The research team examined induction speeches to identify which developers (communities through which people draw their career support) and what kind of support mattered most to career achievement.[16]

This study is interesting in our discussion of authentic gravitas because the researchers defined extraordinary achievement as career-spanning (not just one-off but lasting) excellence, built on objective performance, *and* consensually conferred (recognized by others in the same industry and profession), showcasing an individual's *meaningful contribution* to the field.

The researchers found that those with the highest levels of extraordinary career achievement recognized a *broader range* of developers across and within career communities. They found that these players didn't just have greater career support, but that it was complementary (the support they received from one person would complement the support they received from another). The researchers also found that the players received psychosocial support that went far beyond skills development. The highest achievers had developers from numerous "core" communities: professional (peers, managers, and coaches), family and friends, and, interestingly, a virtual community. The athletes with extraordinary career success didn't have direct access to everyone—they engaged indirectly with virtual developers: heroes or idols whose support was unidirectional (developer to protégé) and was gained by watching them on television or hearing them speak. We must go beyond the norm of our direct managers and peers—because people don't need to be in our game to change our game.

From the findings, the researchers propose that the more exposure one can get to developmental relationships with people from a wide range of communities, including complementary and psychosocial support, the greater the level of extraordinary career achievement.

It's up to us to be intentional about whom we want to influence us, not just whom we want to influence. Who impacts your development now? Who would complement that development? We need to go beyond learning from the people immediately around us and intentionally expand our networks, inviting a broader, more diverse group of people to offer input on our professional lives—the way we work, the way we interact, the way we grow. We need courage to ask people to mentor us, and we need discipline to seek out and make time to engage virtually with those whom we can't access directly. Our developmental networks need to be broad—to be both in, and to go far beyond, our immediate teams and organizations.

The people who add significant value in their field are committed to not only being an *agent* of influence, but also a *target* of (considered and intentional) influence in and beyond their field.

On Being Wise

> By three methods we may learn wisdom: First, by reflection, which is
> noblest; second, by imitation, which is easiest; and third, by experience,
> which is the bitterest.
>
> —Confucius

While being a target of influence can be difficult in practice because it
requires taking time out of our schedule, finding the right influencers,
and broadening our network, it is far from a new concept. Aristotle ad-
vocated a long-term affiliation with a mentor who was known to have
exemplary character and to exhibit good judgment and action. A potential benefit of this mentorship could be an increase in practical wisdom.
He argued that only individuals with good character could acquire excellence in practical wisdom, but that both good character and practical
wisdom *could* be trained.[17]

Why does this matter in our context? One of the common themes
emerging from the research on authentic gravitas is wisdom. Example
reports of people described by others as having a high degree of gravitas
include, "I really admire how wise she is," and "He seems to have wisdom
beyond his years." So if wisdom is a key component of gravitas, a noteworthy question is, how can we develop wisdom? While some consider
wisdom to be a fairly stable individual trait, there is evidence that it can
be developed.

Traditionally discussed in the realms of philosophy and religion, wisdom is increasingly becoming a topic of interest in management and professional development circles. Some researchers broadly define wisdom as
the flexible and appropriate application of pragmatic reasoning to the
challenges of social life.[18] This would include the challenges within the
social context of our professional lives. Much of the research into wisdom
has used the Berlin Wisdom Model, characterizing wisdom in terms of
competence—a system of expert knowledge regarding fundamental life
domains.[19] An alternative approach looks at three characteristics of wisdom: cognitive, reflective, and affective.[20] One executive described people

with high levels of gravitas as demonstrating wisdom by creating genuine connection with other people, showing a strong understanding of the interpersonal. The *cognitive* dimension of wisdom goes beyond just acquiring facts, to being motivated to attain a deep understanding of life (particularly intrapersonal and interpersonal matters) and human nature (including awareness of our inherent limitations, such as the fallibility of human knowledge and the unpredictability of life circumstances).

The *reflective* dimension of wisdom refers to the willingness and ability to invest in self-examination and to look at things from various perspectives. So what matters is not just whether we have the skills to engage in reflection (which we can acquire), but whether we're prepared to do the work. A Dutch study of over seven thousand people examined the relationship between wisdom and happiness and found a moderate positive relationship between the two (regardless of sex and age). The researchers noted that reflectivity tends to reduce self-centeredness, which in turn leads to a deeper understanding of one's own motives and behavior and others'. This, they note, is likely to result in greater sympathetic and compassionate love for others.[21] This takes us on to the affective dimension.

The *affective* dimension of wisdom is concerned with acceptance of, and sympathy for, others, together with a compassionate motivation toward helping and general positivity. A German study of over three hundred people found that wisdom-related knowledge is positively associated not only with valuing personal growth and life insight, but also prioritizing the *well-being of others*.[22] This others-focused component of wisdom relates not only to the people immediately around us, but also to wider society. Ikujiro Nonaka, professor emeritus at Hitotsubashi University in Japan, and Hirotaka Takeuchi at Harvard Business School appeal for leaders who consider what is good, right, and just for society, arguing that wise leaders practice moral discernment about what's good and act on it in every situation.[23]

Being wise is about far more than what we know and how we reason. In a review of the neurobiology of wisdom, researchers at the University of California, San Diego, identify that there is partial overlap in the brain regions linked to the subcomponents of wisdom, and discuss several important characteristics that differentiate wisdom from intelligence and reasoning. They note that wisdom includes domains such as the practical application of knowledge, the use of knowledge for the common social good, and integration of affect and knowledge.[24]

Interestingly, wisdom is often defined in terms of a *motivation*—being motivated to acquire a deep understanding, to reflect, and to give consideration and have concern for others and the wider social good.[25] So perhaps more important than asking ourselves if we have these abilities and behaviors is the question of whether we want them. Whether we're choosing to pursue them. It's about what we're interested in knowing, and how we go about building and making sense of that knowledge through exploration and reflection—mindful of our own limitations and the uncertainties and reality of change, and intentional with having a positive impact on those around us at an individual and wider societal level.

Wisdom *can* be developed. In addition to being a target of influence, taking into account changing contexts, and seeking to have a positive impact on others, here are a few complementary suggestions that studies indicate may be practical ways to develop wisdom:

1. **Practice mind-stretching routines.** Nonaka and Takeuchi recommend that to cultivate the ability to grasp the true essence of a problem, people should engage in three routines that anyone, regardless of their organizational position, can do.[26] The three routines are relentlessly asking what the basis of a problem or situation is; learning to see the trees and the forest at the same time; and continually constructing and testing hypotheses. They offer the example of employees of 7-Eleven stores across Japan personally making decisions on what to order by generating hypotheses about what customers will want, based on the current environment and changing factors in their particular context. Although many of us feel that we regularly generate ideas about why things happen, choosing to construct hypotheses and test them may be a next level of discipline that stretches us and leads to increased practical wisdom.

2. Choose intellectual humility. Researchers at the University of Waterloo in Canada found that people endorse wise reasoning strategies as more useful for resolving other people's social conflicts than for resolving their own. [27] This is Solomon's Paradox: we can be "wiser" when reflecting on other people's problems than our own. Conflicts that are personal to us can stand in the way of our employing wise reasoning, as we're likely to be immersed in our own perspectives and emotions. We might think, *I rarely have conflict.* Conflict, however, can be defined merely as a situation where our wishes differ from the wishes of others—a frequent reality in organizational life where even internally, we often have competing priorities within the broader collective goals. Various researchers discuss the value of intellectual humility—that is, recognizing the limits of our own knowledge, or realizing that our perspective alone may be insufficient to understand our social conflict. Rather than posturing as the one who has all the answers and is objective regardless of the situation (because let's face it, we often think we're being objective and others are being subjective), it seems that when it comes to wisdom, a little humility can go a long way.

3. Develop wise habits. Given what we know of wisdom, rather than seeing it as fixed, we should regard it as fluid, as something we can influence. In different circumstances, we may demonstrate more wisdom or less. While there is some evidence that the dimensions of wisdom are linked to traits that are dispositional and fairly stable over time, the reality that it can be developed means we can influence the extent to which we engage in behaviors associated with wisdom. It may be the case that we need to intentionally introduce the discipline to follow through on what we know of practical wisdom. For example, in a meeting, rather than rushing through the agenda, we can ensure we are engaging in three practices when it comes to issues of importance: seeking a deep understanding—not only of the facts and options, but also being mindful of uncertainty, change, and the interpersonal dynamics contributing to that situation; being self-reflective, considering our own role and influence in the situation; and considering the impact of various options on the well-being of others, and figuring out what is positive, right, and just for those in our wider sphere of influence.

By intentionally choosing these behaviors, having the courage to try out new ways of working and interacting, and committing to the discipline not only of adopting new behaviors but seeking feedback to check if our intention is aligned with our impact, we may increase the extent to which we demonstrate wisdom. It's one thing to be consistent with the new behaviors (be they simple or significant alterations to the way we act) when things are going well and as expected. But what happens when things are stressful or difficult? Research suggests a relationship between wisdom and coping. In one study, conducted over an eleven-year period with 615 participants who had been in military service, researchers looked at whether combat exposure and the perception of benefits from military service were associated with greater wisdom later in life.[28] They found that age was not related to wisdom, nor was it directly predicted by experiencing the extreme stress of combat exposure. Wisdom was predicted, however, by the way in which people looked back on those experiences. The researchers argued that how one interprets experience may be more important for positive experience later in life than the experience of trauma. The ways in which the respondents coped with adversity and developed a broader perspective (their perception of the effects of combat exposure) were positively related to transcendent wisdom. It is not necessarily what happens to us, but how we face, cope with, and reflect on challenges that makes the difference when it comes to growing in wisdom.

Just as wisdom has been positively associated with coping under stress, my research findings suggest that just how authentic our gravitas really is can be seen in the moments and seasons when things are hard. Whether it's intrapersonal or interpersonal stress (at work or elsewhere); challenges with our team, organization, clients, or suppliers; disappointing outcomes or a difficult period in the market in general—how we behave in these moments is likely to shape the extent to which others consider us to have truly authentic gravitas. What matters is not just how we show up when things are going well; how we learn to show up as we intend to, demonstrating authentic gravitas in the midst of adversity, is perhaps of even greater significance. We look at this next in chapter 6.

PRACTICES FOR SELF-LEADERSHIP

The key to effective self-leadership is regularly self-assessing and making tweaks to behavior along the way. We never "arrive" at self-leading. We can slip out of good habits and back into unintentional ones. The following points are offered as a quick checklist that you might want to look at once a quarter.

- Remember that in order to lead the room effectively, you must commit to leading yourself.

- Check if you're caught in any Routines of Exceptions ("I can't today because . . . ," which becomes a daily excuse). Hold yourself accountable if you find yourself making excuses, and be realistic about what you can achieve and intentional about following through on goals that are important to you.

- Build in and maintain your Personal Thought Leadership Window.

- Check your pregame. Are you rushing between meetings without building in even a little time to think before each important encounter? Are you following the Reactive Rule and planning only the percentage of time you actually have control over in a day, or are you filling up 100 percent of your schedule as if others won't make demands on your time? Push the goalposts out—if people need your input sooner, they'll ask; free up time to move quickly on priority items.

- Choose to be curious. We're wired for curiosity, but sometimes we overlook it in the busyness of each day. Create meaningful windows in your schedule for things that are not urgent but are important to you. Stay on top of your industry developments and keep learning—even when nobody is watching.

- How's your commute? Are you using it in the best way possible with prospection (thinking about your workday ahead and making plans about tasks and goals)—or is it often spent on social media and getting a head start on emails? On the way home, remember that reflection has an impact on performance beyond just getting more done. Spend just fifteen minutes at the end of the day to articulate and assess your experiences and learning that day.

- Join your own industry's equivalent of the Baseball Hall of Fame by intentionally becoming both an agent *and* target of influence. Actively keep building a broad, diverse network of people you choose to influence you professionally.

- Choose wisdom! Beyond self-reflection, wisdom is linked to consideration of others' well-being, looking for a deeper understanding of the situations and contexts we're in, and choosing intellectual humility—recognizing our need for others' input, particularly when it comes to our own challenges.

SIX

GRAVITAS IN THE DARK

Taking On Your Gremlins

A coaching client described to me how he felt he had "lost his swagger." He certainly didn't mean he used to come across as arrogant or self-important, but he felt he had lost confidence—he felt "knocked down." Not only had this impacted how he felt, but how he interacted at work and, to some degree, literally how he walked. Jackson was the COO of a start-up in California, and having played a major and challenging role in getting the business to an established, successful place, he was now feeling gradually pushed away by the CEO. He was feeling silently and increasingly rejected. Research using fMRI studies demonstrates that not only does social rejection activate the same parts of the brain as physical pain, but suggests that rejection may even lead to various physical pain disorders.[1] For Jackson, his metaphorically slumped shoulders were starting to take their toll and manifest in actual behavior. He was beginning to question himself, his skills, and his ability to take the business forward, and it wasn't just painful for him—many who knew him well could see a physical change. Jackson, despite his self-described naturally optimistic nature, felt deflated and defeated. He wanted to "get his swagger back."

What to Do About Negative Self-Talk

We've seen the power and importance of self-leadership for authentic gravitas. Researchers have argued that at the core of how individuals lead themselves is their internal dialogue (self-talk).[2] In order to build gravitas, we spend much time considering what we say to others. What also matters is what we say to ourselves. What Jackson needed to do first was address his inner dialogue.

Inner speech has been noted as a critical part of being human.[3] We all have self-talk. The questions to ask are, *What am I saying to myself?* and *What impact is it having?* Most theorists and researchers use dichotomies to categorize self-talk: as constructive (positive) or destructive (negative), or as instructional or motivational. Constructive self-talk is considered to be thoughtful, substantive, motivational, insightful, and self-reflective.[4] Does positive self-talk help us in the moment? Extensive research has shown a positive effect on performance.[5] Does it help us in the long run? Constructive self-talk has been found to be associated with reduced job strain and an increased ability to lead others.[6]

My coaching clients repeatedly disclose that they feel negative self-talk is one of their primary barriers to having greater gravitas. One client, Catherine, said, "It's like there's a little gremlin sitting on my shoulder, saying to me, *You can't; you're not enough. Who do you think you are?* The gremlin whispers at the most annoying times, usually the exact moments when it's important for me to have gravitas, and it pulls the rug out from under me." She was frustrated with her "gremlin" and wanted to know how to "push it off my shoulder for good!"

Destructive self-talk is a tendency to focus on the negative aspects of a challenging situation and to continue thinking about it long after the situation is over. Researchers argue that this type of self-talk does not embrace change or challenge; rather, it shies away and focuses on the obstacles.[7]

If we find that we, at times (possibly more often than we'd like), feel and act as victims of our own negative self-talk, are we able to change it? Yes. Researchers found that when leaders were trained in effective self-leadership and self-talk, they experienced better mental performance, job satisfaction, positive affect, and reduced nervousness.[8] If they could change their self-talk to make it more constructive, so can we.

Here are five practical ways to deal with that annoying, negative self-talk.

1. Take away the gremlin's power. While constructive self-talk has a positive impact on performance, the majority of research suggests that negative self-talk does not impede, impair, or lessen performance. In a study of 189 senior executives in a program designed for professionals with fifteen or more years of management experience and leadership responsibilities for five hundred or more people, researchers found that destructive self-talk was only related to one outcome (decreased leader creativity). It was unrelated to job strain or leadership of others. The extent to which these leaders reported destructive self-talk was not associated with their ability as a leader or how they experienced the job.[9] In a sports context, researchers found negative self-talk was not associated with impaired performance.[10] Other researchers conducting a wide review of the literature found that negative self-talk is not associated with reduced performance.[11] Take the rug out from under the gremlin. When you hear the negative self-talk starting, remember that while it is no doubt annoying and upsetting (it feels bad), it's not going to reduce your actual ability to give and perform at your best. It has less power than you think it does.

2. Talk back to the gremlin. You know it's coming. Many coaching clients disclose that it's rarely a surprise when their negative self-talk pipes up. They expect it, and that's part of the pain—they're disappointed in themselves for having this negative self-talk. Because, let's face it, we look around and can't really see anyone else struggling with it. Other than the few close friends or colleagues who may confess that they also experience negative self-talk, everyone else's shoulders look free of gremlins. And this can be a vicious circle—feeling bad about yourself for having negative self-talk fuels the gremlin. So we try to shut it down or ignore it. Susan David, psychologist at Harvard Medical School, and Christina Congleton, who researches stress and the brain at the University of Denver, note that much research shows that attempts to minimize or ignore thoughts and emotions serve only to amplify them. They argue for what they call "emotional agility," which requires recognizing the patterns, labeling your thoughts and emotions, accepting them, and acting on your values (that is, resolving to be guided by your principles).[12] When it comes to your gremlin, decide in advance, ideally in a non–emotionally charged environment where you don't feel the pressure to "perform" (like your thought leadership window), what you believe to be true *about yourself.* Construct clear sentences that you would throw back to the gremlin so you don't have the experience of thinking of a great comeback only after it's too late to use it. In this case, you know the encounter with the gremlin is coming, so you can be prepared with your great comeback line. And it helps that you know the line happens to be accurate.

3. Acknowledge any truth, and act. Self-leadership can be an answer to negative self-talk. Rarely are the negative internal whispers all accurate, but there may be some aspect of truth fueling them. Examples could be, "I'm not knowledgeable in this area," "I don't have enough experience of this," or "I'm not skilled enough in this." If you can identify any foundations of truth, you can choose to address it. You are not fixed in your knowledge, experience, and skills; you can continue to learn and grow. The groundbreaking work of Stanford University professor Carol Dweck and her colleagues on growth mind-set versus fixed mind-set has highlighted the power on performance and resilience of believing (or being taught) that you are able to develop abilities.[13, 14] You can address those negative whispers if you can honestly say, "I've made a plan, am being proactive, and am gaining more knowledge every week," "I'm actively taking steps to increase my experience," "I'm doing x and y to gain more skills," or simply, "I have the ability to grow in this area. I'm going to start." We can reframe and change negative self-talk to be constructive, knowing the new self-talk is accurate and based on facts (not just a superficial or groundless pep talk). If you're working on the area highlighted in your negative self-talk, you can reduce the power of it.

4. Remember, only mushrooms grow in the dark. Or so my friend Brendan used to tell me. It took me a long time to work out what on earth he was talking about, but eventually I saw the wisdom in his proclamations about fungi. The negative self-talk can become too loud if we're not letting anyone else in on what it's saying. Sense-checking the internal whispers with a trusted friend or adviser is a powerful means of addressing negative self-talk. They will help us explore whether there's any foundation to its claims and give us a different set of ideas for how to move forward. If left unchecked, the gremlin, like the mushroom, can and probably will grow in the dark, stopping us from growing personally and professionally. Proactivity and constructive self-talk are more likely to grow in the open light of conversation with trusted colleagues.

5. Look at others' intentions. As a young doctoral candidate, I had the incredible opportunity to speak with many eminent professors of psychology and organizational behavior. While at Harvard as a Visiting Fellow, I had the privilege of working with the late Professor J. Richard Hackman, who read my work, encouraged me, and constructively challenged me. His input was difficult—it made my work harder—but his intention was to ensure that I offered the very best work possible. Often he would pop into the office I shared with another psychologist, ask some questions, and give me nuggets of valuable advice. After a few minutes, he'd walk away and I would realize two things: I suddenly had a lot more work to do, and the cookies that had been on my desk were now missing! I often compare these encounters with my experience of another professor in a similar position. On the surface, they looked similar, but in truth they were chalk and cheese. While visiting another top-tier university, I met with a professor of leadership. When he asked what I would like to do in the future, I shared a personal aspiration about wanting to be a part of making a significant difference in one major challenge facing our world. I was in my mid-twenties at the time and a PhD candidate, with energy and excitement for what I could be part of. Laughing loudly, he replied, "Sorry, but you're a drop in the ocean" (except he didn't use the word *drop* but rather another four-letter word starting with "p" and ending in "iss"). "Who do you think you are?" I left that office with my shoulders down that day. Thankfully (probably largely due to my parents, who instilled in me the belief that with hard work, I could do anything, as well as my own belief that when working together with a shared purpose, people can make a positive difference in even the most challenging of circumstances), about three minutes into my walk away from his building, I decided, *Who was he to tell me what I—working with others—couldn't do?* He could take his advice and get lost. While Professor Hackman embodied authentic gravitas, the other professor, who shall remain unnamed, demonstrated the toxicity of adverse gravitas. I learned something from both of them. I am a better psychologist today than I would have been without the input of Professor Hackman. And I am a better teacher today than I would have been without my experience with the other professor and my subsequent commitment to never laugh at my students or tell them, with self-importance, what they *can't* do with their futures.

What's important in deciding who we open up to is whether we trust that they have our back—that they have our best interests at heart, will keep our disclosures confidential, and will simultaneously be both honest and constructive. These prerequisites are important because the voices we choose to listen to are likely to shape our own self-talk. When we intentionally seek out these trusted confidantes, we build strength and resilience. We can't stop other people from saying things and we can't stop what we hear, but we can choose whose voices we value.

6. **Count your blessings.** It sounds cheesy, but extensive studies suggest that practicing gratitude has powerful positive effects. This exercise can increase our well-being and resilience to be able to tackle our gremlins. Researchers at the University of California, Davis, and the University of Miami asked participants to engage in exercises to "count their blessings" (weekly for ten weeks or on a daily basis for two to three weeks).[15] During that period, those in the gratitude group reported higher positive affect and physical well-being than those in the control group (who focused on daily hassles, downward social comparisons, or routine life events). Don't let the gremlins keep pointing you to only what you lack.

Take away the gremlin's power and talk back. For Jackson, tackling the growing gremlin on his shoulder was a positive first step. Next we looked at how he could address his growing anxiety, which was creeping regularly into business meetings.

"AN ORGAN HAS BURST": MANAGING NERVES AND ANXIETY

I was a budding young psychologist, on top of the world. At twenty-two, having recently completed my master's in psychology at the LSE, I had temporarily moved back to Australia and taken up my first full-time role in an organizational psychology consultancy. I was excited to wear suits, commute into town, and have a cubicle (now my favorite days are the ones when I can work in jeans, avoid rush hour, and work wherever I like!). I was pretty much excited all the time. I had a job in my field; I had "made it." One of my first projects was to co-create a program that assisted managers in designing good interview questions. Rejoicing that I was valuable enough to be paid to travel, I jumped when asked to go to Melbourne with a senior consultant to present the product to a new client. Lauren would do the general business part of the talk, and I would talk through how the product worked in practice. Simple enough. Once at the client meeting, Lauren presented her part and I remained outside the room for a couple of minutes to organize a few last items. Walking back, I looked down the corridor from reception. I saw Lauren standing there, presenting, with about thirty people staring at her intently. It was at this point that I realized I didn't feel very well. Sitting down on the couch in reception, I quickly came to terms with the fact that something serious was happening to me. The receptionist asked, "Are you okay, honey?" probably surprised to find a young woman lying on their couch with her shoes off and feet on their reception coffee table! I replied (honestly, word-for-word truth), "An organ has burst! Call an ambulance! Here's my mother's phone number in case I die . . ." Before even stepping foot in the room, I was taken away from my first big client meeting in an ambulance and admitted to the hospital. In the ambulance, I asked the paramedic, "Which organ is it?" so certain I was that one had spontaneously combusted. She looked at me somewhat perplexed. "You hyperventilated. It's what happens to teenagers all the time when they get too excited." Complete humiliation. *But I'm a grown-up consultant*, I sadly thought as I was driven to the hospital. Back in the office days later, my colleagues asked, "Are you okay, Rebecca? I heard you went to the hospital!" "I'm fine. Thanks for asking. It was close," I joked, "but I'm all right."

You have probably heard it reported that many of us rank public speaking as our number one fear, even over death. Comedian Jerry Seinfeld joked, "This means to the average person, if you have to go to a funeral, you're better off in the casket than giving the eulogy!"

Although fear of public speaking largely arises when giving speeches and presentations, we have smaller meetings at work that can be just as, if not more, important and therefore nerve-racking. So even if you are not afraid of public speaking, the challenge is that your nerves can still get the better of you on occasions that are especially important to you, when you want your brain to work at its best. Whether it's an important one-on-one meeting, a presentation to a medium-size group, or a speech to a large crowd, how we handle pressure and nervousness can shape our impact and our gravitas. It is not merely about feeling better in the moment. As we discussed earlier, others subconsciously interpret the nervousness evidenced in our body language as a lack of confidence in our message, and then they wonder why we are nervous and question our arguments. We can send messages that lead the people around us to doubt us before we even get going.

So how can we handle pressure in those significant moments and ensure that our nerves don't undermine our gravitas?

We can start by managing our internal dynamics with simple steps to manage the external environment. One useful strategy I adopt with clients is taking them to the place where they'll be presenting or meeting, particularly if they have not been there before, and doing a run-through. For one executive who was giving a talk to peers and potential clients at an industry conference, we booked the venue room for three hours the day before he was due to speak. He delivered his talk a couple of times, in addition to sitting in various audience seats to get an idea of their view. He ended up winning a huge deal from one audience member and attributed his powerful message to his comfort with the scene and stage. If you cannot physically go, ask the receptionist or organizing team beforehand to describe the room or setting to you in detail, so you will not have any surprises on the day.

Give Your Brain a Break

In terms of our mental management, it is important to know one useful insight about the brain. Neuroscience research suggests we have two distinct forms of self-awareness: narrative focus (where we are engaged in reflections, planning, strategizing, forward thinking, aspirations for the future—anything related to what we're going to say or do next, be it the drive home or goals for the week ahead) and experiential focus (centered on our present experience). We habitually integrate these two—wandering between awareness of ourselves and our senses in the present moment and the narrative around our past reflections and of our future. Findings from a research team led by Norman Farb from the University of Toronto suggest we can learn to dissociate these two forms of self-awareness.[16] Doing so means we're able to truly focus on the immediate experience of the moment and *not* think about the future. This is useful because the type of mental stress we're talking about stems from our narrative: how might this meeting go, what may—or may not—happen as a result of it, what will happen if I mess up, what will people think, etc.

A simple activity I recommend to clients is designed to help them generate a "current experience" moment. It sounds simplistic, but it helps. Even doing this briefly can have a positive effect. Breathe in for four slow counts and then out for six to eight slow counts. However, when you are breathing out, count backward from a random high number—for example, "One, two, three, four" on the breath in; then "237, 236, 235, 234, 233, 232, 231, 230" on the breath out. Repeat this at least five times, or more if you need to. The reality is that when our parents told us we should "take a deep breath" when we were nervous or stressed growing up, they lied! Or at least, they just gave us half the answer. Breathing in too much without a full exhale will cause you to hyperventilate (as I sadly found out the hard way!). Breathing out for six to eight counts from a random high number will mean that not only do you not hyperventilate (always useful), but that you must focus your mental attention on the current moment to count backward and exhale longer than it took to inhale. Just for those few seconds, your brain doesn't switch to forward thinking. The tiny break your brain receives gives you surprisingly great relief. Although your mind comes back to the narrative focus the moment you stop, your body has enjoyed the small respite. This can have the wonderful side effect of subtly and subconsciously sending the message to others through your body language that you are calm, potentially giving them greater confidence in your message. Your brain may be yelling, "I'm nervous, I'm stressed, I can't handle this!" but the goal is to get your body saying, "No, I'm okay, I've got this."[17]

Free and released breathing is a fundamental part of gravitas, according to Charlie Walker-Wise from London's RADA (Royal Academy of Dramatic Arts) Business. In my interview with Walker-Wise, he highlighted the importance of how you manage your body, your breath, and your voice in relation to the time and space you have to speak. He noted that many people are too quick to speak (or occasionally overcompensate by being too slow), and take up too little space physically, as if they are being apologetic (or occasionally overcompensate by taking up too much space). "When I feel comfortable with myself, I'm relieved of excessive and unhelpful tension, and I'm able to manage my self and my environment well," he explained. "The fundamental thing is to breathe effectively. To do this, take some time out to leave the stress of the day, from previous encounters, at the door rather than rushing in and bringing the baggage with you. If you need to slow your pace down, try to take a slow walk around the block. Or if your next meeting requires higher energy, go for a brisk walk. Manage yourself proactively to be in the right state to show up with gravitas for your next encounter." He also noted that deep breaths shouldn't sit in your chest (like a puffed-up Roman or Greek god), but in your belly (picture Buddha). It's at this point that Walker-Wise switched to Latin. "*Inspirare*," he declared, "of which the modern derivation is *inspiration*, means 'to breathe life into' or 'breathe upon.' The connection between a thought or idea and the communication of it is *breath*. Think of a pub quiz: a question is asked and we respond with, 'Ah!' on a big breath in, 'I've got it!' The physical connection between a thought and how we communicate it is so clearly linked in that moment of inspiration, on a breath."

How to Keep Calm and . . .

As I'm writing this, I look over at my tea and smile—the mug I've coincidentally chosen this morning was given to me by a friend and has the phrase *Keep Calm and Carry On* printed on it (he also gave me a second mug that says, *Now Panic and Freak Out!*).[18] Nowadays it's rare to find a gift shop in the UK without a "Keep Calm and . . ." message printed on some kind of merchandise. The message resonates with many around the world, but as I've come to learn after twenty years living as an Australian in the UK, this is a particularly British sentiment. I laugh again as I pause from writing to put on some hand cream from a little "de-stress kit" gift box that has this message printed on it: *Learn to be calm and you will always be happy*.[19] Okay, okay, I get the message. The question is, how do we choose to be calm? One useful approach is reappraising the situation rather than trying to suppress any anxiety.[20]

For those of us who do feel anxiety at times, in some contexts, we might think, *I shouldn't/don't want to feel like this*, and try to squash any feelings of anxiety. But much research suggests that suppressing emotions actually leads—paradoxically—to an increase in the unwanted emotional experience. Researchers at Boston University looked at anxiety levels of students asked to give an impromptu speech, assigned to one of three different conditions: reappraisal (reassess or reframe the situation and realistic likely outcomes), acceptance (embrace your feelings), and suppression (don't let your feelings get in the way).[21] They found that reappraisal was the most effective strategy for reducing the experienced level of anxiety.

Rather than just trying to "make the feelings go away," the research suggests reframing how you think about the situation. Yes, it might be a more "important" presentation than usual, there might be a larger or different audience than you're used to, or it might be an opportunity that rarely comes up to present to your management team, but anticipate the feelings of anxiety (which you might feel even when you're just thinking about or preparing for the presentation) in advance and decide what you rationally believe to be true about the situation. Are you likely to fall on your face? Probably not. Are you prepared? Be prepared, and then you can say, "Yes!" Rather than ignoring the feelings or mentally highlighting the feelings, try to reappraise. For example, "It's normal to feel increased emotions—this is important to me. I've been asked to do this (or have the opportunity to do this) because I'm the right person for it." An interesting approach to reappraisal comes from Alison Wood Brooks of Harvard Business School. She suggests reappraising anxiety as excitement, using simple strategies such as self-talk: *I am excited* or *Get excited*. In the research, this led participants to improve their performance as a result of feeling more excited and adopting an opportunity mind-set rather than a threat mind-set.[22] You're most likely nervous because this situation matters. And it matters because it's an opportunity that could lead to positive outcomes. Wanting to show up well and demonstrate authentic gravitas is a good thing, so "get excited."

These are all skills that can be learned. You are not born a public speaker or not. You are not born as someone who handles significant encounters well or not. You choose to develop and learn the skills. And even when a lack of confidence screams at you to stay in your comfort zone, forget about desiring confidence and instead choose courage. Continue proactively putting yourself in scenarios where you get exposure to different contexts that might terrify you at first. We should regularly be nervous. People who do not get nervous are not stepping out of their comfort zone, which is required for growth. Gravitas is reserved for those who continue to challenge themselves and increase their skill, regardless of whether it feels good in the process.

Let's come back to Jackson, our defeated COO. Once he introduced some practices to manage his anxiety, we looked at his strengths and started to make a plan to proactively drive positive change in his career.

NATURAL FUEL FOR RESILIENT GRAVITAS: YOUR UNIQUE STRENGTHS

Chris, my friend and colleague who specializes in leadership and professional development, and I were debriefing at lunch after running a business simulation with some master's degree students. "Passion," Chris said emphatically. "People with gravitas are passionate. That looks different for different people, but you can see it. Now, someone might be in a role or environment that is not fulfilling and they're not excited about it, and you wouldn't describe them as having gravitas. Then the next week, they might have started a new job and be showing up completely differently, full of passion, and with gravitas." Gravitas is not something that happens in a vacuum: it is influenced by the situation we're in and the people around us. And if, as Chris and many other interviewees believe, passion is a requirement of gravitas, we need to be aware of two things: first, what it is we personally really care about (a key to authenticity); and second, which situations bring out our natural energy. Understanding our own unique strengths is a key part of starting this process.

When we talk about "strengths," we tend to think about what we're skilled at. But strengths are different from skills. Strengths, in this context, are what we're naturally *energized* by (which we also may be good at or likely to become good at because we enjoy these things and naturally spend time on them). There is power in awareness and commitment to fostering strengths—individually and collectively. Strengths experts Tom Rath and Barry Conchie discuss research findings that show that when leaders adopted a deficit focus (focusing on what people need to do differently or improve) in their approach, only 9 percent of staff were engaged, compared to 73 percent of staff when leaders focused on their strengths.[23] Following from Rath and Conchie's findings, researchers from the University of Houston and the University of Richmond found that employees whose managers supported them in using their strengths at work were more likely to show higher levels of performance as well as "positive organizational behaviors"—collaborating with and supporting colleagues.[24]

We have a tendency to see our weaker areas as unique—I'm rubbish at this (personal and specific to me)—but to gloss over our strengths, thinking, *Lots of people are good at this* (collective and widespread). The reality is, our particular combination of strengths is unique. Mathematically, the Strengthscope® model of twenty-four work-based strengths, which highlights for each individual their "seven significant strengths," shows that the likelihood of anyone having the same significant strengths as you is 1 in 346,000![25] It even suggests that if you were to order these by what most resonates with you as your greatest strengths, the likelihood of anyone having the same order as you would be 1 in 1.7 billion! You will never meet anyone with the same exact combination of strengths as you. You are unique. As Paul Brewerton, PhD, managing director of the company that developed the Strengthscope® model, shared with me, "By providing an insight into their strengths, we always encourage leaders to own their uniqueness—their strengths and their vulnerabilities. Wherever you go, whatever challenges you face, *you* are the one constant. When a leader is clear on the strengths that they can bring to each encounter, each challenge, each conversation, this can help build a far deeper level of confidence and resilience because that leader feels more in control of the situation and better equipped to choose their response to it."

For *authentic* gravitas, we want real, natural passion, not forced, false excitement. When it comes to building natural energy, two things are important. The first is identifying our strengths. Think of a time when you were naturally energized recently. It might have been challenging, but you felt an excited "buzz." Start to look across your career and life for times when you felt natural passion and identify patterns. Yes, it will be shaped by the macro—whether you care about the overall goals—but the micro behaviors also matter: what specifically were you doing? We all have numerous natural strengths, but you will be able to find some common themes.

The second is being proactive about building a career in which you have regular opportunities to utilize and grow these strengths. Yes, there are parts of any role that we won't particularly enjoy, but as Chris noted, context matters. If we're in a context where we have the chance to draw on our natural strengths, we will bring more genuine passion, and thereby authentic gravitas, to the table. But there isn't a one-size-fits-all environment for people to flourish. Just as we all have different strengths, the environments that give us natural energy and opportunities to have authentic gravitas are equally diverse. We need to be intentional in seeking out or creating contexts that bring out our natural strengths and, if necessary, have the courage to make a change to our role or environment. There may be significant weaknesses that you know are holding you back from having a positive impact, and certainly it's important to address these issues. But many of us spend a lot of time and energy working on every little weakness in order to have an incrementally greater impact, when we would have a much more significant impact if we focused on developing our unique strengths.

The Power of a Reframe

One of the most powerful things I've seen for building, or getting back, natural energy is applying our strengths to reframe a situation—here are two examples.

Carlette is a deputy director in business development for a consulting firm. When we met, she described how she was shooting herself in the foot. Generating new ideas, collaborating with others, and driving change were all things that came naturally to her. As such, she felt well-suited to her role. But she quietly disclosed, "I'm overwhelmed. I constantly start all these new projects and ventures. But look at my desk—I feel like I'm drowning with all the endeavors I'm meant to be moving forward, all of which I've created for myself." When looking at her Strengthscope® profile, I could certainly see how this resulted from her combined strengths going "into overdrive"—natural energizers over-played, too much of a good thing, so to speak. I see strengths applied in overdrive as potentially more dangerous than nonstrengths or weaknesses. We tend to be aware of the latter but rarely give consideration to how our strengths (or the way we're *over*working them) may be doing us a disservice. When Carlette and I looked at her profile, another strength stood out to me: critical thinking. I suggested that if I'd brought Carlette to my desk and shared with her the same challenge, she would have been able to systematically guide me through the mountain of work in front of me to evaluate each project in order of priority, and help me make some tough decisions about how to move forward. "Yes," she said, and smiled in agreement, knowing where this was headed. Carlette decided to apply one of her other strengths to tackle the challenge she was facing. It enabled her to reframe the idea that she had created a monster that was out of control, to the realization that she naturally had within her exactly what she needed to make the monster work for her.

A mentor whom I truly value shared with me that he is not at all energized by efficiency. I was shocked, because in the many years I've known and worked with him, I'd never experienced a lack of efficiency. In fact, I found it hard to imagine that any of the friends and colleagues we had in common would experience him as inefficient. And he wasn't. But rather than focusing on the need to be efficient to get through his endless emails and administrative work associated with managing dozens of employees and responding to his global clients' continual demands, he reframed these tasks. Given that his natural strengths lie in relationship building and having compassion for others, he explained, "I choose to see these tasks as being about the people on the other side of them, not just as something I have to get done. When I focus on the people I empower by doing these tasks, I'm energized and passionate about them." How we see the things on our to-do list for the day shapes how we show up that day. A reframe can help bring authentic passion and be a natural fuel for gravitas.

Drawing Others Toward You

"People are drawn toward them." Leaders and professionals describing others with gravitas repeated this phrase over and over again in our research. We are drawn toward people who bring out the best in us. Understanding strengths enables us to not only bring our own natural energy, but equips us with the skills to help others bring theirs. People are attracted to others who can see and appreciate their unique strengths—not as baseless cases of flattery, but grounded in observation, experience, reflection, and exploration. Sometimes we assume that people are energized by the same things we are, but as we see from the research, everyone is different. If we take an interest in identifying the situations and opportunities that naturally energize others, we learn to value their strengths and adapt our ways of working with them to activate their strengths.

For Jackson, our COO with the slumping shoulders, these practices helped him, in his words, "regain his swagger." Feeling that it was time to move on, he took on an exciting role in a new firm and was pleased when he had the opportunity to build coaching others into his role. This would fuel his ability to sustain his authentic gravitas.

MITIGATING POWER STRESS TO SUSTAIN AUTHENTIC GRAVITAS

This shift to focusing on others and their strengths can have a powerful, positive impact not only on the people around us, but also on ourselves. We need this mentality not only to build but also to sustain authentic gravitas because one of the things that may happen as we increase authentic gravitas is that we may take on greater responsibilities and subsequently experience more "power stress." Eminent professor Richard Boyatzis and his colleagues from Case Western Reserve University argued that leaders experience psychological and physiological effects from chronic power stress that adversely affect their sustainability as leaders.[26] The researchers didn't restrict "leadership" to positions of power (i.e., the boss), but included other forms, like thought leadership in introducing innovation. What matters is that the person is influencing others. Power stress comes with the demands of increased responsibility over others. It can involve working on things that are personally important and therefore risky, often while others are watching or critiquing. These conditions can cause stress. Chronic power stress can mean that a person loses some ability to adapt, learn, and stay healthy, meaning they have "difficulty sustaining the mental, emotional, perceptual, and behavioral processes that enabled him or her to be effective."[27]

People with authentic gravitas take responsibility for ensuring they add positive, significant value, often amid uncertainty. The value they add is substantive, and with that comes power stress. The irony is that while we work through dark or difficult moments to build authentic gravitas, authentic gravitas can also be responsible for some of those dark moments because of the self-determined pressure to positively influence others. This, in turn, can reduce one's ability to continue adding substantive value. How can we manage stress to ensure we not only build authentic gravitas but also sustain it?

Boyatzis and his colleagues offer a valuable approach to ameliorate power stress in the workplace. Taking into consideration the many psychological and physiological responses to stress, they highlight the power of what they call *coaching with compassion*: "helping others in their intentional change process (i.e., achieving their dreams or aspirations or changing the way they think, feel, and act)."[28] Sound familiar? In chapters 2 and 3, we looked at the golden gravitas question: *How do I want them to think, feel, and act as a result of this encounter with me?* Coaching with compassion aligns with the principles of authentic gravitas.

Coaching is more complex than we may think. In addition to the many forms of coaching outside the workplace (e.g., life coaching, sports coaching), there are various interpretations of coaching within the working environment. While executive coach training is largely focused on equipping people with skills in active listening, questioning, facilitation, and goal-setting, usually people who ask for a "coach" at work are looking for someone to give them advice in a specific area. I call this a coach-adviser, who acts as the former *and* the latter, offering guidance on a particular professional area of which they have expertise, yet grounded within the powerful methodologies of traditional executive coaching. This can be within an internal or external workplace coaching relationship. This is different again from leadership coaching. In today's workplace we expect leaders to act as a coach, and this is perhaps the most complex form of coaching because leaders simultaneously wear four hats—they are a:

- Coach (in the traditional sense of listening, questioning, facilitating, and goal-setting)

- Adviser (offering guidance as to how to address challenges and achieve those goals)

- Leader (sharing vision and motivation; influencing and facilitating to develop another's potential and maximize their contribution towards achieving collective team/organizational goals)

- Mentor (sharing personal experiences and recommendations based on what did and didn't work for them on their own professional journey)

This is my CALM Model of Leadership Coaching, which we use to train leaders in moving flexibly, often within a single conversation, between the various components required of one relationship.

Whether the coaching relationship is formal or informal, being *others-focused* is an important factor in attaining the psychological and physiological benefits of coaching with compassion that ameliorate power stress. A coachee doesn't need to report to us—coaching is not restricted to hierarchical lines. But coaching does need to include three components to be considered coaching *with compassion*: noticing another's need or desire; empathic concern; and supporting another's desire to grow or develop.[29] And that is without an expectation of anything in return from the person being coached. Coaching with compassion is centered on helping the person being coached to be their "ideal self" (that person's vision of who he or she wants to be, including his or her goals, values, and deepest aspirations for the future), which then guides the change process. Coaching with compassion also involves strengths-based development, with a focus on looking at strengths before weaknesses.[30] In the framework of authentic gravitas, we can see that coaching with compassion is a method by which we can facilitate others' personal vision for how they show up and make their own positive impact and add their own substantive value.

Boyatzis and his colleagues noted that compassion can act like an antidote to stress. Coaching with compassion stimulates "positive emotional attractor" (PEA), not only in the mentee, but also in the mentor. PEA is a state of positive emotional arousal and activation of the parasympathetic nervous system, which slows down the heart rate and triggers the release of hormones such as oxytocin and vasopressin. According to the researchers, that arousal of positive emotions and PEA are conducive to cognitive openness, improved cognitive performance, and openness to behavioral change. They argued that individuals in this state could experience greater physical wellness, a calmer and more elated state, and neurogenesis (the generation of new neural tissue). Importantly, this can be a self-reinforcing, self-perpetuating cycle, as positive emotions lead to positive cognitive bias, creating positive feedback loops.[31]

While we can, of course, experience compassion through many other activities, coaching is relatively easy to build into our regular working life, enabling us to continue building gravitas and mitigate the effects of power stress. If we can sustain the practice of coaching with compassion, we can offset the potential power stress caused by increased responsibility and continue adding substantial value (i.e., *sustain* our authentic gravitas).

It's not always easy in practice. The times when we need these positive psychological and physiological benefits coincide with the times when we feel busiest and under the greatest pressure. Taking time out just to focus on the needs of another can feel like something we would *like* to do, but in the moment cannot possibly manage. So again, we need to be intentional—deciding in advance that we will engage in this positive activity not only when we find it most convenient but also in the midst of the busyness, and to be disciplined in following through on that decision. Those who build this challenging habit into their regular working lives are better able to sustain their authentic gravitas. In helping others to build their personal authentic gravitas, it seems we may be better able to sustain our own.

PRACTICES FOR GRAVITAS IN THE DARK

Perhaps you're doing well and feel pretty good in the current moment, as you're reading this book. In case there are moments further down the line when things become trickier, harder, or just downright disheartening (which, let's face it, happens to all of us at times), here are a few reminders of how to bring out your best in those darker moments:

- Getting down with negative self-talk? Remember that it's unlikely to be negatively impacting your actual performance (though it certainly is annoying!). Have your comebacks ready for the gremlin you know will pop up on your shoulder at the very moments you don't want it there. Decide what you believe to be true about yourself, and if there's any question that some part of the gremlin's message is true, make a commitment to grow in those areas. Seek out trusted advisers and friends who will challenge you and be honest with you, but who have your best interests at heart, and check your negative self-talk with them.

- Practice gratitude (daily or weekly). It can lead to higher positive affect and physical well-being. It's easy to focus on all the difficult situations that may justifiably take up your attention and energy, but don't forget the research-proven power of counting your blessings.

- Manage anxiety proactively. If it's anxiety about a particular event, it can be useful to go to the location of the event beforehand to get a sense of the environment. Remember to build in current experience moments to give your brain a break from all that narrative thinking. Reframe "I'm anxious" to "I'm excited"—this isn't a silly pep talk; you probably *do* have reason to be excited, because it's an important opportunity for you.

- Identify your own unique strengths. What energizes you? Be proactive about creating conditions and opportunities where you can apply and develop your strengths. Growing them is likely to give you much greater returns than the incremental gains of only addressing weaknesses.

- Practice coaching with compassion to mitigate your own power stress and build resilience. Set yourself up for taking long-term responsibility and having a lasting positive impact by remembering to take time out to focus on the needs of others—benefiting both them and you.

SEVEN

ADAPTING MY STYLE

True to Me, Tailored to You

"Rebecca, you're stubborn," Chris said to me. I was in Texas, getting feedback on a 360-profile I had undertaken from someone I now consider to be one of the best coaches globally. *"No, I'm not."* The words instantly came out of my mouth before I could notice the irony in them. He smiled. "Really, Chris," I persisted, "I'm just not."

Absurd as this conversation is on reflection, I fully believed in my position, stating it as a fact. "Okay, how about asking three people who work with you for feedback? Ask them on a scale of one to ten how stubborn they would say you are," Chris suggested. "Sure," I replied, happy to have the opportunity to show him I was right. A few weeks later I was in central London with a long-standing colleague and friend. We were putting on our coats in a café, getting ready to go out into the cold and walk over to a client's office for a meeting. Out of the blue I asked, "Hey Sarah, on a scale of one to ten, ten being the highest, how would you rate me on stubbornness?" "Ten," she said, without even a breath between my question and her answer! It was as if she had been waiting for years to tell me and this was her chance.

That feedback and consequent conversation changed my life. Sarah, one of the most incredible professionals I know, felt that I didn't truly value her, even though I did. She experienced me as someone who didn't allow her space to have different opinions—mine were always so ready, strong, and loud. I discovered that, unknowingly and unintentionally, I wasn't giving her space to challenge my ideas. I now recognize this stubbornness as one of my key risk areas, something I need to constantly watch out for and catch myself on—not because it's "right" or "wrong," but because it's not how I want to be, it's not aligned with my intent. I would not say the experience was pleasant, but it has positively impacted all my relationships since, both personally and professionally.

I saw firsthand that my natural style is not always the best one. Sometimes it's completely fine. My wonderful dad—a seasoned lawyer who loves a good argument—wouldn't negatively experience me as "stubborn" because he has a similar style and preferences for interacting. If I follow my natural style, I would talk to Sarah the same way I talk to my dad—some would equate this consistency with authenticity. But my goal is to add value to a situation and to make others feel empowered to make a positive contribution as well. In encounters with my dad, we often debate the "best" way forward, each of us strongly advocating our position. This is the case regardless of what we're discussing—be it business or investment decisions, the current political climate, or the best way to get to our destination. In these interactions, we both feel that we're adding value and making a positive contribution to the situation— healthy debate that leads us to better outcomes. But I now know that if I engage with Sarah in this "natural" style, then while I may feel like I am adding value to the situation, I am certainly not making her feel empowered to make a positive contribution, too, so my value is limited. Being authentic is not about being rigid with our natural styles, but about being true to our intention and outworking our values—which often means adapting our natural style to the person with whom we're interacting. This benefits ourselves (by aligning our action with our intention), others (by creating conditions for them to make their best contribution), and the situation at hand (by adding significant value). The Gravitas Myth would have us believe there is one right way of behaving and interacting that we typically associate with surface gravitas, but adding real value lies in being flexible in how we show up with others. It takes courage to try out new styles of interacting that don't come naturally to us. Even when it makes sense to adapt, behaving differently makes us feel vulnerable and uncomfortable.

Studies have highlighted the power of being prepared and able to adapt your style. One group of studies suggested that there is a positive relationship between overall *effectiveness* of leaders (as rated by superiors, peers, and direct reports) and the ability to be *versatile* (to move freely between different styles, in particular between forceful and enabling leadership styles and between strategic and operational leadership styles).[1] For leaders, this ability to be versatile relates to "social intelligence"—the capacity to understand the situation, including the politics and social relationships involved. Leaders who demonstrate social intelligence are intentional in selecting appropriate responses and varying their behavior in the face of changing conditions. Researchers have argued that social intelligence is an important quality that separates leaders from non-leaders.[2] This matters regardless of where you're at in your career journey; to have gravitas, you need to be able to effectively demonstrate leadership, regardless of hierarchical position.

If we are to increase our skill in adapting behavior to the circumstances and social situation around us, we need to develop self-awareness, which includes not only an understanding of our values and goals but also of our effectiveness in influencing others.[3] It is something that many studies have shown can be developed—for example, through multisource feedback, assessment, coaching, training, and developmental assignments.[4]

We might worry that adapting our style means we're not authentic. *Should I really pretend to be someone I'm not?* But I would rather adapt my style and be true to my intention for how I want to be with other people than be true to my natural style if it means unintended and undesirable consequences in how I make others feel.

Being someone who adds value means we close the gap between our intention, our action, and our impact. We may have positive intent toward those we work with, but our impact is limited by a lack of self-awareness and flexibility in how we interact with others. People who have the greatest authentic gravitas have been vulnerable in proactively seeking feedback about the gap between their intent and impact, and have the courage to try out different styles and ways of working. Furthermore, if we have authentic gravitas, we recognize that others also have a gap between their intention and their impact on us, which, in turn, impacts how we think, feel, and act toward them. This feedback and recognition goes beyond the context of meetings and presentations; it is relevant to all our daily interactions with those around us.

Catching a Ball

"We just clicked." Camille recalled how she felt about her working relationship with colleagues at her former Paris-based hedge fund. "We were such a tight group and all in sync. The work was hard but the people were easy." When another European fund approached her, Camille decided it was time to move on, having spent seven years at the Paris-based firm. However, she soon discovered that the dynamics at her new professional home were complicated. She described to me strong personalities, complex relationships, and her sense that after only three months, she had not made the strong first impression she had hoped for. Her new boss, whom I knew well and respected, had asked me to coach her. He felt she lacked the gravitas he'd observed in her when they first met, and echoed her views regarding the first impression she'd made on the wider team. His two partners were questioning his decision to bring her on board.

Camille herself was questioning whether the move had been a bad decision. I asked her to describe the people she worked with at her new fund. Then I asked her to describe the people she'd worked with previously, one by one, and how she'd interacted with each of them. Over the course of our conversations, I challenged her view as to whether her new colleagues were indeed (in her words) "stronger personalities," and she discerned that the difference lay in her understanding of her colleagues' preferences for working and interacting, rather than with the people themselves. Her former colleagues were not more similar to her or more easygoing. They were just known. Over her many years of working there, she had picked up habits of how to work well with the various people there. She'd adapted her style with each almost subconsciously. Camille needed to now adapt her style consciously—to generate the same flow and ease in her new working relationships.

In considering how to adapt our style to increase our gravitas when working with others, it is not about trying to become somebody else. Nor is it about pretending to *be* somebody else. It is about understanding our impact on others and being intentional in adapting our behavior so that our intention and actual impact are aligned. And while personality—our unique combination of preferences, biases, habits, and feelings—is relatively stable over time, we are not fixed beings and can change our behaviors. A simple example is, if I prefer to throw a ball underarm, but my six-year-old son prefers to catch a ball that's been thrown overarm, I can throw it to him overarm. My preferences for throwing underarm won't change, but I can adapt for him.

Here's why authentic gravitas requires us to adapt. Gravitas isn't just about how we believe ourselves to be adding substantive value; when other people are involved, it's also in the eye of the beholder. Adverse gravitas—self-serving, loud dominance—is less subject to personal interpretation; people tend to perceive it in the same way. It may vary in strength, depending on how loud and assertive the other voices are, but it is typically clearly seen (or more likely heard). But authentic gravitas, the level to which someone has a positive impact and adds significant value to a situation and the people in it, is subject to personal interpretation by the people in that scenario. And those people are all different.

Whether your comments and actions add significant value to them personally and to the situation as a whole is determined, in part, by them. They regard our interaction through the lens of their own personality and preferences, just as we regard them through our own.

Embracing Cognitive Dissonance

When it comes to our professional development, we can spend a great deal of time thinking about our own personality and preferences for interacting, but rarely do we discuss others' preferences. Perhaps we're concerned with putting them in a box; perhaps it's just more interesting to think about ourselves! But following on from "target assessment" (as discussed in chapter 3), adding value requires giving greater consideration to others—including their relatively fixed preferences for interaction. Certainly, we should not fall into the trap of putting people in a box. Many times, I have jumped to conclusions about a colleague or client, only to discover, after spending more time getting to know them, that I was wrong. When it comes to others, we must choose to embrace cognitive dissonance: two contradictory ideas at the same time (as mentally uncomfortable as it may be). This means holding informed beliefs about their personality and preferences for interaction so that we can use those beliefs to guide our behavior, and simultaneously remaining open to being proven wrong and needing to change our understanding of them. Not only do we have to hold these two contradictory ideas about each person, we also need to act on both. We adapt our style in line with our beliefs about their preferences and simultaneously seek novel information to possibly contradict that understanding. However, because cognitive dissonance is uncomfortable, we actively seek to reduce it, often by avoiding or not attending to contradictory information. In other words, our natural tendency is to note signs and actions that reinforce our existing beliefs about people. We need to intentionally choose to be open to cues that we are wrong, which can be both uncomfortable and counterintuitive. We naturally reduce the gap between how we regard others and how they actually are as we get to know them, and we can do this proactively by seeking clarity. In other words, ask them!

The research findings support the notion that gravitas is not reserved for those with certain personality types, but for those who are able to adapt their style with skill. Far from being disingenuous, adapting requires the courage to try out new ways of engaging and the conviction to impact others in a positive way.

Here are some examples of how we can effectively adapt our style to minimize the intention-impact gap and increase our authentic gravitas, all in just one working day.

To build gravitas, the research highlighted three key areas for adapting our style—pace, idea generation, and critique—regardless of our personal preferences in these areas.

CHOOSING OUR SPEED SETTINGS: THE POWER OF PACE

Marco sighed silently as Anita walked into his office. *There goes my work,* he couldn't help but think. Marco liked Anita. She was smart, good with clients, and easy to get along with. But she had a tendency to talk on and on, and Marcus liked to get things done. "Yes, Anita, how can I help?" He didn't need a fifteen-point plan, and he didn't want dozens of questions. He liked it when people came in and got straight to the point. Smiling, Anita calmly walked in and took one of the two leather chairs on the other side of his desk. "I've been looking at how we should move forward on the Monetty case and have come up with three options. The first is that we could go back to the developers . . ." Anita went on and described each option in turn. She walked through her three well-thought-out plans, waiting to get positive reinforcement, hoping that at last she would impress Marco and show him that she could take the lead on the Monetty account. It would be by far her biggest account, and she felt ready to oversee it. Marco never showed her that he was pleased, she wasn't sure what he thought of her, and some evenings she left the office with a niggling concern that he didn't like or respect her. After all, sometimes he would walk straight past her without even saying hello. Still, she was determined to show him that she was ready.

Anita: Take One

Having thoroughly explained the three options, Anita was pleased when Marco suggested option three, advising the client to make changes to the plan, which she felt was the best choice. "Yes, great. I was thinking that was the best as well because . . ." she went on happily. "So if we go with this option, should we go back to the client first or check in with Jim in the real estate team? I think Jim could add a lot of value here. Maybe I'll go and speak to him and come back to you with what he says. Is it best to wait for the next planned client catch-up meeting, or should I meet with them as soon as possible? Or you could, or we could both go? I think this really is the best option for them. It might be a good case study for the firm's newsletter. I'm looking forward to it." Anita hoped that Marco would see she was ready and suggest she handle the next phase alone. He didn't.

Marco wished Anita would live up to her potential. He just didn't feel she had the gravitas to carry off being the lead on the Monetty account. He wished she was ready, because he certainly could do with having it off his very full plate, and for him, it was a relatively small account.

Let's give Anita a do-over.

Anita: Take Two

Having briefly explained the options and answered Marco's questions on a couple of points, Anita was pleased when Marco suggested option three, advising the client to make changes to the plan, which she felt was the best choice. "Great, that's what I thought. Thanks, Marco." Anita gathered her things quickly, stood up, and walked back to her desk.

Later, she would find Jim from the real estate department and seek his advice on changing the plans. She'd then email the client to find out when they'd be available to meet. Anita wasn't sure if Marco would want her to go alone or if he'd want to go, too (or by himself), so once she had the client availability, she planned to send him a brief email asking what he'd prefer. Anita hoped that Marco would see she was ready and suggest she handle the next phase alone. He did.

Marco was pleased. Anita had confidently walked out of his office without taking up much of his time, and when he got a three-line email explaining her actions since their conversation and asking if he wanted to go to the meeting, he realized he didn't need to. She was ready to be the lead on the account.

Clarity, Brevity, and Haste

Some professionals have a strong preference for moving things forward quickly—both on projects and in conversation. They may appear assertive, direct, and goal-oriented. When working with people who have this preference, it's easy to make the mistake of simply talking too much. Whether we're excited about the options or calmly walking through what we see to be many important details, we can be thorough in making our point. If you ever feel like someone is curt in response to you, take that as a red flag—an indication of a possible interaction preference. They may prefer their colleagues to be direct and to the point, particularly if they're in the middle of something else. It may sound obvious, but it's easy to miss the signs to stop talking.

You might think, *Surely that person needs all the details to make a good decision? Surely it's okay to keep asking the questions I need answered?* Yes and yes. But they'll ask you for more details if they want them. And they'll appreciate you just getting the key questions out of the way, and coming back when necessary (and again, in short, punchy interactions—be they face-to-face or by phone or email). When I ask clients with these preferences how they would describe someone with gravitas, they highlight the importance of being to the point and direct and having the facts and figures to support their argument if needed. They appreciate clarity in communication. The way Anita concluded her meeting with Marco in take two made him believe she was assertive, confident in her views, and certain about her ability to carry out the work. Anita's gravitas, for Marco, was revealed in how and when she walked away.

People who prefer brevity are not careless in their work or decision-making. Far from it. Kathleen Eisenhardt at Stanford University, writing in the *Academy of Management Journal*, proposed that in high-velocity environments, fast, high-quality, strategic decisions can actually lead to superior performance.[5] The findings, from research with top management teams across eight firms, suggest that fast decision-makers used more, not less, information and developed more, not fewer, alternatives. The key was to have as much information in real time as possible and to identify as many alternatives as possible. Eisenhardt highlights that having simultaneous alternatives can reduce the escalation of commitment to any one option given their lower psychological stake in any one position, and it can allow executives to shift quickly if one alternative fails, given they have a fallback position. She found that conflict resolution was crucial; fast teams actively dealt with conflict, whereas teams that made slower decisions tended to delay until external events forced them into action. Eisenhardt describes a simple two-step process whereby a team attempts to reach consensus. If they have it, the choice is made. If they don't, the CEO and relevant VP make the choice, guided by others' input.

Adapting your style for others who like speed certainly doesn't mean rushing and leaving work unfinished or producing lower-quality work than you otherwise would have presented. It's not an excuse to turn up unprepared in the name of getting a lot of things done quickly. We actually need to be more prepared and systematic to be able to engage in "speed" effectively. And it's of course not about the pace at which we speak or rushing through conversations. It's a reflection of some professionals' strong preference for clear and concise interactions that are focused on moving a project or situation forward. This does not mean they won't ask for details or want longer conversations at times—especially when those things are needed in order to make the right decisions about how to quickly move things along.

Anita could identify cues to Marco's preferences for interaction. His communication was direct, straight to the point, and focused on making decisions to get things done. Here are some keys as to how Anita could adapt her style:

1. Be clear about her goal—ideally just one (e.g., know the one question she most needed answered).

2. Have evidence and detail to support her argument, *should she need it.*

3. Be direct with her objective or questions—share/ask them and then stop talking after a clear, punchy, confident ending: "Great, that's what I thought. Thanks, Marco."

4. Follow up with more minor comments or questions at a later date, unless they can be quickly covered in the meeting.

Let's look at the flip side. Shouldn't Marco adapt as well? If he wants to create an environment where he's respected, bringing out the best in others to bring out the best in the situation overall—to have authentic gravitas—then yes. Anita notices that sometimes he walks past without saying hello, making her feel uncertain about his view of her rather than instilling confidence *in* her. Marco knows that Anita likes to take time to talk through options and ideas, and he, too, could adapt and proactively manage their interactions to make sure he's bringing the best out of her and adding the most value (consider the ideas discussed in the "Silent Messages of Value" section in chapter 2 for more on how Marco could adapt his style and proactively manage their relationship given Anita's interpersonal preferences). He could adapt by proactively managing timing (when they talk) so he feels he is able to slow down and give her the time she wants (how they talk).

Having a preference for "speed" is not a requirement for authentic gravitas. What does help is looking for cues that suggest people have this strong preference, combined with the discipline and skill to adapt if we're not naturally oriented this way when we work with people who are. Or if we have this preference, to be mindful when working with people who are different from us. It's about adapting our style, throwing the ball a different way.

GENERATING BRIGHT IDEAS

"So if we don't move on this without the Acorn deal sewn up, we risk delaying the rest of the project. Okay, let's hear it. What do you think?" Anita caught only the last part of Rowena's briefing as she walked in. One of the founding partners of the firm, Rowena was known for her brainstorming meetings—they could go for hours and always involved a lot of coffee, sometimes pizza, and Anita knew numerous people who pinpointed one of these meetings as being pivotal in their career. She knew the context well and was happy to jump in and discuss ideas, quickly getting filled in on some of the information she'd missed.

Shaun: Take One

As Anita took in the room, she saw Jim, and made a mental note to catch up with him afterward. She saw his clear enthusiasm, aware that he loved a good brainstorm and debate. Anita had heard Jim contribute many strong ideas in such meetings. She glanced across at her colleague and friend Shaun, who was clearly not as enthused. Shaun sat quietly, examining the many documents in front of him, rarely contributing. Anita knew he was taking it all in, and was conscious that he was one of the brightest people in the room, but wished, for his sake, that he'd speak up.

When Rowena asked Shaun which of the possible directions he felt they should take, Anita watched him go for it. He talked through the pros and cons of each option, finally contributing, seemingly comfortable to share his take on each. Anita sighed—if only Shaun had answered Rowena's question.

Shaun felt defeated. He was starting to resent the fact that he seemed to need so much more time than everyone else. He couldn't just jump in with great ideas and certainly wasn't prepared to throw out a recommendation when he hadn't had the opportunity to seriously consider all the options. All he felt he could do was talk through how he saw all the options; but that didn't seem to be what Rowena (or often others) wanted. He wanted to have time to think through things and oscillated between self-defeat (*I just can't do it; I'm not like them*) and annoyance (*Why don't people ever give me time to think things through properly?*).

Let's give Shaun a do-over.

Shaun: Take Two

As Anita took in the room, she saw Jim, and made a mental note to catch up with him afterward. She saw his clear enthusiasm, aware that he loved a good brainstorm and debate. She glanced across at her colleague and friend Shaun, who was clearly not as enthused. Shaun sat quietly, with many documents in front of him that Anita knew he would be eager to go through in detail. Although he wasn't saying much, she could see that he was fully engaged—focusing his eyes on the person speaking, showing his clear interest in the topic. Anita knew he was taking it all in, and was conscious that he was one of the brightest people in the room, but wished, for his sake, that he'd speak up.

When Rowena asked Shaun which of the possible directions he felt they should take, Anita watched him gracefully navigate what she knew to be his reluctance to make a call when he hadn't had time to carefully go through the options. He smiled and said, "There's a lot here, Rowena.

We've got a lot of options now and I'm mindful that we need to make a decision by the end of today. How about if I make some time to look over the options, do a sense-check of what we have on the table, pull together some of the final numbers to bring back to everyone, and we all regroup mid-afternoon to make a final decision?" Anita admired his ability to make known his desire for time to think through things and simultaneously show he was adding value for the team by taking the weight off others, contributing in a way that suited his strengths, all while being mindful of the real and immovable deadlines. On other occasions, she had seen him directly answer questions posed by members of the executive team and clients, sharing his point of view in a way that he was comfortable with. "I think our second option is the right way forward. What I'll do is take this offline, go through the details in light of the new information we've discussed today, and come back to you by Tuesday morning with confirmation so we can quickly move ahead."

Courage, Vulnerability, and Owning Your Preference

Can Shaun adapt his style? Though he could choose to give an answer quickly, Shaun is likely to not be able to shift his natural *preference* from wanting time to go through details and think things through independently to suddenly coming up with ideas on the spot. He might have some ideas but be uncomfortable sharing them without his considered due diligence. So what can he do? In his second take, he adapted by acknowledging and accepting, rather than resenting, the fact that some people, like Rowena and Jim, do work best in this environment. Shaun fought his desire to put his head down and stayed fully engaged in the conversation and ideas, using his body language to show respect for the contributions others were making. He maintained silent gravitas. He knew the brainstorming, on-the-spot decision-making culture of his workplace, and had developed a strategic way of bringing his best work. When there was space for it, he expressed his preference for independently going through the details in order to contribute to the team, while still acknowledging the tight timelines. When he needed to, he did make a call, even though he didn't feel comfortable, giving himself a post-meeting strategy to ensure he was doing his best work and happy to take full ownership of his recommendation.

Furthermore, he could go to Rowena and others to communicate his preferences for coming up with ideas and making decisions after having some quiet time to think alone. He may feel vulnerable doing so, particularly with people who are different from him in this way. Nonetheless, he could share his perspective on how he can best contribute—recognizing it's not always possible, but wherever it is, he'd appreciate an opportunity to go through information before group meetings so he can think through the options and be prepared to bring his ideas to a meeting. When that isn't possible, he would like to take away the information from the meeting and come back with reflections and possibly new ideas—this is the way he contributes best. Without data to the contrary, it's easy for us to assume that people's preferences for thinking, decision-making, and interacting are the same as ours. Rowena may never have known Shaun's preferences if he wasn't bold enough to tell her and to ask for more time to think through things.

What about Rowena? Could she adapt? Her desires for brainstorming and group decision-making aren't preferences she's likely to be able to change, just as Shaun couldn't change his. But with authentic gravitas, the goal is to bring out the best in other people, not just be your personal best. So when working with others, consider their preferences for thinking, coming up with new ideas, and making decisions. For Rowena, she would get the best out of Shaun and therefore get a better outcome by giving him the information and challenge before the meeting. This isn't always possible, but many organizations don't even take into account different work styles when they give information, generate options through brainstorming and debate, and make decisions all in one meeting. This works well for some professionals, but certainly not for all, and not for all tasks, problems, or decisions, either. Having the headspace, even for just an hour or two, to look through and review the information and generate options beforehand would enable Shaun to put his best foot forward in the meeting, making a stronger outcome for the team overall more likely.

SEEING THE HOLES IN THE BOAT

Jim had enjoyed the brainstorming meeting. That afternoon, he went by Angus's office. A new technology director, Angus had only been at the firm for a few weeks, but his reputation preceded him. He was known for being one of the best in the industry—creating new technical models that supported their work, enabling them to offer potential clients solutions that were both faster and more reliable. Jim had been working on an exciting new project. He had taken the initiative to redesign a client service offering, known internally as "Ex-cap," and had received positive feedback from many across the firm—he couldn't wait to take it to clients. "Angus!" Jim beamed as he walked through the open door. "How's it all going? Your office is looking great!" "Hi, Jim," Angus replied, moving some papers around on his desk. Jim jumped straight to the reason he was there: "You've probably heard about my Ex-cap development project? I'd love for you to get involved, Angus. I think it could make a big difference for clients—everyone's pretty excited. Having your input would be amazing. We'd be unstoppable!"

Angus: Take One

Having seen some of the draft materials, Angus asked, "How are you planning to deal with the fluctuations in the independent variables? I don't think the model will hold up with the continuing changes. And if you look at the second phase . . ." Angus went on and shared all his concerns, highlighting the numerous issues that needed to be fixed in order to make the project successful. He was pleased that Jim had come to him with this. The partners had mentioned it with a great deal of excitement, and it would be good to have his name associated with such an important project so early on. He wanted to make sure they had worked through all the technical challenges so all would run smoothly when they took it to market.

Jim couldn't believe it. Angus went on and on, listing one challenge after another, all of them seemingly small in Jim's mind—surely these things could be fixed? That was why he'd come to Angus. But Angus didn't seem to understand how exciting this project was, or see its potential. After all, it was a groundbreaking approach and the partners had almost said as much. Jim felt deflated and defeated. He'd given this project his all, and here was the new guy beating up on him with an endless stream of, "This is wrong." Angus's tone was flat—it was almost as if he were bored by the whole idea. Jim wished he hadn't come to Angus—he could have worked out the glitches with the team he usually worked with. He certainly wouldn't bring his best ideas to Angus again.

Let's give Angus a do-over.

Angus: Take Two

Angus was pleased that Jim had come to him with this. The partners had mentioned it with a great deal of excitement, and it would be good to have his name associated with such an important project so early on. He had seen some of the draft materials and wanted to make sure they had worked through all the technical challenges so all would run smoothly when they took it to market.

"Thanks for thinking of me for this, Jim," Angus said with a smile. "I've heard the partners talking about this, and they seem pretty excited. Why don't you talk me through your main goals and challenges and how I can help?" Jim took him up on this offer to share all his plans and some of his concerns. Angus realized that Jim hadn't seen all the potential problems, such as changes to the independent variables and phase two. "Would it help if I went through the technical details and came up with a list of things for us to look at? I want to make sure it's all smooth when you take it to market." "Yes, great!" declared Jim. He was thankful to have someone on board who could spot the gaps. Any technical glitches would really frustrate the clients. This was exactly the reason why Jim had come to Angus. He felt more confident than ever that Ex-cap II would be a hit.

Not Just What, but How

The *way* we offer our critiques, not just what critiques we offer, shapes how much value we add to a situation. It changes the way others hear us, what they do with the information and comments we share, and whether they come back to us again. In order to lead the room, we have to be welcomed into it first.

People differ in how they offer, and prefer to receive, critique. Critique is a necessary part of business success. When heavily invested in a new venture or plan, we want feedback that is encouraging, not challenging. But we know that's not necessarily all that's needed. Greater value lies in challenges to improve our initiatives. And people with authentic gravitas add value. Adapting here doesn't mean we *don't* find the holes in the boat. It is about being mindful of how people prefer to receive a critique and adapting how we give it, not what we're saying.

When working with people who tend to be optimistic and big-picture oriented, it's important to respond with energy if they are sharing an idea. Explain why you like the ideas (be authentic, and only communicate what you genuinely feel positively about), or comment on how much work they've clearly put into it, or the interesting nature of the project or topic. And share that with energy—not silly, over-the-top excitement, but at least *some* energy. People with this interactive preference can feel particularly deflated when new ideas are received with immediate criticism or simply a lack of vitality. People with authentic gravitas not only develop their own confidence but also instill confidence in others. Immediately critiquing a new idea delivered by someone with high energy can decrease his or her confidence. Alternatively, it can decrease your gravitas in their eyes. You may feel you're adding significant value to the content, but if it is at the expense of the one who owns the content, you are not making a positive impact on that person. Furthermore, professionals with this preference, particularly if paired with high self-confidence, can self-protect by responding with a critical approach themselves—not of the content but of the messenger. They may regard the messenger as lacking sophisticated social skills or the ability to see the big picture.

The goal is certainly not to flatter without substance, instill false confidence, or overlook problems. It is to instill confidence in others, to match their energy levels and communicate a commitment to making a project work—by highlighting strengths and asking if pointing out challenges would be useful. If your initial response is phrased well, constructive challenge will almost always be well-received. It will enable you to make a significant and positively received contribution.

Having recognized Jim's energy and enthusiasm, Angus was able to adapt his style well in the following ways in take two:

1. He was clear (and genuine) about what he appreciated about the project/conversation and why.

2. He delivered his messages with matching energy.

3. He asked if Jim would like to hear challenges and constructive input, highlighting why this would make a significant, positive difference in the bigger picture, thus letting Jim take the lead in *inviting* challenge and constructive criticism rather than having it forced upon him.

If Angus were giving feedback to Marco rather than to Jim, he would need to adapt differently—still focusing on the big picture, but perhaps requiring less positive energy and being more direct. Offering a critique is one of the key areas where we need to adapt to others' preferences to build authentic gravitas.

It's not only how we highlight the holes in the boat that matters but also how we *respond* to them. Let's look at how Marco could increase or decrease authentic gravitas when responding to a critique offered by Angus.

Curry with a Side of Recognition

"The vegetable curry, please." Marco heard Angus order from the spot in front of him in line. They had arrived at the corner shop at the same time and decided to have lunch together. Marco was pleased to have this opportunity to speak with Angus. A founding partner had poached Angus from their biggest competitor, and Marco knew Angus was regarded as an important addition to the firm. He was certainly the strongest technical adviser they now had, and he'd only had one chance to work with him so far. Knowing that Angus would be in great demand across the firm, Marco wanted to build a solid relationship with him and have him work on his larger client cases.

Marco: Take One

"Did you get a chance to look at my report on Stellar-Beatty?" Angus asked Marco. He had put in long hours on this report, finding a lot of problems with the current plans and highlighting many changes he felt needed to be made. He had enjoyed throwing himself into the case and was proud of the work he had done, knowing that if his suggested changes were made, they would have a significant impact on the way the firm handled the Stellar-Beatty merger. "Yes, I had a quick look and think we have it all covered. If we make just a couple of changes, it will be fine," said Marco. "What I really want is to talk with you about the new Scotcher case. It will be a big one for us. You've probably seen the . . ." He went on to give an overview of the case.

Angus couldn't believe how little Marco appreciated his work. He also doubted Marco's ability to manage the large Scotcher case well, given that he clearly couldn't manage the smaller Stellar-Beatty one. *"If we make just a couple of changes, it will be fine."* Angus marveled at Marco's words, mentally rolling his eyes at Marco's clear lack of understanding of just what was required to make it work. With many partners asking for his involvement on projects, Angus was reluctant to get involved on the Scotcher case, or any others with Marco, for that matter.

Let's give Marco a do-over.

Marco: Take Two

"Did you get a chance to look at my report on Stellar-Beatty?" Angus asked Marco. He had put in long hours on this report, finding a lot of problems with the current plans and highlighting many changes he felt needed to be made. He had enjoyed throwing himself into the case and was proud of the work he had done, knowing that if his suggested changes were made, they would have a significant impact on the way the firm handled the Stellar-Beatty merger. "Yes, I've gone through it. Thanks for all your work, Angus. You obviously put a lot of time into it," offered Marco. "I noticed you suggested a lot of changes. I particularly appreciated your observations regarding the technical challenges in section three." He paused, sensing Angus was keen to discuss something. Angus went on to describe what he saw as the main challenges in section 3, also drawing Marco's attention to two other findings he wanted to make sure weren't overlooked. Marco nodded in agreement. "Okay, thanks, Angus. Would you be open to working with Anita to make some of the changes and then come back to me with any remaining issues?" "Sure," replied Angus, pleased that his work had been appreciated. "Great," said Marco. "I'd like your input on another case, a bigger one—the Scotcher client—if you're happy to talk through it now?" Angus smiled. "Yes, great, what's it about?"

Noting the Value of a Critique

Seeing the detailed work Angus had provided, Marco should have picked up on how important it was to Angus to offer a thorough critique.

When working with someone whose tendency is to offer in-depth critical analysis, authentic gravitas means we show that we notice and appreciate the value they add. Again, the goal is not to offer false confidence in the work, but rather to recognize the effort made by the contributor and to highlight where real value is added. If the person offering the critique has little confidence, that person can turn their natural strength for critical thinking into criticism of themselves, particularly if they routinely experience a lack of appreciation for their work. Their self-identity and sense of their own gravitas can be reduced because they feel that they can never offer contributions that are valued and taken seriously by others. Alternatively, their focus can turn to the recipient who has not demonstrated—in their mind—that they possess the critical capacity required for the project. That person's gravitas is reduced in their mind.

Having observed Angus's detailed critique, Marco adapted his own style effectively in take two in the following ways:

1. Marco offered genuine appreciation for the amount of work Angus had undertaken and highlighted specific parts of particular value.

2. He gave Angus space to talk through what he saw as being important parts of his work.

3. He identified a way to tangibly address Angus's concerns without transgressing on his own need to strategically focus on a different project.

Let's flip it around, though. What if Angus were giving feedback on work Marco had done? Marco would likely be looking for Angus to recognize and value his work as well, and then follow it up with a simple instruction on next steps and further clarity *if needed*, before moving on to discuss the next case. Gravitas is not only about adding value, but recognizing that people experience value in different ways.

Camille

Let's wrap up by coming back to Camille, who was struggling in her new position at a European hedge fund, and look at how she built authentic gravitas at the new firm. Camille looked for cues to the interpersonal and thinking preferences of her colleagues. She sought to adapt her style to each one, particularly along the lines of how they preferred to work when it came to pace, generating ideas, and identifying holes in the boat. Sometimes she didn't get it quite right, but she stayed open to further cues, and with some colleagues, she went ahead and asked them how they preferred to work, particularly when it came to generating ideas and identifying holes in the boat, which she found more difficult to gauge from observation. She continued to adapt, and within a few months, both she and her boss were happier with her position at the firm. Camille was committed to, and increasingly skilled at, tailoring her approach to her colleagues while staying true to herself.

PRACTICES FOR ADAPTING YOUR STYLE

We all naturally adapt to some extent when interacting with different people. We wouldn't survive long professionally if we didn't. But people regarded by others as having a great deal of authentic gravitas have mastered adapting their style while staying true to themselves. They are not rigid in their behavior but act in line with their values and their intention for impact. For the moments when you're finding interactions with someone tricky, the following points may help:

- First, it's useful to identify your own preferences for interacting, including pace, how you like to come up with new ideas, and how you prefer to give and receive critical feedback at work.

- Think of people who you believe are different from you on each of the above points. List two or three people for each (they'll be different people for each of the three areas) and describe how you think they prefer to work and interact.

- Consider how you have adapted your style successfully to work with those people in the past (or conversely, times when things didn't go as well and how you think you could have done something differently).

- If there is a particular person you're finding it difficult to work with, consider what their preferences might be for how they work and interact. What examples of their behavior made you come to these conclusions?

- Could you ask them how they prefer to work? Perhaps share that you're keen to build a good working relationship and would genuinely like to know if there is anything they would like you to do differently, particularly in terms of how you work together.

- Make some decisions about how you could flex your style when working with them. Have the courage to try out some new behaviors and reflect afterward on whether you feel it made a positive difference. If it did, is there anything else you could do? If it didn't, seek feedback (from that person or others) and try something different. Even if you don't get it right the first time, hopefully the other person will notice your willingness to be flexible and your attempts to build a stronger relationship. Evidence that you are prepared to adapt can be as important as the behavior of adapting itself.

EIGHT

INFLUENCE WITH INTEGRITY

Creating Professional Chemistry

"They can lead the room, regardless of their position in it." This was the sentiment relayed (in various forms) by many senior executives, professionals, and practitioners who participated in my research when asked to describe someone with gravitas. An ability to influence the way others think, feel, and act, regardless of one's place in the organizational hierarchy, was considered a clear marker of gravitas. But people with high levels of gravitas didn't always act in the same way—rather, they were reported to have different approaches in how they influenced different people across various situations. Authentic gravitas involves successfully influencing others in line with your values and intention for impact, in order to make a noteworthy contribution to a situation or the people in it. People with gravitas lead positive change, taking ownership and helping others navigate challenging contexts, regardless of whether they are tasked with it or not.

Influence is the ability to change the thinking, feelings, or actions of others in some intended fashion.[1] Gravitas is not restricted by hierarchical position. In this chapter, we'll look at how people have influence beyond authority—not relying on hierarchical power to shape the thinking, feelings, and actions of others. This is not about a disregard or lack of respect for authority—far from it. Rather, it's about not waiting for a certain job title in order to take ownership of driving positive change.

In so much of business today, we have to influence not just our immediate team but vertically, horizontally, diagonally, and externally to achieve collective goals. To be effective, we are called to influence across the business and outside our business. So how do we influence beyond hierarchical lines?

EXECUTIVE INFLUENCE

Aria works for a global branding and marketing agency in a senior finance role, supporting two key areas of the business. When we met, she had been with the agency for three years, and her boss (who brought me in for coaching) told me how well-regarded Aria was by the wider management team, but that she needed more gravitas with her peers. "She just doesn't seem to have chemistry with them," he said with some level of resignation, as though, because chemistry didn't seem to come naturally, it was unlikely to change. But I knew he must have some faith in Aria's ability to turn it around or he wouldn't have sought out coaching for her.

When Aria and I met, she shared how much she loved her job. She was confident in her work with the leaders of both business units she supported and with the team who worked for her. Then she disclosed how one context made her nervous and doubt herself: finance team meetings, chaired by her boss and attended by the senior finance professionals across the business. They didn't work together on a daily basis, but her relationships with them were important and shaped her ability to contribute to the wider financial strategies of the business. Initially, she would walk into meetings with her peer group feeling fine with speaking up, but she would experience a verbal punch in the gut when they responded critically to her. Over time, such encounters had taken their toll. When we met, Aria had not only lost confidence, but was critical of herself for *not* having confidence. She kept trying to tell herself to have more confidence—but, as she discovered, telling yourself to have more confidence doesn't give you more confidence, and typically just makes you feel worse for not being confident. It can become a vicious cycle. Her reduced confidence made Aria want to withdraw from conversation and challenge. Doing so reduced her ability to influence others.

Influencing your peers can be particularly challenging. Your boss is typically the person who hired you, or at least decided to keep you in that position, so presumably, he or she is open to your contribution and influence. The people who report to you are partially influenced by hierarchical lines (you can choose to influence them in ways other than through positional power, but it still remains a factor in their response to you). Your peers, however they may like and respect you, most likely did not choose to work with you. Nor do they need to accept your attempts to influence them. And often—even in the strongest peer groups—there is competition for power and resources. Peers can be our toughest audience.

While there is a wide range of influencing techniques available to us, we often draw on only a few of these, based on three factors:

- What we've seen modeled or been socialized at work to see as the "normal" way of approaching situations

- What comes naturally to us

- What has worked previously

Where we have awareness of, and skill to access, a wider range of techniques, we are better positioned to influence others effectively, adapting our approach to the situation and the people involved. Authentic gravitas grows with our ability to move flexibly between different techniques.

So how do executives effectively influence their peers? One study examined sixty-two cases where executives attempted peer influence.[2] The researchers found that three things were important in this lateral process: target assessment, executive preparation, and influence tactics. As we discussed in chapter 3, target assessment is the evaluation we make of the person we want to influence. What are *their* resources, goals, personality, and preferences for interacting? Who has been successful in influencing them in the past? Executive preparation is the amount of time and effort put into the development and delivery of the proposal that is being communicated to those peers. Finally, influence tactics refers to matching the right tactic(s) for the situation and person. We tend to just use two or three—for example, always drawing on "rational persuasion" (using logical arguments), "inspirational appeals" (appeals to values and ideals), and "exchange" (reciprocity).

The researchers found that of these three factors, target assessment appears to matter a great deal, as it tends to drive both executive preparation and influence tactic choice. They suggest that target assessment may shape which influencing techniques executives choose, and speculate that executive preparation may have an impact on executives' ability to successfully carry out their chosen influencing strategies. So our success in influencing comes not only from being prepared to be versatile and drawing on a variety of techniques, but also from our preparation for these encounters and, in particular, engaging in target assessment. The greater consideration we give to the people we are trying to influence, the more successful we are likely to be in having an impact that's in line with our intention. Once you've done your target assessment, use your preparation time not just to think about what you're going to say, but begin by considering which influencing techniques you may wish to draw upon.

In this chapter, we'll look at some of the influencing techniques examined by the researchers: rational persuasion, legitimating tactics, personal appeals, apprising, exchange, inspirational appeals, ingratiation, and consulting.[3] As you read through some of the influencing techniques, think about which of these you use frequently, sometimes, and rarely.

INFLUENCING TECHNIQUES

Before we get started, let's just do a quick mind-set check. Speaking recently at a conference for business leaders, I was reminded that we sometimes have a natural hesitation toward the notion of wanting more influence. Some people may have the niggling thought, *Is influence something I* should *want?* We need to remember that wanting greater influence is not a bad or selfish thing in and of itself. What separates influence from manipulation is the goal: are we seeking to drive change to take steps toward achieving collective goals with integrity, or are we self-serving? Influence is a foundational part of leadership. So if we're looking to lead the room and add significant value, it's a good thing to want more influence.

"It's Logical": Rational Persuasion

"Show me the numbers. Show me the evidence." Rational persuasion involves using logical arguments and factual evidence, which are clearly important in business. Many professionals are primarily influenced by seeing numbers, reviewing data, and receiving evidence of why what we're saying will work *will* actually work.

Kevin excelled at research and analysis. There was no question as to his outstanding technical capability, yet clients would choose other consultants to work with. Clients liked having him on the project, but as Kevin's senior partners repeatedly noticed, they didn't want him as their main contact. They felt he was a great number two, but lacked the gravitas to lead projects. This came as a surprise, as he was often seen as the smartest person in the room, and his talent for analysis was certainly valued. Upon exploration, it became apparent that Kevin's confidence in his analytical abilities led him to over-rely on rational persuasion. As important as it is to have the evidence and interpret it accurately, some people rely on it as their *only* approach, and why wouldn't they? The data surely speaks for itself. Well, it doesn't always, and reason alone won't necessarily persuade others. So it's all the more important to be intentional about using other techniques in addition to rational persuasion, especially when we feel uncertain or under pressure, and are more likely to default to what we feel most comfortable with. If we have strong evidence and expertise in a certain area, it makes perfect sense to come to the table with our logical arguments to make our case: "You should buy into what I'm saying because here's the data that tells you to listen to me." If this is our area of expertise, then we may feel safer taking the personal out of the conversation. But gravitas almost always involves courage, and it requires connection.

Let's take a closer look at Kevin, who is confident in his numbers but not in his relational persuasiveness. Kevin told himself, *This isn't about me and them, our relationship; it's about the numbers and the data on the table.* But business is also about relationships, and sometimes we overuse rational persuasion when other techniques may be more influential. Or we may have greater success if we partner our logic with another appropriate influencing style. Research shows that our reasons and logic, our facts and evidence don't sit in isolation in our relationships. One study looking at relationships in the manufacturing industry showed how trustworthiness enhances the positive effects of rationality.[4] Rationality alone may be influential, but it is more effective when we focus not only on showing *why* someone should make a deal/buy into a new initiative/work with us, but also give energy to building a foundation of interpersonal trust.

Kevin committed to up-skilling in other influencing techniques and connecting with clients. He had to acknowledge that building strong relationships with people was just as important to his job as coming up with the right information for them. He needed to understand the context of the situation, and the needs and preferences of the people he was with. It is what you do *before* trying to influence someone (executive preparation) that can make the difference. By taking time to look at the context and conditions of the situation, Kevin was able to introduce new complimentary influencing techniques into his approach. This enabled him to add more substantive value. He increased his gravitas, and within a few months, he had become the lead on numerous client projects.

"Because X Says So": Legitimating

"The boss told me you need to do it." Legitimating tactics are where we draw on a source of authority to influence others in some intended fashion. However, just as authentic gravitas is not about drawing on one's own hierarchical power to make a difference in a situation, likewise it is not rooted in borrowing the hierarchical legitimacy of others. People with authentic gravitas can certainly have positional power, but do not need to continually rely on the argument "because I'm in charge," and rarely does "because *they're* in charge" have the desired effect, either. Another reason for being wary of legitimating in this way is that rarely do leaders appreciate having their name used by others to get someone to do something. Borrowing the weight of someone else's authority does not give us authentic gravitas and, in fact, can lead to difficulties with the person whose authority we are trying to invoke.

When trying to gain support for an idea, it's worth considering your relationship with the person you are seeking to influence. A study looking at organizational change and managerial influencing tactics argued that when employees have a positive relationship with their manager, they might be less likely to resist changes, as they see the use of legitimating tactics as a result of the situation at hand.[5] However, if employees don't have as positive a relationship with their manager, they may view the use of such legitimating more suspiciously and be even more likely to resist the requested changes than they would have been had the manager not tried to legitimize the changes. This suggests that whether legitimating tactics (drawing on a source of authority) have a positive or negative effect depends on the relationship between the person using that tactic and the person or people they're trying to influence. The findings highlight that in deciding which influencing tactics to apply, it's not enough to consider the situation, but we also need to reflect on our own relationships with those involved. Legitimating may not be the best approach (and it can even have unintended negative consequences). But when we don't have strong relationships, legitimating can feel like the easiest, most comfortable, and "safest" influencing technique that we can slip into if we forget to be intentional. However, as we've discussed, comfortable isn't the short-term priority.

Some forms of legitimating, however, can be powerful when preceded by thorough consideration of those you are trying to influence: who/what have they chosen to be a legitimate source of authority for them? It might be the client. It might be information from a journal or industry experts. There are many sources of authority that we can draw upon to support our arguments and recommendations. Keep in mind that legitimating is not about who is in a position of authority but who, or what, the people you're working with regard as a source of authority.

"One for Me, One for You": Favors and Exchange

"Rebecca, can you do me a favor?" I was in a taxi on my way to a breakfast meeting with a client across town when I received Lorraine's text. After breakfast, I would jump in another cab to meet an executive team and facilitate a development program on leading change. While the participants were breaking for lunch, I would race over to the LSE to host an introductory session for our incoming master's degree students. It was a busy day. Lorraine was having a busy day herself. While planning a meeting for more than one hundred volunteers at our church, she had just discovered there was an issue with the event organization. Because I hadn't had any involvement in this event, it would have been easy for me to let her know I was busy but that I hoped it worked out okay. She would have understood. But her text caught my attention. I couldn't remember the last time Lorraine had asked for a favor, though I could remember her helping me out on numerous occasions. I found windows in between my meetings (mainly in cabs) to call a few people and make some arrangements for help. I reflected later that had she not specifically asked for a favor, in the busyness of my day, I might have responded differently. Asking for a favor can be the last thing some of us want to do. But there is power in the vulnerability of needing someone else's help. Contrary to what we may believe if we focus on surface gravitas, authentic gravitas is not reduced by relying on the input of others. Asking for a favor shows trust in the relational proximity (being close enough to ask), clarity around the goal, and a belief in the other person's ability to have a positive impact, and it creates equilibrium in a relationship that is built on give-and-take.

Apprising is the flip side of asking for a favor—it's demonstrating how something is going to be favorable for the other person. It's me doing a favor for you. We apprise by suggesting to another that being involved in a project and following a suggested path will prove beneficial for them. Consider how your goal could benefit the others you would like involved. They may not be able to see the connection before you point it out. But in order to point it out, you need to know what is important to them, bringing us back to the need for target assessment and discovery to understand the environment, context, and conditions.

Exchange is often implicit in business. But as with rational persuasion, exchange is more effective when occurring within a strong relationship. We may think that the evidence of a valuable exchange is enough, but research shows that the positive effects of exchange are enhanced by the trustworthiness of the person suggesting the exchange.[6] Relational strength builds influencing effectiveness, even in the seemingly simplest forms.

Happy, Sad, or . . . : Inspirational Appeals (Emotions)

As we saw in chapter 2, emotions play a powerful role in decision-making. They have a greater role than we give them credit for. Be conscious of the emotional state of those you're with. Heightened emotions will have an impact on how someone responds to your appeal. It may mean they have a different response than they would have had if they were in a different emotional state. We've all had a peer, client, or customer respond in an unexpected way. Often this is a result of increased emotions, brought on by pressure or stress (or by favorable events leading to a more positive response, though we attune more to unexpected negative responses).

The emotions of the person we're speaking to shape our persuasiveness. Researchers explored the impact of message recipients' moods and "source likeability" on persuasion.[7] Source likeability refers to the degree to which a recipient finds the message's source likeable (that is, how likeable they find you, if you are the one attempting to persuade them of your argument or position). Building on previous research indicating that being in a good mood affects people's ability to process information, the researchers found that happy people are more likely to take into account your credibility and the extent to which they like you when making decisions about what you say. People who are sad are less likely to be influenced by your likeability and credibility and are more likely to scrutinize your message. This research reinforces what we instinctively know: having a happy audience does make a positive difference.

It's worth considering the mood of the people you are working with as you think about how to move forward. If you are looking to influence someone and find he or she is not in a good mood when you pop in to discuss an important idea or a particularly challenging issue, do not push it. You may even need to have a quick alternative question up your sleeve to justify your interruption. They will be less likely to take into account how much they like you or how credible you are, and will be more likely to scrutinize your proposal. Similarly, when it comes to meetings, sometimes it is not the right time to "just push through." If you sense anything emotionally out of the ordinary, do ask what, if anything, is going on, or recommend taking a break and coming back together at a later stage wherever possible. A well-advocated "time-out" is often more powerful in the long run than serving as a slave to the agenda. Of course, often we just have to continue as planned. Being aware of others' emotions means we're able to adapt accordingly (as I should have done with the lawyers who had just been given challenging news about the future of their firm, right before I launched into an upbeat talk about leadership). We need to remember that we're also able to influence others' emotions. A well-placed humorous opener or getting them energized through participation or framing the interaction in a positive way could also open up positive emotional pathways.

To make the most of inspirational appeals, recognize the power of emotion in shaping others' thinking and decision-making and consider the emotive elements of your interactions. Be intentional about which emotions you aim to invoke in others through your message and delivery.

Beyond the Banner: Inspirational Appeals (Values)

Years ago, I had the unusual experience of sitting on a client board to assist them in choosing a service provider. My client, an IT company, was seeking a consultancy to work on a large rebranding project. Four executives and I sat and listened to multiple agencies walking us through their slides and pitching to us on why they were the right fit. Then two women walked in. They sat down opposite us and asked us some questions. I kept waiting for the impending slide deck to emerge, to be handed hard copies and spoken *at*. But it never happened. They facilitated a discussion with us. The women had done their research and knew the values of the client company, but went further to identify what that meant and looked like in practice. They then went on to ascertain the values of the executives, asking what they appreciated about the company, what they valued, and what was most important to them in the project. They crafted a model throughout the discussion that highlighted to us how their values and the client's values were aligned. At the end of that pitch, we felt like we knew them and what they stood for. Making the decision to go with them was an easy one.

Inspirational appeals go beyond invoking emotions and include values-based messaging. In our day-to-day life at work, we can overlook the immense power of shared values. Jim Kouzes and Barry Posner have spent decades researching and writing about leadership, highlighting the importance of clear and shared values.[8] In a study of 711 members of the American Management Association, Posner found that high levels of congruence between personal values and organizational values, and high levels of clarity of organizational values, were both significantly related to higher commitment, satisfaction, motivation, and ethics, as well as lower job anxiety and less work stress. This was regardless of age, gender, and function area.[9] And we can see the power of values alignment around the world. A study of over four hundred professionals across seventy-two corporate teams in Taiwan found that teammates' shared work values were positively related to team member performance and satisfaction with cooperation.[10]

Often we forget to highlight and draw on shared values. While we're happy to work with people who have different styles and areas of expertise and experience from ours (this difference is usually why we seek them out in the first place), we want to work with people who share our values. Knowing that your core principles are aligned is perhaps the most powerful foundation for influencing.

We readily talk about what I call "banner values"—those displayed on the walls in reception and the homepage of the company's website. But when it comes to the values we live and breathe at work, and the values we hold personally, we can be more reserved. This can be because we think others aren't interested, because it makes us feel vulnerable if we share, or because we're just not in the habit of talking about values at work. If all else is equal with your competition—your expertise, offerings, price points, etc.—but you convey shared values in your presentation or pitch, you will stand out. And even if everything else is not equal, you may still find values to be the key differentiator that sways a final vote. This is especially (but not exclusively) relevant to the context of business to business. But also within an organization, colleague to colleague, regardless of hierarchy, having a genuine interest in what matters to others and choosing to share your aligned values can significantly increase your influence.

Instilling Confidence in Others: Ingratiation

Early in my career, my boss asked me to run a team day. I hadn't run one before. "I can't," I told him, "I don't know what to do!" "You absolutely can do this," he said. "I know you can. You'll be good at this because …" He went on to list four reasons he thought I personally was a good fit for this project. Ingratiation is about using praise to express confidence in someone's ability to carry out a challenging task or request. While flattery can be associated with insincerity, genuine praise is not just nice to have, but an actual necessity at times. We can have more confidence in another's ability than they have in themselves. Share with others specific reasons you believe they would be a good person to do what you're asking of them. People with gravitas not only build confidence in themselves by engaging in courageous behaviors, but also instill confidence in others around them.

Telling someone what you like, respect, or appreciate about him or her can also be a great way to adjust your perspective of a person you don't "click" with. You can find that one thing about them that you do like, such as the way they present or pull together a proposal. While this can be hard, it shifts your perception of them and ultimately has a positive impact on your relationship.

Participation Gains Buy-In … or Does It?: Consulting

Consultation is one of the most powerful influencing techniques available to us because we naturally are more attached to things we create. When others contribute their intellectual energy and professional expertise to a project or proposal, they are more likely to regard it positively.

Getting others involved to suggest improvements or to help plan our projects can mean they are more likely to give a positive assessment of it.

People have a desire for social consistency. It's the reason we are more likely to follow through on our goals if we share them with other people—we want to be seen as consistent with what we have said. If others suggest some part of our project is worthwhile by engaging and participating in it, they are more likely to stick with that idea.

So, participation gains buy-in. Or does it? A study of organizational change found consultation tactics to be associated with less resistance.[11] Research we conducted at the London School of Economics, however, suggests that while participation may increase buy-in, what matters is *if* it's genuine—if it's something we sincerely want and plan to take into account in decision-making, and if we have the potential to change based on their contribution.[12] The danger is in asking people to contribute, but failing to act on their input. It sounds obvious, but it happens regularly. Think of employee surveys. People get extremely frustrated when they share their ideas and feelings about the company, team, and work, but nothing is done to address their concerns. In our study, we looked at change leadership and found that while change leaders (those responsible for change strategy and/or implementation) received ideas and suggestions, employees often did not feel their ideas were given genuine consideration, and rarely were these ideas implemented. Similarly, if we invite contribution and then do nothing with it, we can unintentionally put ourselves in a worse position than if we had never sought feedback in the first place. This can decrease our influence and increase resistance to our plans. I am certainly not saying we should adopt others' ideas just to make them feel valued. They may not come up with the best idea, or there may be reasons their good ideas won't work or can't be implemented. But we do need to be genuine in our desire to hear others' feedback if we're asking for it. Be clear about the boundaries of what others can and can't shape, and invite participation within those boundaries. And if you choose not to follow through with their contribution, explain why.

Coalitions and Forward Influence

Consider who could make or break your project or proposal and request their contribution—their ideas, input, and alterations. Knowing that you have the support of a few key people will increase your confidence in your message. And when people perceive this message confidence, they will be more open to your ideas and suggestions. Having this support additionally allows you to draw on what I refer to as "forward influence"—whereby others, regardless of position and hierarchy, extend your influence beyond your own direct interactions. They go before you in positioning your proposal, behind you in reinforcing it, and beside you in influencing a wider sphere, and they take it beyond the people or spheres you could access alone.

Research supports the importance of identifying and gaining the support of key people for this form of influence. Bernard Caillaud at the Paris School of Economics and Jean Tirole at the University of Toulouse explored strategies that a proposal's sponsor may use to build consensus and persuade a majority of the group's members to accept their proposal.[13] Imagine you are the one making a proposal to a group. The research indicates that factors such as the size and governance of the group, and the extent of congruence among group members and between you (as the sponsor) and the group members, will affect your ability to build consensus. In addition, it is imperative to inform certain key group members individually of the idea or proposal. By distilling information in this way, members who approve of the proposal are able to sway the opinions of other members of the group. The study highlights the importance of identifying and bringing on board key members who possess credibility within the group and align with you, the sponsor. Key members' endorsements could turn out to be pivotal in influencing the receptivity of a majority of the group members in favor of your proposal. Getting key members' endorsements, through consultation or other means, requires us to take time out to engage them, and with sufficient lead time to offer real opportunities for a contribution that can meaningfully impact the plans.

It seems that influencing to get an idea or proposal accepted can work in a similar way to leading change successfully—getting other champions on board makes a tangible difference. This is yet another way we can be intentional when it comes to influence. This forward influence can be as powerful, if not more powerful, than your own direct influence.

Practically Applying the Influencing Techniques

We can increase our influence by being intentional with which techniques we choose to apply in a particular situation, based on our target assessment and thorough preparation. Remember, it is what you do before you go into the room that largely shapes how successful you are likely to be in influencing others once you're in the room. We can be strategic about how we influence directly and how we build forward influence.

There is much evidence to suggest the power of proactively utilizing various influencing techniques. One study of two thousand firms in Malaysia found that transformational managers tend to use inspirational appeals, consultation, and ingratiation to increase organizational citizenship behavior (OCB).[14] OCB is voluntary action and mutual aid without a request for pay or formal rewards—for example, accepting extra duties and responsibilities at work, working overtime when needed, or helping junior staff with their work. The researchers note that while most previous research attributes differences in OCB to leadership styles, appropriate choice and successful use of influence tactics (specifically, inspirational appeals and consultation) also play an important role in generating positive outcomes.

Rather than relying on habit, natural style, or what's been modeled to us to get others on board with our work, we need to first get clarity on the goal and then choose the best technique(s) available. A study in the public administration and public policy realm found the most effective techniques for influencing participants varied according to the type of decision being made.[15] In the visioning process, coalition tactics (other people supporting your idea with forward influence) and inspirational appeals were most effective. Where they needed to make more concrete decisions about current issues, rational persuasion, inspirational appeals, and consultation effectively influenced decisions.

Consider whether you use each of the techniques outlined above on a frequent, occasional, or rare basis. Given your influencing goals, are there other techniques you could try? If you're unsure of how they could be applied in your context, consider how those around you with gravitas influence key people in their sphere. Observe which techniques they apply in various situations and assess whether it is worth challenging your own influencing habits and expanding your toolkit. Look around you and see what naturally exists in your environment. Influence is like a muscle: if you don't use it, exercise it, and condition it, it won't get bigger and stronger. The best influencers reflect on and practice their techniques—they spend time giving great consideration to the context they are working in and the people they are trying to influence.

BEING PRODUCTIVE AT THE WATER COOLER AND HAVING INFLUENCE AT THE COFFEE MACHINE

We increase influence with intention, but what happens in the context of unplanned encounters in our day-to-day? Many of the people we seek to influence are in our world on a regular basis. In this case, influence isn't determined by a one-off event, but by their perception of us, built up over time through each encounter. So how can we prepare to influence in moments we didn't know were coming and couldn't possibly prepare for?

Professor Alex "Sandy" Pentland and his research group at MIT conducted research to challenge the notion that time spent informally chatting around the office is unproductive. They found that the cohesion of one's group, or "tribe," was a central predictor of productivity (where cohesion is defined by how connected work friends are with one another, how tight and interconnected their personal network is).[16] Pentland calls it the "Water Cooler Effect," arguing that much of the important information about how to be productive at work is found in informal conversation around the office. We find out how to be "successful" in our jobs here. Beyond productivity, we can also increase our influence around the coffee machine or the water cooler, or waiting for the elevator, or sitting at a large table with just one other person who also arrived a few minutes early for the meeting, while waiting for everyone else to show up. The list goes on. There are three ways in which the informal chat at the coffee machine can increase our influence.

The first comes as our general organizational knowledge increases— some of the questions on our target assessment list are answered in casual conversation (even when we don't explicitly ask the questions). We find out directly or indirectly about others' goals and challenges, resources, personalities, and positions.

Secondly, we deepen relationships and build trust. Influence is about much more than our ability to prove our case. Research suggests relationship building is crucial to successfully garnering support for new initiatives.[17] As we strengthen relationships, we are able to build trust, and this increases our ability to influence others through the techniques discussed earlier to ultimately add greater value. Research confirms what we see in our day-to-day work—a high degree of trust in the person proposing an initiative is more likely to elicit support from peers. In the busyness of our rush from one twenty- to thirty-minute meeting to the next, and the next, we cover much ground and can feel we get a lot of things done, but this habit of working can be at the expense of relationship building and trust. Research shows us that time at the coffee machine is not wasted.

Thirdly, we can be prepared for small encounters that can lead to great change. We need to recognize that we can prepare. These encounters seem spur of the moment, and indeed, we don't know whom we'll bump into and when. But it's likely we'll bump into someone. And if there's someone or a group of people we're trying to influence, it's likely we'll encounter them at some point, particularly if we are regularly getting out and about around the office. So while we don't know when an opportunity may arise, we can prepare for the brief encounters that can happen several times a day. We prepare for meetings and plan our work, but we just walk around bumping into people, shaping their perception of us with little, if any, forethought. Be ready for these brief encounters with content that would be important or interesting to the people you most seek to influence. Let's take a look at how this can play out in practice.

Jessel is in the office kitchen getting a mid-morning coffee. Chip, an executive who is not usually on his floor, walks in. "Jessel, how are you?" Chip asks. "Oh, yes, great, thanks, Chip. Really busy, you know. You?" Jessel replies, missing a rare opportunity to shape Chip's perception of him. Chip may, of course, interpret the "busy" comment to mean that Jessel is hardworking and in demand. He could also, however, take away that Jessel isn't coping well with his workload. Chip could interpret Jessel's off-the-cuff response in multiple ways, since Jessel offers no useful content. So let's give Jessel a second take.

"Jessel, how are you?" inquires Chip. "Oh, hi, Chip. I'm well, thanks," Jessel replies. "We're busy with a new project around sustainability. We think this can really drive some positive change. We're seeing a lot of interest from clients. How are things with you?" This response is a few short sentences that leave Chip with an understanding of Jessel's current work and its importance to the wider executive team, including Chip ("a lot of interest from clients"). If Jessel delivers it casually, it won't sound staged or over the top for a coffee machine conversation. It's simply about being ready to talk about what you're working on in two to three short sentences. Here are two things that might happen. First, Chip could ask more questions, find out more about Jessel's work, and note that he's making an important contribution. Second, Chip may pass this information on to others, thereby becoming a forward influencer on Jessel's behalf. Jessel could have gone one step further in the chat and applied another influencing technique such as consultation: "Actually, Chip, it would be great to get your input, if you have ten minutes anytime in the next couple of weeks?"

If you've left the house and there are other people where you work who at least know your face, it's very likely someone *will* ask, "How are you?" or "How are things going?"—those sweeping questions that give you the reins to respond with whatever you like regarding your health, personal life, work in general, current emotions, or what you're working on now. Of course, it's only about being prepared for encounters with people you are looking to influence (you don't need to be ready to chat with your friend Pete, who sits next to you and engages in nonstop banter with you!). But do take advantage of that inevitable generic question by being ready with one or two key messages (just a couple of sentences) for those potentially important, unplanned encounters. Not only can you positively shape key individuals' perceptions of you, you may create champions for forward influence that stretches far beyond the coffee machine.

INFLUENCE FROM A DISTANCE

But how do I have influence when it comes to virtual working? How can I apply the water cooler/coffee machine principles when I'm not actually in the office or regularly in the same space as the people I most want to influence? Virtual working is a growing part of most of our professional lives—we looked at some of the challenges and opportunities around virtual authentic gravitas in chapter 4. When it comes specifically to influence, research has shown that influencing techniques applied face-to-face are also successfully applied in virtual contexts.[18] One factor that plays an important role in virtual influence is ambiguity reduction. Researchers note that this requires empathy and perspective-taking, reinforcing our need to not only acquire knowledge and understanding of the people we're working with, but also to consider and be clear about potential areas of miscommunication.

As we wrap up this chapter, let's come back to Aria, our finance professional within the global branding and marketing agency, struggling with gravitas among her peer group. I was pleased that within a few short months, Aria became much happier and more confident at work. However, she didn't suddenly walk into their finance group meetings one day with more confidence. Aria's confidence built up gradually from the increased positive peer responses she received to her ideas and proposals for the wider financial strategies at the agency. These improved responses came after her assessment of key peers (remembering that assessment here is about giving greater consideration to others, their personal preferences for interacting, their goals, their resources, their challenges, etc.). This led to not only more, but also better, preparation for her encounters with them and being intentional in choosing which influencing techniques to apply. Aria was most comfortable using rational persuasion, but it was simply not working on its own with her peers. She chose to be courageous and try out different techniques that she was initially unsure of and which, at times, didn't work. But Aria bravely persisted and found various combinations of different techniques that worked for different people. It was certainly more work and required more energy, but it led to greater influence and authentic gravitas within her peer group. Working with Aria, I once again saw firsthand how confidence can be a by-product of being intentional and choosing courage.

We tend to rely on habit when trying to influence our management team, direct reports, peers, stakeholders, and clients. These habits may include styles that come more naturally to us, or that we've seen successfully modeled by people we respect. But there is a wide range of techniques available to us. Our greatest barriers to successfully influencing others can be not taking the time to think about how we currently influence, and how we want to influence. It requires thinking about how we work, not just what we have to do for work. If we are being intentional, we then need to be courageous enough to try out new styles and disciplined in seeking feedback and continuing to adapt. In doing so, we reduce the gap between intentions, action, and impact. Being prepared to use the full toolkit and being intentional about which tools to pull out at which time, with which people, fuels professional chemistry and equips you for greater authentic gravitas.

PRACTICES FOR CREATING PROFESSIONAL CHEMISTRY

We influence on a daily basis, yet it's easy to slip into unintentional habits and inherited behaviors that we've seen modeled, without considering if they're the *best* approach for the situation we're in, and in line with our goals for impact. If you're in a situation where you want to increase your positive influence, here is a reminder of two key points for creating that professional chemistry:

- Remember, there is a wide range of influencing techniques available to you. Most of us are not using our full toolkit. Try to identify at least one person whom you see using each of the influencing approaches effectively in your working environment: rational persuasion, legitimating, favors and exchange, inspirational appeals (emotions and values), ingratiation, and consulting. Reflect on what it is they do well and if there are any behaviors (sometimes this can be as small as a phrase or way of questioning) that you could try to adopt in your own way.

- Be ready to balance inquiry and advocacy, not just in the meeting room, but also in passing. Make time for small encounters around the office—sometimes just a couple of powerful open or focused questions can lead you to a much better understanding of another person or a particular situation. Also, be ready to share in these encounters. We think of them as unexpected, given that we don't know when and with whom they're going to happen, but these encounters aren't really a surprise. On any one day, assuming we've left the house and are headed to work, it's likely we'll meet at least a few people. Be ready with a couple of sentences that highlight what you're working on right now and why it matters. It's certainly not the goal to deliver a rehearsed speech at the coffee machine! But it is about being able to articulate what you're doing and why it matters succinctly—because one thing we do know is that people will ask. What we make of those brief encounters is up to us.

NINE

THE JOINT ADVENTURER

Creative Collaboration over Silent Competition

In chapter 1, we saw that rather than focusing on how to stand *out* from the crowd, authentic gravitas comes when we're able to focus on the people *in* the crowd. Instead of trying to be the superhero who stands apart and saves the day, people with authentic gravitas move toward others. While they often have the spotlight, they don't need it or focus on attaining it—rather, they focus on adding genuine value. As such, they are better able and more likely to promote collaborative effort. Driving collaboration means we are able to add greater value by drawing on collective energy, input, and creativity. In this chapter, we'll look at some of the reasons why collaborative efforts can fail or undermine authentic gravitas, and examine strategies for collaborating well.

WHY TWO (OR MORE) HEADS ARE BETTER THAN ONE

Here's the seeming irony: gravitas can be shared. We might find ourselves asking, "What is it about them—that person who stands out?"

Here, gravitas seems like a unique, individual quality. But those professionals with authentic gravitas are not afraid of sharing the spotlight. Sitting behind their spotlight, what makes them stand out is an ease that emanates from knowing that they don't need to keep the spotlight to themselves. They are focused on how they can make a positive, substantive contribution, and they are aware that they are better equipped to do that with others than to do it alone.

We collaborate when we intentionally choose humility—a belief that two, or more, heads really are better than one.[1] By humility, I do not mean putting yourself down or undervaluing your own skills, strengths, and potential contribution, but adopting a mind-set that *I alone cannot do what I have the potential to do with others who add different expertise, skills, and strengths*. It is a belief that *I can add more value when I'm collaborating with others*. Humility not only enables you to collaborate with others, but it also creates the conditions for others around you to collaborate. While humility is often regarded as a fairly stable trait, it is something that can change, through experience or training.[2] How can we train ourselves to be humble? Researchers highlight three factors that are essential for humility in a workplace context: willingness to obtain accurate self-knowledge, a tendency to keep an open mind and continuously learn and improve, and appreciation of others' strengths and contributions. In a study of CEOs, their top management teams (TMT), and outcomes at 105 US firms, researchers found that when a *humble* CEO runs a firm, its TMT is more likely to collaborate and share information.[3] They noted that this enables the CEOs to make the most of the firm's talent. In another study of sixty-three private companies in China, including 328 TMT members and 645 middle managers, findings revealed that CEO humility was positively associated with empowering leadership behaviors, which, in turn, was related to the level of TMT integration.[4] When people demonstrate humility and intentionally choose not to stand alone, their impact goes far above and beyond their direct interactions.

It also requires courage to invite collaboration—much more than it does to act alone or delegate. Because true collaboration is intimate and uncertain. It's now not just about me and how I show up, which I can control to some degree. It's about you and me. It's the *and* that is risky. I know me. I'm not perfect, but I'm known (of course I have blind spots, but I feel I know me more than I know you). I have a sense of what I'm capable of doing and delivering in this situation or with these clients or for my boss. I invite collaboration because I know that another person has the potential to add something different—something I don't know. Perhaps my expertise does not stretch to their area of expertise. Perhaps their strengths are not like my strengths. So even if I know that person, I don't know what they know and I can't add what they can. And there's the risk: the unknown. It takes courage to invite and drive collaboration with others—to trust them to co-deliver in situations and projects and meetings where others trust us. It is a counterintuitive idea, but in order to stand out, I need to stand alongside.

WIN-WIN OR DIE: THERE IS NO PIE

In all situations, we can unconsciously adopt either an exclusive or a collaborative approach. With the exclusive approach, we protect our projects and relationships and keep others at a distance. We protect our piece of the pie. We might do it with good intent, and we may be working alongside others in a team, but we don't truly drive collaboration. When we use the collaborative approach, we proactively bring in others to achieve our goals. This goes beyond—and is often confused with—compromise. At work, we often label our efforts as "collaborative," but really all we achieve, or had aimed for in the first place, is compromise. When it comes to our competing priorities and objectives, we win a bit and lose a bit. In collaboration, on the other hand, both parties win and tie success to their ability to collaborate, even when they started with conflicting ideas. You courageously create codependency for success. It's "win-win or die"—there is no pie to divide.

To offer collaboration is also a commitment to increased proximity and to building "relational capital": *I know that to truly collaborate, we must work well together, and I am prepared to be proactive in building our relationship, even though at times this is likely to be difficult.* It is a commitment to being more vulnerable with you and, perhaps even more poignantly, opening up the people who trust me to be vulnerable with you. In the creative process of working together, I will need to be transparent with my thinking and open with my motivations, and you will see not only my strengths at work, but more of my flaws as well. Collaboration never works without vulnerability. And if I have invited you in—whether you are my colleague or an expert from outside my immediate sphere—I am opening myself up to risk. But I am also opening up the potential for great gain. I may add value by myself, but we have the potential to be invaluable together. This is evidenced in the current shift in leadership thinking from individual to shared/collaborative leadership.

There is clear, strong research evidence for the benefits of increasing collaboration at work. Heidi K. Gardner from Harvard Law School has conducted extensive research showing that collaboration is a powerful driver of both financial and people-related benefits for firms.[5] Organizations globally are eagerly seeking help in building collaborative leaders and professionals. An openness to genuine collaboration and the skills to execute it are highly valued. Given that professionals with authentic gravitas lead the room, we'll look here at the requirements and enablers of collaborative leadership.

COLLABORATIVE LEADERSHIP

In organizational psychology, we no longer consider only the distinctions of "the leader" and "the followers," but also a collective, inclusive model where leadership is shared. And everywhere I turn, I hear leaders talking about their need for collaborative leadership. It's being identified as a fundamental differentiator in achieving strategic objectives. It's recognized as being a key foundation of how leaders can add substantive value. I think of real collaborative leadership as facilitating constructive interpersonal connections and activities between people and between heterogeneous groups to achieve shared goals. It is proactive and purpose-driven.

There is increasing evidence making the case for collaborative or shared leadership that showcases how this approach to work enables us to add greater value. Research into new venture performance found that shared leadership was positively related to new venture performance. Measuring performance by the growth rate of the firm, researchers found performance was positively related to leadership being shared in the top management team, regardless of their particular style of leadership.[6] Other research suggests shared or collaborative leadership is positively related to:

- Greater team interaction[7]

- Broader collaboration and coordination[8]

- Novel and more innovative solutions[9]

- Team effectiveness and performance[10, 11]

In order to make a difference, though, collaborative leadership has to go beyond the polite, thoughtful behaviors of involving others, sharing information, and lending strength when it's needed.

Dubai Airports offer a case study. When I interviewed the leaders there, they were being incredibly proactive in their collaborative leadership efforts, with a very clear purpose. While already running the world's busiest airport for international travel (passenger traffic grew to over 88 million in 2017), they recognized that to achieve their vision of becoming the world's leading airport company, they needed to drive a new service culture through the 3,400-person organization.[12] But they knew they couldn't make a meaningful change in their culture alone. To change customers' real experience of Dubai Airports, they needed to engage their vendors and partners as well.

One of the outcomes was a customer service training program that was rolled out over a three-year period across many stakeholder organizations and 43,000 employees. The Dubai Airports team was investing in training for more than 39,000 people outside of their own organization, aiming to ensure behavioral consistency and therefore customer experience consistency at every possible touch point. Samya Ketait, Dubai Airports' VP for learning and development, said, "This is a huge project, but a worthwhile one. It means that regardless of who you meet at Dubai Airports—a police officer, a cleaner, an immigration officer—you should have the same positive customer experience. Collaborating with our stakeholder leaders has made this possible."

While it's spoken of highly in organizational life, collaborative leadership is not something that necessarily comes easily. It may seem like a lovely, generous gesture of Dubai Airports to offer customer service training for so many other organizations' employees, but the leaders of those outside organizations had to weigh the costs of their employees' time out of work to participate, and to trust Dubai Airports with training their teams in a way that would match their own organizations' values and objectives. To sustain the three-year collaborative process and achieve its goals, these leaders recognized the behaviors that would make it work.

When it comes to collaboration, these factors can drive success:

- Focusing on interests rather than positions. As with negotiations and conflict resolution, one of the most important keys to successful collaboration is focusing on interests rather than positions. When we are "collaborating," we are typically not from the same team— otherwise, we would most likely frame it as "teamwork." What makes teamwork different from collaboration is the goal. In collaboration, the goals may be different—we may have different positions, yet common ground can almost always be found at the level of interests. In collaborating with others, ask, "What's most important to you here? What really matters?" Encourage their openness and foster trust by sharing personally what your main drivers are.

- Being an agent *and* a target of influence. In the last chapter, we looked in great detail at how to increase influence (i.e., to be a more successful *agent* of influence). This is important, as influence (e.g., influencing people toward common goals) is at the core of what constitutes leadership, and people with authentic gravitas, regardless of their position, lead the room. Of equal importance when it comes to collaboration is being prepared to be a *target* of others' influence, as discussed in chapter 5. This requires *openness* to alternative ideas, *inquisitiveness* to understand the foundation of others' arguments before pushing back and asserting one's own ideas, and *recognition* of the other party's value and what they add to the collaborative venture.

- Sharing ownership of the goal, but dividing roles and responsibilities. Explore and understand one another's strengths and expertise, then go through a detailed process of agreeing who is responsible for what. After studying multiple corporate examples of shared leadership, James O'Toole, Jay Galbraith, and Edward E. Lawler suggest that shared leadership is much more likely to be successful with clear and agreed-upon differentiation.[13] Map out roles and responsibilities early, but remember that this isn't a one-off conversation. Make collaborative efforts sustainable by regularly reevaluating your respective roles and effectiveness in delivering on those roles, being prepared to hold one another accountable.

- Carving out space and time to collaborate—and identifying a mission worthy of that effort. Too often in organizational life, we know we should be collaborating, and so try to squeeze it into our schedules when really we just want to get the pressing things on our to-do list done, or collaborate simply to the point of meeting our own immediate priorities. In order for collaboration to be purposeful and sustainable, it needs to meet all parties' true interests, warrant their time, and help them achieve their core objectives. We need to high-light why this particular collaboration matters (not just extol "collaboration" in general), what difference it will make, and encourage the project's participants to create the time and space it deserves. Only then can we find creative ways forward that have the potential to exceed our initial plans and expectations for what we can achieve.

One of the most exciting parts of the collaborative journey is that while it is purpose-driven (there are clear goals and objectives in mind to achieve along the way), the end is unwritten: we never know where our collaborative efforts may take us. One door opens another possibility, and one creative venture prequels another. And in being courageous enough to risk sharing the effort and the ending, you position yourself to make a more important contribution and add greater value, thereby increasing your gravitas.[14]

THE CHALLENGES OF BEING SIDE BY SIDE

When we choose to collaborate, we can increase our gravitas by increasing the value of our contribution. But what happens when collaboration is almost forced upon us?

In order to lead the room well, we need to acknowledge that today we rarely lead alone—we lead with others. The days of the "Great Man" theory of leadership—where one leader rules over the masses from an ivory tower—are long gone.

Some of us quite literally lead with others—we co-lead a project, a team, or an organization with a peer. Others informally co-lead with colleagues. Although sharing leadership can be energizing and rewarding, the arrangement can easily become draining and frustrating if the relationship isn't strong. We might have divided responsibilities, but the reality of leading alongside others is that it's often tricky, messy, political, and hard. In the intricacies and difficulties of leading together with others, we can also risk reducing our authentic gravitas. What if their contribution derails our goals, or their behavior does not reflect our values—does this behavior misrepresent our own values given our collaboration?

Success begins with commitment. When colleagues and I designed and facilitated the first collaborative training between the police forces of two countries with a decades-long history of conflict, we had the opportunity to see shared leadership in its most intense and most powerful form. Not merely putting the past aside, but rather prioritizing a peaceful joint future, the leaders from each of the forces ensured a successful training that rolled out across the two countries. Their joint success was not only a result of their commitment to the program and its objectives, but their visible commitment to one another, which began with a steeled choice and ended with a valued relationship that would go on to impact countless others.

Whether we are recruited or promoted into a role to lead with others, start a new project or venture with chosen partners, or actively bring others on board to lead alongside us, collaborative leadership is both an opportunity and a challenge that most of us will face. And in order for our authentic gravitas to be increased in the process of leading with others, rather than put at risk, we need to be proactive in making collaborative leadership work in line with our values. Here are a few keys for building and maintaining authentic gravitas through the challenges and complexity of collaborative leadership.

- Be transparent from the outset about what matters to you. We often assume others have the same professional values as us. But while they may sound the same at a big-picture level (e.g., trust, respect, innovation, etc.), how these values play out at a behavioral level can be very different and trigger frustration or concern. Equally, find out what matters to your co-leaders—don't settle for throwaway value statements, but seek to understand what their values look like in practice. Ask for examples and explore what success would look like for them, not just in terms of what is achieved, but the process of getting there. If there's tension in the collaborative efforts, check in to see if your co-leaders feel their values are being accurately represented . . . and share if you feel yours aren't. With transparency and respect, most differences can be resolved; but if there is both clarity and conflict at a values level, it may be time to consider ending or changing the collaboration. In collaborating, we still have to own the gap between intention and impact, even if that impact is coming from our co-leaders.

- Remember that there are more people affected by shared leadership than just those who are leading. As leaders, we tend to focus on how we navigate this relationship for ourselves, but it can be equally tricky for others to navigate us. With your co-leaders, be mindful of your joint impact on others. Clients, our managers, and especially our combined team can find shared leadership arrangements challenging and confusing, especially at first. Be clear about communicating your roles and responsibilities to others, and seek regular feedback on how they experience you not just as individuals, but also as a collective leadership group.

- Be first to reallocate praise for successes and to take responsibility for failures. Check in on who is being given credit for what. Acknowledging our own part in a problem, even if it's taking a small portion of the blame, alleviates tension during conflict and leads to faster reconciliation. The flip side is true of facilitating collaborative success. Acknowledging others' contributions, be they big or small, in the success of our ventures, energizes them in our collaborative efforts. Nothing undermines collaborative leadership like one leader taking all the credit—whether actively or by passively allowing others to attribute success to them. Because our brains interpret perceived unfairness as a threat, tensions between co-leaders could be coming from a sense (even a subconscious one) that they are not receiving due credit for their contributions. Whether others correctly or incorrectly assign success to you personally, offer praise to your co-leaders for any success. And when failures happen, own and address them together, regardless of your direct input into the situation.

- Be open to renegotiating your roles based on changing circumstances and ambitions. Over time, our skills grow and we want to expand our capability. A task that may once have been unappealing to your co-leaders may eventually become a stretch goal they would like to embrace. Whether it's directing part of the business function, taking the lead on large client projects, fronting presentations and pitches, or owning one-to-one development meetings for the team, there are endless ways both you and your co-leader may want to change the dynamic of your relationship. Be open to these changes, and share your own evolving goals.

- Recognize that of all people, it's likely that you personally have the greatest impact on your co-leader's experience of work, and that they have the same impact on yours. Honest conversations exploring the reality of this impact—what's great, what's challenging, and what feels limiting or restrictive—may be emotional and very likely uncomfortable, but will be worth it.

These points may seem obvious, but in the daily busyness, and sometimes messiness, of collaboration, it can be difficult to prioritize these practices. Investing time and energy into the collaborative relationship beyond just the scope of your role will almost certainly make it a better one. It will also mean that for both the organization and the co-leaders personally, two heads—or more—really can be better than one.[15]

CLOSE ENOUGH TO FIGHT

I often get calls from executives about facilitating management team days, and when asked what their number one goal is, some offer the intruiging response, "to be able to argue more." They'll describe their team positively, but know there's a deeper level of connection missing. "We're nice, we have fun together, we like each other and trust each other on some level, but it needs to be deeper. We need to be able to disagree with one another more openly." To be people who foster collaboration, we need to create a team culture where people choose to challenge one another—on their thinking, their behavior, and their decisions. We need to be more than just "nice." It's easier to choose to sweep a lot of things under the rug. It's easier to go to someone else and complain about a person rather than confront them. And it's easy to oscillate between two extremes of not bringing up anything challenging most of the time and then having the odd explosion. We might feel comfortable yelling at a driver who has just cut us off, or complaining to a random service provider about a terrible experience, but most of us find it hard to choose confrontation when it comes to people we have continuing, close working relationships with. But conflict isn't necessarily a bad thing, and it should be expected given that for most of us, there is no "right answer" in business. Conflict in business can be constructive or destructive— what matters is how we handle differing positions and points of view. Disagreements about the way forward in particular can be healthy, productive, and lead to better outcomes. Fostering an environment of being "close enough to fight" with peers is one of the trickiest challenges we face in developing a healthy collaborative culture. The peer relationship can be simultaneously the most comfortable and the most threatening. Time after time, I've encountered successful professionals whose core barrier to authentic gravitas seems to be building genuine trust and practical collaboration with peers. Why is it that we can feel less sure of ourselves with peers? And what can we do about it?

Peers tend to be the people in the organization with the same level of specialist knowledge that we have. Often they come from a similar background and have the same amount of experience. They know what we know. So when a peer has a more assertive or aggressive style than you do, or simply comes to different conclusions from the same set of facts, it can feel like a personal attack on your way of doing things. Our internal monologue oscillates between negative self-talk (*Why didn't I think of that?*) and defensiveness (*That'll never work anyway!*). This common monologue hinders our gravitas. Moreover, there's a natural competitiveness between people at the same level in the organization—you're often competing for the same resources and promotions. Letting this turn into a negative cycle can be destructive, eroding your own confidence, undercutting your attempts to come across as calm and competent, and limiting the value you're able to add.

People with authentic gravitas have learned the skills and committed to the disciplines and strategies for making relationships work well in order to truly be "close enough to fight." These commitments include:

1. Recognizing your own uncertainty about others' intentions. We focus on the gap between our own intent and impact, and feel bad when we have an unintended negative impact on others. Through the pure acknowledgment of this difference, whether stated to others or just a self-whisper (e.g., "I didn't mean to come across like that"), we are shifting the focus from our impact to our intention. With others, it's easy just to focus on their impact, as that's all we can see or experience. Let's be gracious enough to others to assume they also have a gap between their intention and impact on us, and not just examine their impact but also explore their intention.

2. Choosing courageous conversations rather than silent competition. To have an honest conversation about your dynamic and relationship with that one person who particularly intimidates you takes a huge amount of vulnerability, personal risk, and interpersonal skill. The easy option is to continue without having the difficult conversation. The courageous conversation is more likely to lead to collaboration and better outcomes. When you're less intimidated, you don't just feel stronger—you're able to give more in terms of both quantity and quality.

3. Realizing that in business, for most of us, there is no right answer.
This little mantra has helped some of my most intimidated clients to share
their views with strong-minded peers. When I ask them to recall the last
time they offered an opinion that was ridiculed (openly or silently), they
can't give one example. Speaking up is almost always worth the risk.

4. Recognizing there actually is no pie. Working with peers is not a
winner-takes-all game; more wins for you does not mean fewer for me.
Not adopting an idea doesn't mean the idea wasn't valuable, particularly
if it was a springboard for others' contributions. Conversely, getting your
proposal accepted doesn't necessarily mean that you gain an edge over
your peers.

The goal is not to reduce the frequency with which we disagree
with our peers or vice versa. It's to change how we feel about these
conversations. Whether it's with peers, our boss, people who report
to us or are more junior, customers, clients, or other stakeholders—
these steps can help us to foster deeper relationships in even the
most challenging contexts. Ironically, it's by stepping further into the
uncomfortable—by having courageous conversations, carving out seemingly impossible time to think, being more willing to say and hear a variety of opinions, and being "close enough to fight"—that we are able to
fuel real collaboration. Even when we have difficult messages to deliver
or when we outright disagree, we can have positive connection and add
significant value.[16]

A FOUNDATION OF TRUST

Perhaps the most important requirement for creative collaboration is
one that sits at the very heart of authentic gravitas: trust. It's not enough
to be open to, and proactive about, inviting others to collaborate. We
need to create conditions for them to want collaboration, because rarely

is it easy—it often requires more time and has great risks attached not just for us but for others. The key is building trust. Researcher Gloria Barczak and colleagues at Northeastern University explored antecedents of creativity within teams.[17] They looked at two parts of team trust: affective trust (the confidence an individual places in a team member based on empathy or concern shown by that team member) and cognitive trust (the confidence a person places in another based on that team member's competence and reliability). They found that team trust helps to create a culture of collaboration, which in turn enhances team creativity. Cognitive trust also moderates the relationship between collaborative culture and team creativity. We need to foster trust—a willingness of others to be vulnerable with us.

What is likely to influence another's decision to take a chance and trust us? Trust researchers from the Kellogg School of Management at Northwestern University highlighted various factors that will shape a person's choice: their own propensity to trust; their emotions; and their perceptions of our trustworthiness (based on such factors as assessments of our interests and advantages, social roles and groups, relationship history, social norms, and third-party reports). They argue that people naturally assess others' trustworthiness before they engage in trusting actions.[18] For mutual trust, one person has to take the first step. The researchers noted that this subjects that person to risk—of intentional or unintentional exploitation, embarrassment, or other negative outcomes. If we are serious about building authentic gravitas, which is grounded in trust, we are called on to take the first step.

Interestingly, collaboration and trust appear to exist in a positive cycle. Where we actively collaborate, we foster greater trust. A Canadian research team found that not only did fostering collaboration help build trust and manage conflict, but that *without collaboration, trust had no bearing on performance.*[19] This again highlights the promise and power of collaboration in practice. It may be that collaboration is the greatest opportunity we have for adding positive, significant value.

PRACTICES FOR BEING A JOINT ADVENTURER

The reality is, the people who stand out for the positive, significant value they add are those who are prepared to stand alongside others. Collaboration requires us to be *humble* (recognizing that two or more heads can add more value than one), *courageous* (it's normal to feel risk—by inviting others in, we're bringing in an element of the unknown), and *vulnerable* (others will see more of our flaws, as well as our strengths, and we have to be okay with that). If you're not feeling prepared to be vulnerable with the people you're collaborating with, it's likely they're not willing to be vulnerable with you, either. But a willingness to be vulnerable is a core component of trust, and without trust, we can't genuinely collaborate. Here's a summary of some useful behaviors and habits to practically build collaboration:

- Move beyond positions to understand interests (what is most important to your collaborators when it comes to the area you're discussing). Be transparent from the outset about what matters to you. If you miss this step in the collaboration process, if you don't feel understood or things have changed, be prepared to open up and have these conversations. It might feel awkward, but true collaboration requires transparency when it comes to our interests. Be open to renegotiating your roles based on changing circumstances and ambitions as a result of that conversation. You might want to change your goals as your collaborative project evolves; check in to see if your colleagues would like to change theirs, too.

- Be prepared to be a target of your colleagues' influence, rather than simply focusing on influencing them. If you are truly sharing ownership of the goal, make sure you have clearly allocated roles and responsibilities. This will help guide the process for who takes the lead and influences whom at various stages and decisions along the way. Regardless of the allocation, be first to reallocate praise for successes and first to take responsibility for failures. If you see others giving credit to you and not your partner(s), or highlighting their failings at no cost to you, direct some praise to them or shoulder some of the responsibility for those failings.

- Make sure you're building real time to collaborate into your schedules and give your efforts the space and energy they need to be successful. It's easier to build this time in at the beginning, when we're excited about where the collaboration could go. But rarely is it our only responsibility. We can get caught up in other tasks that require our time, but the potential of collaboration can only be realized if we continue to (psychologically and practically) commit to it.

- See if you really are "close enough to fight"—in a good way, that is—going beyond the niceties and being prepared to be honest and challenge one another. Our uncertainty about others' intentions can hold us back from really opening up. Think about the people you're working alongside. Do you know their intentions? If you're not sure, it's worth asking them—just go in prepared to share yours, too (probably first).

Ultimately, for collaboration, we need trust. If we are committed to building genuine trust, then we need to follow through with the behaviors outlined above to ensure it's mutual, based on a strong understanding, and grounded in an ongoing commitment. Remember that for mutual trust, one person has to take the first step—be prepared to take it.

THE AUTHENTIC GRAVITAS JOURNEY

The Myth of the Gravitas Gift would have us believe that some people are "naturals" when it comes to having other people take them seriously. These people seem to carry the most weight, regardless of hierarchy, and effortlessly command respect from those around them. But in reality, they have most likely worked very hard at developing skills and behaviors that allow them to credibly have a positive impact and add significant value. As a result, their contributions are in line with their values and are taken seriously, engendering feelings of respect and trust in others.

The Myth of Confidence would have us believe that people with gravitas wake up feeling confident every single day. They don't—or at least, not every day. And certainly, as they continue to step into new opportunities and take on new challenges, their confidence wavers just like everyone else's. We all want confidence, but courage precedes it. Don't wait to feel confident; clarify your goals for impact and commit to courage, connection, and curiosity. As you do so, regularly seeking feedback and continuing to adapt, you minimize the gap between your intention and your impact. The Myth of Charisma would whisper, if we let it, that we just don't have what it takes—*I'm not enough*. But we know that authentic gravitas isn't reserved for people with a certain personality. You can have gravitas and still be you.

There are so many areas about who stands out and why yet to be explored with future research. Let's take a final look at the truths about authentic gravitas, as we know them so far:

- It's more about courage than it is about confidence. Courage precedes confidence.

- It's about leading—taking ownership of and responsibility for a situation to influence and facilitate others to achieve collective goals. It's not about waiting for a position of leadership.

- It's more about a commitment to developing skills than it is about natural style. It's not something you're born with, and there's no fixed personal characteristic requirement for gravitas.

- It's not about being serious and self-important. It's about being taken seriously and considered important—being valued—because you're making a valuable contribution.

- It's as much about inquiry as it is about advocacy. It's not being the loudest voice in the room that counts. It is about clearly and persuasively explaining your thinking, offering insights, and not shying away from expressing your point of view. It's about having conviction without being dogmatic. Equally, your understanding of the situation and others' motivations and perspectives matters. Curiosity counts. The people who stand out in the crowd are those who move toward the crowd, not those who focus on standing apart from it.

- It's about credibility with a commitment to learning and increasing knowledge, as well as how you use that knowledge, but also remembering that knowledge alone is not enough. Inspiring people live inspired.

- Anyone can authentically have gravitas. Being authentic isn't about staying the same, defaulting to "natural," unintentional habits. It's about adapting and growing to increasingly act in ways that align clear intention with actual impact. Authenticity requires agility.

- Rather than being an invincible superhero, gravitas demands vulnerability, discipline, and humility. It requires vulnerability to get feedback about ways in which your impact may not line up with your intention, discipline to keep trying out and sticking with new behaviors to achieve the impact you're after, and humility to accept that two or more heads really are better than one. People with authentic gravitas are collaborators, not independent heroes.

We want to add great value, but habits and busyness can get in the way. My hope is that as you've come with me on this gravitas journey, some of the ideas and practical steps have stood out and been useful to you. Most of all, I hope that you intentionally and courageously implement those practices in the midst of the pressures and realities of daily organizational life, and that when you reflect on the question, *Did I add the most value that I could today?* your answer will be increasingly and authentically *yes*.

ACKNOWLEDGMENTS

I'm thankful to be surrounded by outstanding people who make a positive, significant difference to my life. They have made an incredible contribution to my personal and professional journey.

First, I'm grateful to my clients. While I have changed names and some details, the accounts in this book are all based on the experiences of real people. Thank you for inviting me into your worlds and sharing your stories. We often believe that our challenges are unique to us and our strengths are commonplace. By being vulnerable and open with what you find hard, you help us see that our challenges are largely shared, and it is our strengths that are unique. By having the courage to try out new things, you have paved the way for others to discover strategies and behaviors that may equip them. My sincere thanks to the research participants for sharing your time, insights, and experiences. Thank you to my many colleagues and friends passionate about leadership and professional development for your wisdom, ideas, and relentless encouragment, and to the researchers globally whose dedicated work has informed the ideas in this book.

I have the wonderful opportunity to wear both a practitioner and an academic hat. It has been twenty years since I first walked into the London School of Economics and Political Science, and I still learn something new every day. Thank you to all those in the Department of Management with whom I have the privilege of working. My particular thanks to Paul Willman, Saul Estrin, Jackie Coyle-Shapiro, Connson Locke, and Joanne Hay for welcoming me into the Department of Management, and to Sandy Pepper and Emma Soane, who have guided me so wisely for many years, who encouraged me to write, and who demonstrate authentic gravitas every day. Thank you also to my LSE students—I am inspired by your energy and determination to make a significant difference in your world. During my time at Harvard University, I was amazed by the generosity of so many incredible people, particularly Jeff Polzer, the late J. Richard Hackman, and Paul R. Lawrence. Thank you for your welcome, and your input and challenges to my ideas.

To my incredible team at CoachAdviser, thank you for being on this book journey with me, and for allowing it to take such a central place in our working life. Particular thanks to Tia Aitken, Kimberley Rayman, and especially Patrycja Sowa—for helping me navigate the vast research literature and for your enthusiasm for this project, which at times surpassed my own. I'm also thankful to the executive education teams at LSE, the University of Cambridge Møller Centre, and Duke Corporate Education, who have invited me to facilitate development programs with some of the world's largest, industry-leading organizations. These opportunities enabled me to partner with and learn from the very best, and to explore what is most useful to global organizations in preparing leaders for the future.

This book was a thought in my mind for many years, but it only came to life because of my incredible literary agent, Giles Anderson. Thank you for seeing the potential in, and for your commitment to, both this book and me. Your advice and guidance have been invaluable. To the teams at TarcherPerigee and Orion, thank you for your excitement about my book and your superb direction. Particular thanks to my excellent editor, Joanna Ng—I am so grateful for your advice, patience, and encouragement from beginning to end. Thank you to the teams at *Forbes*, particularly Fred Allen, and at *Harvard Business Review* for giving me the opportunity to share and test my ideas. In particular, thanks to Sarah Green-Carmichael at *HBR*. Your writing and editorial skills are exceptional, your insights always spot-on, and I have learned so much from you.

I have many friends who are also my most trusted advisers and mentors—thank you all for your fierce belief in me. Particular thanks to Elsbeth Johnson, Meghan Oates-Zalesky, Lea Waldron, Vicky Rough,

Flip and Susan Flippen, James Prior, Ana Loback, Melanie Backe-Hansen, Rosalie Audoin, and Sal Dennis—I have navigated the opportunities and challenges of this professional adventure much better thanks to you. I am extremely grateful to Paul Brewerton, who has been my closest mentor for nearly twenty years, and whose detailed critique made this book better. I am thankful to Gary and Cathy Clarke for encouraging me to always "look up," and to Kris and Kalleigh Mikkelson, who show me what it is to lead with authenticity every day.

Finally, thanks to all who walked this book journey with me—you know who you are, my "besties." Apparently, there are some people in the world who would say, "It can't be done. You're crazy," to a mum of two, signing a book deal while eight months pregnant with her third child and launching a new business. I'm glad I don't know them. Thank you to my dear friends who tell me I can when I feel like I can't. My faith and my friends are two of the biggest parts of who I am, making me feel like my version of "normal" is actually exciting, meaningful, and fun. And to my incredible family—thank you to the Newton-Darbys for your wise counsel and everyday fun; to the van Dijk family for your encouragement; and to my parents, Ray and Lesley Newton, for telling me all my life that I could do anything (and practically enabling me through being the best grandparents in the world). Above all, I am so grateful for the unwavering love, patience, and support of my husband, Stephan, and our three little munchkins, Saskia, Sam, and Amélie—you are my rock, my reason, and my smile. Thank you.

CHAPTER 1: THE MYTHS OF GRAVITAS

1. Definition of *gravitas* from the *Cambridge Advanced Learner's Dictionary & Thesaurus*, https://dictionary.cambridge.org/dictionary/english/gravitas.

2. Definition of *gravitas* from the *English Oxford Living Dictionary,* https://en.oxforddictionaries.com/definition/gravitas.

3. T. Brosch and D. Sander, "Neurocognitive Mechanisms Underlying Value-Based Decision-Making: From Core Values to Economic Value," *Frontiers in Human Neuroscience* 7 (2013): 398. Definitions of *value* from the *Oxford Dictionary of English*, https://en.oxforddictionaries.com/definition/value (accessed December 13, 2018).

4. Adapted from R. Newton, "What Kind of Leader Do You Want to Be?" *Harvard Business Review,* January 26, 2015, https://hbr.org/2015/01/what-kind-of-leader-do-you-want-to-be.

5. M.E. Palanski, K.L. Cullen, W.A. Gentry, and C.M. Nichols, "Virtuous Leadership: Exploring the Effects of Leaders' Courage and Behavioral Integrity on Leader Performance and Image," *Journal of Business Ethics* 132, no. 2 (2015): 297–310.

6. J. Ménard and L. Brunet, "Authenticity and Well-Being in the Workplace: A Mediation Model," *Journal of Managerial Psychology* 26, no. 4 (2011): 331–346.

7. U.B. Metin, T.W. Taris, M.C.W. Peeters, I. Van Beek, and R. van den Bosch, "Authenticity at Work: A Job-Demands Resources Perspective," *Journal of Managerial Psychology* 31, no. 2 (2016): 483–499.

8. A.M. Wood, A.P. Linley, J. Maltby, M. Baliousis, and S. Joseph, "The Authentic Personality: A Theoretical and Empirical Conceptualization and the Development of the Authenticity Scale," *Journal of Counseling Psychology* 55, no. 3 (2008): 385–399.

9. M.M. Koerner, "Courage as Identity Work: Accounts of Workplace Courage," *Academy of Management Journal* 57, no. 1 (2014): 63–93.

10. C.R. Rate, J.A. Clarke, D.R. Lindsay, and R.J. Sternberg, "Implicit Theories of Courage," *Journal of Positive Psychology* 2, no. 2 (2007): 80–98.

11. C.R. Woodard and C.L.S. Pury, "The Construct of Courage: Categorization and

Measurement," *Consulting Psychology Journal: Practice and Research* 59, no. 2 (2007): 135–147.

12. D. van Dierendonck and I. Nuijten, "The Servant Leadership Survey: Development and Validation of a Multidimensional Measure," *Journal of Business and Psychology* 26, no. 3 (2011): 249–267. The authors describe the theory of servant leadership, first introduced by Greenleaf (1997), as ethical and people-centered, including a moral component with emphasis on the needs of followers. The idea of service is embedded in the leader–follower relationship, whereby leaders have a genuine concern for followers.

13. J.J. Sosik, W.A. Gentry, and J.U. Chun, "The Value of Virtue in the Upper Echelons: A Multisource Examination of Executive Character Strengths and Performance," *Leadership Quarterly* 23, no. 3 (2012): 367–382.

14. A. Bandura, *Self-Efficacy: The Exercise of Control* (New York: W. H. Freeman and Company, 1997).

15. R.M. Tipton and E.L. Worthington, "The Measurement of Generalized Self-Efficacy: A Study of Construct Validity," *Journal of Personality Assessment* 48, no. 5 (1984): 545–548.

16. B. Amos and R.J. Klimoski, "Courage: Making Teamwork Work Well," *Group and Organization Management* 39, no. 1 (2014): 110–128.

17. L.E. Sekerka, R.P. Bagozzi, and R. Charnigo, "Facing Ethical Challenges in the Workplace: Conceptualizing and Measuring Professional Moral Courage," *Journal of Business Ethics* 89, no. 4 (2009): 565–579. Even when looking at courageous efforts as having trait-like qualities, which are relatively stable over time, researchers argue that these features of one's personal character can be developed in most people.

18. D. Putman, "Philosophical Roots of the Concept of Courage," in *The Psychology of Courage: Modern Research on an Ancient Virtue,* eds. C.L.S. Pury and S.J. Lopez (Washington, DC: American Psychological Association, 2010), 9–22.

19. W.I. Miller, *The Mystery of Courage* (Cambridge, MA: Harvard University Press, 2002).

20. R. Reed, *If I Could Tell You Just One Thing . . .* (Edinburgh: Canongate Books, 2016).

21. M.E. Palanski et al., "Virtuous Leadership."

22. T. Thompson, P. Foreman, and F. Martin, "Imposter Fears and Perfectionistic Concern over Mistakes," *Personality and Individual Differences* 29, no. 4 (2000): 629–647.

23. D. Malhotra and F. Lumineau, "Trust and Collaboration in the Aftermath of Conflict: The Effects of Contract Structure," *Academy of Management Journal* 54, no. 5 (2011): 981–998.

CHAPTER 2: CONNECTION OVER CHARISMA

1. "The World's 100 Most Powerful Women (2010)," *Forbes*, https://www.forbes .com/lists/2010/11/power-women_2010.html.

2. Adapted from R. Newton. "What Kind of Leader Do You Want to Be?"

3. J.S. Lerner, Y. Li, P. Valdesolo, and K. Kassam, "Emotions and Decision Making," *Annual Review of Psychology* 66 (2015): 799–823.

4. M. Seo and L.F. Barrett, "Being Emotional During Decision Making—Good or Bad? An Empirical Investigation," *Academy of Management Journal* 50, no. 4 (2007): 923–940.

5. B. Seymour and R. Dolan, "Emotion, Decision-Making, and the Amygdala," *Neuron* 58, no. 5 (2008): 662–671.

6. The first definition is from the *English Oxford Living Dictionaries*: Oxford University Press, https://en.oxforddictionaries.com/definition/charisma (accessed December 13, 2018). The second is from the *Cambridge Advanced Learner's Dictionary & Thesaurus*: Cambridge University Press, https://dictionary.cambridge.org/diction ary/english/charisma (accessed December 13, 2018). Italics added.

7. S. Plous, *The Psychology of Judgment and Decision-Making* (New York: McGraw-Hill, Inc., 1993).

8. P.R. Wheeler and V. Arunachalam, "The Effects of Decision Aid Design on the Information Search Strategies and Confirmation Bias of Tax Professionals," *Behavioral Research in Accounting* 20, no. 1 (2008): 131–145. Although confirmation bias is typically regarded as occurring in non-expert decision-makers, various studies such as this one show us that professionals do exhibit confirmation bias.

9. J. Park, P. Konana, B. Gu, A. Kumar, and R. Raghunathan, "Confirmation Bias, Overconfidence, and Investment Performance: Evidence from Stock Message Boards," *McCombs Research Paper,* Series No. IROM-07–10 (2010).

10. E.J. Carter and K.A. Pelphrey, "Friend or Foe? Brain Systems Involved in the Perception of Dynamic Signals of Menacing and Friendly Social Approaches," *Social Neuroscience* 3, no. 2 (2008): 151–163.

11. T. Masuda, P.C. Ellsworth, B. Mesquita, J. Leu, S. Tanida, and E. van de Veerdonk, "Placing the Face in Context: Cultural Differences in the Perception of Facial Emotion," *Journal of Personality and Social Psychology* 94, no. 3 (2008): 365–381.

12. A. Tanaka, A. Koizumi, H. Imai, S. Hiramatsu, E. Hiramoto, and B. de Gelder, "I Feel Your Voice: Cultural Differences in the Multisensory Perception of Emotion," *Psychological Science* 21, no. 9 (2010): 1259–1262.

13. S. Mineyama, A. Tsutsumi, S. Takao, K. Nishiuchi, and N. Kawakami, "Supervisors' Attitudes and Skills for Active Listening with Regard to Working Conditions and Psychological Stress Reactions Among Subordinate Workers," *Journal of*

Occupational Health 49, no. 2 (2007): 81–87. In particular, the researchers were looking at Listening Attitude and Listening Skill, both of which constitute a central part of the Active Listening concept.

14. K. Izuma, D.N. Saito, and N. Sadoto, "Processing of Social and Monetary Rewards in the Human Striatum," *Neuron* 58, no. 2 (2008): 284–294.

15. M. Sliter, S. Withrow, and S.M. Jex, "It Happened, or You Thought It Happened? Examining the Perception of Workplace Incivility Based on Personality Characteristics," *International Journal of Stress Management* 22, no. 1 (2015): 24–45; citation, page 25.

16. J.T. Cacioppo and L.C. Hawkley, "Perceived Social Isolation and Cognition," *Trends in Cognitive Science* 13, no. 10 (2009): 447–454.

17. R.C.K. Chan, D. Shum, T. Toulopoulou, and E.Y.H. Chen, "Assessment of Executive Functions: Review of Instruments and Identification of Critical Issues," *Archives of Clinical Neuropsychology* 23, no. 2 (2008): 201–216.

CHAPTER 3: THE IMPACT MODEL

1. Of course, this is assuming it's within the responsibilities and expectations of your role, you're clear about legal limitations, and there is insurance in place, where appropriate.

2. Obituary for Paul Lawrence, https://www.hbs.edu/news/releases/Pages/paullaw renceobituary110311.aspx.

3. P.R. Lawrence and N. Nohria, *Driven: How Human Nature Shapes Our Choices* (San Francisco: Jossey-Bass, 2002), 107.

4. N. Nohria, B. Groysberg, and L.E. Lee, "Employee Motivation: A Powerful New Model," *Harvard Business Review* 86, no. 7–8 (2008): 78–84.

5. H.G. Enns and D.B. McFarlin, "When Executives Successfully Influence Peers: The Role of Target Assessment, Preparation, and Tactics," *Human Resource Management* 44, no. 3 (2005): 257–278.

6. T. Dietz, A. Fitzgerald, and R. Shwom, "Environmental Values," *Annual Review of Environment and Resources* 30 (2005): 335–372.

7. A. Bardi and S.H. Schwartz, "Values and Behavior: Strength and Structure of Relations," *Personality and Social Psychology Bulletin* 29, no. 10 (2003): 1207–1220. This weak link may be because while values do motivate our behavior, the researchers note that the relationship between values and behaviors may be partly obscured by norms: we experience norm-related pressures to behave in certain ways.

8. M. Sliter et al., "It Happened, or You Thought It Happened?"

9. S. Vazire and M.R. Mehl, "Knowing Me, Knowing You: The Accuracy and Unique Predictive Validity of Self-Ratings and Other-Ratings of Daily Behavior," *Journal*

of Personality and Social Psychology 95, no. 5 (2008): 1202–1216. Some research suggests that some biases are so strong that at times people can be even less accurate than close others about their own personality, particularly for evaluative traits. See, for example, a discussion of this in K.L. Bollich, K.H. Rogers, and S. Vazire, "Knowing More Than We Can Tell: People Are Aware of Their Biased Self-Perceptions," *Personality and Social Psychology Bulletin* 41, no. 7 (2015): 918–929.

10. See B. Brown, *Daring Greatly: How the Courage to be Vulnerable Transforms the Way We Live, Love, Parent and Lead* (New York: Avery, 2012) and *Dare to Lead: Brave Work. Tough Conversations. Whole Hearts.* (New York: Random House, 2018).

CHAPTER 4: TECHNIQUE

1. J.K. Burgoon, L.K. Guerrero, and V. Manusov, "Nonverbal Signals," in *The SAGE Handbook of Interpersonal Communication*, eds. M.L. Knapp and J. Daly (Thousand Oaks, CA: Sage Publications Inc., 2011), 239–280.

2. For an excellent resource on this, see A. Cuddy, *Presence: Bringing Your Boldest Self to Your Biggest Challenges* (New York: Back Bay Books, 2015).

3. S. Bonaccio, J. O'Reilly, S.L. O'Sullivan, and F. Chiocchio, "Nonverbal Behavior and Communication in the Workplace: A Review and an Agenda for Research," *Journal of Management* 42, no. 5 (2016): 1044–1074. This is a useful review of the nonverbal behavior literature, including of workplace studies. The authors' discussion of the relationship between nonverbal and verbal communication is taken from V.A. Richmond and J.C. McCroskey, *Nonverbal Behavior in Interpersonal Relations*, 5th ed. (Boston: Pearson, 2004).

4. C.S. Areni and J.R. Sparks, "Language Power and Persuasion," *Psychology & Marketing* 22, no. 6 (2005): 507–525.

5. J.R. Sparks, and C.S. Areni, "Style versus Substance: Multiple Roles of Language Power in Persuasion," *Journal of Applied Social Psychology* 38, no. 1 (2008): 37–60.

6. A. Shapira, "Breathing Is the Key to Persuasive Public Speaking," *Harvard Business Review*, June 30, 2015, https://hbr.org/2015/06/breathing-is-the-key-to-persuasive-public-speaking.

7. J. Cesario and E.T. Higgins, "Making Message Recipients 'Feel Right': How Nonverbal Cues Can Increase Persuasion," *Psychological Science* 19, no. 5 (2008): 415–420.

8. Z. Semnani-Azad and W.L. Adair, "Watch Your Tone . . . Relational Paralinguistic Messages in Negotiation: The Case of East and West," *International Studies of Management and Organization* 43, no. 4 (2013): 64–89.

9. W.J. Mayhew, C.A. Parsons, and M. Venkatachalam, "Voice Pitch and the Labor Market Success of Male Chief Executive Officers," *Evolution and Human Behavior* 34, no. 4 (2013): 243–248.

10. C.A. Klofstad, R.C. Anderson, and S. Peters, "Sounds Like a Winner: Voice Pitch Influences Perception of Leadership Capacity in Both Men and Women," *Proceedings: Biological Sciences* 279, no. 1738 (2012): 2698–2704.

11. C.A. Klofstad, "Candidate Voice Pitch Influences Election Outcomes," *Political Psychology* 37, no. 5 (2016): 725–738.

12. N. Kock, "Media Naturalness and Compensatory Encoding: The Burden of Electronic Media Obstacles Is on Senders," *Decision Support Systems* 44, no. 1 (2007): 175–187. The research findings were regarding perceived cognitive effort, perceived communication ambiguity, and perceived compensatory encoding effort.

CHAPTER 5: INSPIRING PEOPLE LIVE INSPIRED

1. A.D. Boss and H.P. Sims Jr., "Everyone Fails! Using Emotion Regulation and Self-Leadership for Recovery," *Journal of Managerial Psychology* 23, no. 2 (2008): 135–150.

2. Adapted from the definition of *leadership* offered by G. Yukl in *Leadership in Organizations,* 6th ed. (Upper Saddle River, NJ: Prentice Hall, 2005).

3. M.R. Furtner, U. Baldegger, and J.F. Rauthmann, "Leading Yourself and Leading Others: Linking Self-Leadership to Transformational, Transactional, and Laissez-Faire Leadership," *European Journal of Work and Organizational Psychology* 22, no. 4 (2013): 436–449.

4. C.P. Neck and C.C. Manz, *Mastering Self-Leadership: Empowering Yourself for Personal Excellence,* 6th ed. (Upper Saddle River, NJ: Prentice Hall, 2012).

5. Definitions adapted from M.R. Furtner et al., "Leading Yourself and Leading Others," 437.

6. U. Konradt, P. Andreßen, and T. Ellwart, "Self-Leadership in Organizational Teams: A Multilevel Analysis of Moderators and Mediators," *European Journal of Work and Organizational Psychology* 18, no. 3 (2009): 322–346.

7. S. Amundsen and Ø.L. Martinsen, "Linking Empowering Leadership to Job Satisfaction, Work Effort and Creativity: The Role of Self-Leadership and Psychological Empowerment," *Journal of Leadership and Organization Studies* 22, no. 3 (2015): 304–323.

8. M.R. Furtner, J.F. Rauthmann, and P. Sachse, "The Socioemotionally Intelligent Self-Leader: Examining Relations Between Self-Leadership and Socioemotional Intelligence," *Social Behavior and Personality* 38, no. 9 (2010): 1191–1196.

9. B.J. Zimmerman, "Attaining Self-Regulation: A Social Cognitive Perspective," in *Handbook of Self-Regulation,* eds. M. Boekaerts, P.R. Pintrich, and M. Zeidner (San Diego, CA: Academic Press, 2000), 13–39.

10. J.D. Creswell, J.K. Bursley, and A.B. Satpute, "Neural Reactivation Links

Unconscious Thought to Decision-Making Performance," *Social, Cognitive, and Affective Neuroscience* 8, no. 8 (2013): 863–869.

11. M. Bar-Eli, O.H. Azar, I. Ritov, Y. Keidar-Levin, and G. Schein, "Action Bias among Elite Soccer Goalkeepers: The Case of Penalty Kicks," *Journal of Economic Psychology* 28, no. 5 (2007): 606–621.

12. S.H. Harrison, D.M. Sluss, and B.E. Ashforth, "Curiosity Adapted the Cat: The Role of Trait Curiosity in Newcomer Adaptation," *Journal of Applied Psychology* 96, no. 1 (2011): 211–220. The researchers here looked at "trait curiosity"—individuals with strong dispositional tendencies with an attraction to a broad array of novel stimuli. People with greater trait curiosity experience the state of curiosity more often, more intensely, and for longer than people who are less trait curious. While some people are higher on this dispositional tendency, all of us are able to choose curiosity as a mind-set and engage in corresponding regular behaviors, thereby accessing benefits associated with curiosity.

13. S.R. Covey, *The 7 Habits of Highly Effective People* (New York: Simon & Schuster, 1989).

14. J.M. Jachimowicz, J.J. Lee, B.R. Staats, J.I. Menges, and F. Gino, "Commuting as Role Transitions: How Trait Self-Control and Work-Related Prospection Offset Negative Effects of Lengthy Commutes," *Harvard Business School Working Paper*, no. 16–077 (revised January 2017).

15. G. Di Stefano, F. Gino, G.P. Pisano, and B.R. Staats, "Making Experience Count: The Role of Reflection in Individual Learning," *Harvard Business School Working Paper*, no. 14–093 (2014; revised June 2016).

16. R.D. Cotton, Y. Shen, and R. Livne-Tarandach, "On Becoming Extraordinary: The Content and Structure of the Developmental Networks of Major League Baseball Hall of Famers," *Academy of Management Journal* 54, no. 1 (2011): 15–46.

17. P.B. Baltes and J. Smith, "The Fascination of Wisdom: Its Nature, Ontogeny, and Function," *Perspectives on Psychological Science* 3, no. 1 (2008): 56–64.

18. A.C. Huynh, H. Oakes, G.R. Shay, and I. McGregor, "Corrigendum: The Wisdom in Virtue: Pursuit of Virtue Predicts Wise Reasoning About Personal Conflicts," *Psychological Science* 28, no. 12 (2017): 1848–1856.

19. S. Etezadi and D. Pushkar, "Why Are Wise People Happier? An Explanatory Model of Wisdom and Emotional Well-Being in Older Adults," *Journal of Happiness Studies* 14, no. 3 (2013): 929–950.

20. V.P. Clayton and J.E. Birren, "The Development of Wisdom Across the Life-Span: A Reexamination of an Ancient Topic," in *Life-Span Development and Behavior*, vol. 3, eds. P.B. Baltes and O.G. Brim (New York: Academic Press, 1980).

21. A. Bergsma and M. Ardelt, "Self-Reported Wisdom and Happiness: An Empirical Investigation," *Journal of Happiness Studies* 13, no. 3 (2012): 481–499.

22. U. Kunzmann and P.B. Baltes, "Wisdom-Related Knowledge: Affective, Motivational, and Interpersonal Correlates," *Personality and Social Psychology Bulletin* 29, no. 9 (2003): 1104–1119.

23. I. Nonaka and H. Takeuchi, "The Wise Leader," *Harvard Business Review* 89, no. 5 (2011): 58–67.

24. T.W. Meeks and D.V. Jeste, "Neurobiology of Wisdom: A Literature Overview," *Archives of General Psychiatry* 66, no. 4 (2009): 355–365.

25. S. Etezadi et al., "Why Are Wise People Happier?"

26. I. Nonaka et al., "The Wise Leader."

27. A.C. Huynh et al., "Corrigendum: The Wisdom in Virtue."

28. P.A. Jennings, C.M. Aldwin, M. R. Levenson, A. Spiro III, and D.K. Mroczek, "Combat Exposure, Perceived Benefits of Military Service, and Wisdom in Later Life: Findings from the Normative Aging Study," *Research on Aging* 28, no. 1 (2006): 115–134. Participants in the study were all male and predominantly European/American. The researchers note the need for further research, particularly with women and people of other ethnicities, to generalize the findings.

CHAPTER 6: GRAVITAS IN THE DARK

1. E. Kross, M.G. Berman, W. Mischel, E.E. Smith, and T.D. Wager, "Social Rejection Shares Somatosensory Representations with Physical Pain," *Proceedings of the National Academy of Sciences of the United States of America* 108, no. 15 (2011): 6270–6275.

2. C.C. Manz and C.P. Neck, "Inner Leadership: Creating Productive Thought Patterns," *The Executive* 5, no. 3 (1991): 87–95.

3. C. Fields, "Why Do We Talk to Ourselves?" *Journal of Experimental & Theoretical Artificial Intelligence* 14, no. 4 (2002): 255–272.

4. S.G. Rogelberg et al., "The Executive Mind: Leader Self-Talk, Effectiveness and Strain," *Journal of Managerial Psychology* 28, no. 2 (2013): 183–201.

5. D. Tod, J. Hardy, and E. Oliver, "Effects of Self-Talk: A Systematic Review," *Journal of Sport and Exercise Psychology* 33, no. 5 (2011): 666–687.

6. S.G. Rogelberg et al., "The Executive Mind."

7. S.G. Rogelberg et al., "The Executive Mind."

8. C.P. Neck and C.C. Manz, "Thought Self-Leadership: The Impact of Mental Strategies Training on Employee Cognition, Behavior, and Affect," *Journal of Organizational Behavior* 17, no. 5 (1996): 445–67.

9. S.G. Rogelberg et al., "The Executive Mind."

10. A. Hatzigeorgiadis and S.J.H. Biddle, "Negative Self-Talk During Sport Performance: Relationships with Pre-Competition Anxiety and Goal-Performance Discrepancies," *Journal of Sport Behavior* 31, no. 3 (2008): 237–253.

11. D. Tod et al., "Effects of Self-Talk."

12. S. David and C. Congleton, "Emotional Agility: How Effective Leaders Manage Their Negative Thoughts and Feelings," *Harvard Business Review* 91, no. 11 (2013): 125–128.

13. D.S. Yeager and C.S. Dweck, "Mindsets That Promote Resilience: When Students Believe That Personal Characteristics Can Be Developed," *Educational Psychologist* 47, no. 4 (2012): 302–314.

14. C. Dweck, *Mindset: Changing the Way You Think to Fulfil Your Potential* (New York: Random House, 2006).

15. R.A. Emmons and M.E. McCullough, "Counting Blessings versus Burdens: An Experimental Investigation of Gratitude and Subjective Well-Being in Daily Life," *Journal of Personality and Social Psychology* 84, no. 2 (2003): 377–389.

16. N.A.S. Farb, Z.V. Segal, H. Mayberg, J. Bean, D. McKeon, Z. Fatima, and A.K. Anderson, "Attending to the Present: Mindfulness Meditation Reveals Distinct Neural Modes of Self-Reference," *Social Cognitive and Affective Neuroscience* 2, no. 4 (2007): 313–122.

17. A useful resource on the benefits of such attention training and the practices of mindfulness is Oxford University emeritus professor Mark Williams and Dr. Danny Penman's *Mindfulness: A Practical Guide to Finding Peace in a Frantic World* (London: Piatkus, 2011).

18. McLaggan Smith Mugs, Scotland, www.msmugs.com.

19. De-Stress Kit by Neom Organics London, www.neomorganics.com.

20. The discussion here of anxiety relates to managing temporary states of feeling anxious, related to particular contexts or situations. If you are experiencing extreme or sustained anxiety, I encourage you to speak to your medical professional or mental health practitioner.

21. S.G. Hofmann, S. Heering, A.T. Sawyer, and A. Asnaani, "How to Handle Anxiety: The Effects of Reappraisal, Acceptance, and Suppression Strategies on Anxious Arousal," *Behavior Research and Therapy* 47, no. 5 (2009): 389–394.

22. A. Brooks, "Get Excited: Reappraising Pre-Performance Anxiety as Excitement," *Journal of Experimental Psychology: General* 143, no. 3 (2014): 1144–1158.

23. T. Rath and B. Conchie, *Strengths Based Leadership: Great Leaders, Teams, and Why People Follow* (New York: Gallup Press, 2008).

24. D.T. Kong and V.T. Ho, "A Self-Determination Perspective of Strengths Use at

Work: Examining Its Determinant and Performance Implications," *Journal of Positive Psychology* 11, no. 1 (2016): 15–25.

25. See www.strengthscope.com.

26. R.E. Boyatzis, M.L. Smith, and N. Blaize, "Developing Sustainable Leaders Through Coaching and Compassion," *Academy of Management Learning and Education* 5, no. 1 (2006): 8–24.

27. R.E. Boyatzis et al., "Developing Sustainable Leaders," 9–12.

28. Definition in R.E. Boyatzis et al., "Developing Sustainable Leaders," taken from R.E. Boyatzis, *Notes from a coaching workshop* (Cleveland: Weatherhead School of Management, Case Western Reserve University, 2003), unpublished paper.

29. R.E. Boyatzis, M.L. Smith, and A.J. Beveridge, "Coaching with Compassion: Inspiring Health, Well-Being and Development in Organizations," *Journal of Applied Behavioral Science* 49, no. 2 (2012): 153–178.

30. R.E. Boyatzis et al., "Coaching with Compassion," 155.

31. R.E. Boyatzis et al., "Coaching with Compassion," 161–162, 167.

CHAPTER 7: ADAPTING MY STYLE

1. R.E. Kaplan and R.B. Kaiser, "Developing Versatile Leadership," *MIT Sloan Management Review* 44, no. 4 (2003): 19–26. In this overview of three research studies, the authors describe strategic leadership as setting long-term direction, thinking broadly about the organization, seeking ways to grow the business, and aligning people with the vision and strategy. They describe operational leadership as focusing on short-term results, getting involved in operational detail, being grounded in the realities of implementing strategy, and using processes to keep people on track. They describe forceful leadership as taking charge, taking stands, having leadership presence, being decisive, setting challenging expectations for people, holding them accountable, making tough calls, and asking probing questions. The authors describe enabling leadership as empowering people, being receptive to where others stand on issues, being responsive to the needs of others, being understanding when others don't deliver, and sharing the limelight.

2. S.J. Zaccaro, J.A. Gilbert, K.K. Thor, and M.D. Mumford, "Leadership and Social Intelligence: Linking Social Perspectives and Behavioral Flexibility to Leader Effectiveness," *Leadership Quarterly* 2, no. 4 (1991): 317–342.

3. S.J. Zaccaro, R.J. Foti, and D.A. Kenny, "Self-Monitoring and Trait-Based Variance in Leadership: An Investigation of Leader Flexibility Across Multiple Group Situations," *Journal of Applied Psychology* 76, no. 2 (1991): 308–315.

4. G. Yukl and R. Mahsud, "Why Flexible and Adaptive Leadership Is Essential," *Consulting Psychology Journal: Practice and Research* 62, no. 2 (2010): 81–93.

5. K.M. Eisenhardt, "Making Fast Strategic Decisions in High-Velocity Environments," *Academy of Management Journal* 32, no. 3 (1989): 543–576.

CHAPTER 8: INFLUENCE WITH INTEGRITY

1. Adapted from C. Anderson, S.E. Spataro, and F.J. Flynn, "Personality and Organizational Culture as Determinants of Influence," *Journal of Applied Psychology* 93, no. 3 (2008): 702–710.

2. H.G. Enns and D.B. McFarlin, "When Executives Influence Peers: The Role of Target Assessment, Preparation, and Tactics," *Human Resource Management* 44, no. 3 (2005): 257–278.

3. The researchers drew on the influence tactics and definitions offered by G. Yukl in *Leadership in Organizations,* 5th ed. (Englewood Cliffs, NJ: Prentice Hall, 2002).

4. A.W. Joshi, "Salesperson Influence on Product Development: Insights from a Study of Small Manufacturing Organizations," *Journal of Marketing* 74, no. 1 (2010): 94–107.

5. S.A. Furst and D.M. Cable, "Employee Resistance to Organizational Change: Managerial Influence and Leader-Member Exchange," *Journal of Applied Psychology* 93, no. 2 (2008): 453–462.

6. A.W. Joshi, "Salesperson Influence on Product Development."

7. R.C. Sinclaire, S.E. Moore, M.M. Mark, A.S. Soldat, and C.A. Lavis, "Incidental Moods, Source Likeability, and Persuasion: Liking Motivates Message Elaboration in Happy People," *Cognition and Emotion* 24, no. 6 (2010): 940–961.

8. See, for example, "Practice One: Model the Way" in the sixth edition of Kouzes and Posner's international bestseller *The Leadership Challenge* (San Francisco: Jossey-Bass, 2017).

9. B.Z. Posner, "Another Look at the Impact of Personal and Organizational Values Congruency," *Journal of Business Ethics* 97, no. 4 (2010): 535–541. This study was a replication of earlier work by Posner and W.H. Schmidt, "Values Congruence and Differences Between the Interplay of Personal and Organizational Value Systems," *Journal of Business Ethics* 12, no. 5 (1993): 341–347. The 2010 study was done to determine if the findings of the earlier study were still valid, given new economic realities and changing human resource assumptions.

10. L. Chou, A. Wang, T. Wang, M. Huang, and B. Cheng, "Shared Work Values and Team Member Effectiveness: The Mediation of Trustfulness and Trustworthiness," *Human Relations* 61, no. 12 (2008): 1713–1742.

11. S.A. Furst et al., "Employee Resistance to Organizational Change."

12. R.van Dijk (Newton) and R. van Dick, "Navigating Organizational Change:

Change Leaders, Employee Resistance and Work-Based Identities," *Journal of Change Management* 9, no. 2 (2009): 143–163.

13. B. Caillaud and J. Tirole, "Consensus Building: How to Persuade a Group," *American Economic Review* 97, no. 5 (2007): 1877–1900.

14. L.K. Lian and L.G. Tui, "Leadership Styles and Organizational Citizenship Behavior: The Mediating Effect of Subordinates' Competence and Downward Influence Tactics," *Journal of Applied Business and Economics* 13, no. 2 (2012): 59–96.

15. J.L. Jensen, "Getting One's Way in Policy Debates: Influence Tactics Used in Group Decision-Making Settings," *Public Administration Review* 67, no. 2 (2007): 216–227.

16. A. Pentland, "The Water Cooler Effect," *Psychology Today,* November 22, 2009, https://www.psychologytoday.com/blog/reality-mining/200911/the-water-cooler-effect.

17. H.G. Enns et al., "When Executives Influence Peers."

18. M.B. Wadsworth and A.L. Blanchard, "Influence Tactics in Virtual Teams," *Computers in Human Behavior* 44 (2015): 386–393.

CHAPTER 9: THE JOINT ADVENTURER

1. Section subtitle from J. O'Toole, J. Galbraith, and E.E. Lawler III, "The Promise and Pitfalls of Shared Leadership: When Two (or More) Heads Are Better Than One," in *Shared Leadership: Reframing the Hows and Whys of Leadership,* eds. C.L. Pearce and J.A. Conger (Thousand Oaks, CA: Sage Publications, Inc., 2003).

2. A.Y. Ou, A.S. Tsui, A.J. Kinicki, D.A. Waldman, Z. Xiao, and L.J. Song, "Humble Chief Executive Officers' Connections to Top Management Team Integration and Middle Managers' Responses," *Administrative Science Quarterly* 59, no. 1 (2014): 34–72.

3. A.Y. Ou, D.A. Waldman, and S.J. Peterson, "Do Humble CEOs Matter? An Examination of CEO Humility and Firm Outcomes," *Journal of Management* 44, no. 3 (2018): 1147–1173.

4. A.Y. Ou et al., "Humble Chief Executive Officers' Connections."

5. For an excellent resource on the power and benefits of collaboration, see H.K. Gardner, *Smart Collaboration: How Professionals and Their Firms Succeed by Breaking Down Silos* (Boston, MA: Harvard Business Review Press, 2016).

6. M.D. Ensley, K.M. Hmieleski, and C.L. Pearce, "The Importance of Vertical and Shared Leadership Within New Venture Top Management Teams: Implications for the Performance of Startups," *Leadership Quarterly* 17, no. 3 (2006): 217–231.

7. See, for example, A. Seers, "Better Leadership Through Chemistry: Toward a Model of Emergent Shared Team Leadership," in *Advances in Interdisciplinary*

Studies of Work Teams: Team Leadership, vol. 3, ed. M.M. Beyerlein and D.A. Johnson (Greenwich, CT: JAI Press, 1996), 145–172; and A. Seers, T. Keller, and J.M. Wilkerson, "Can Team Members Share Leadership? Foundations in Research and Theory," in *Shared Leadership: Reframing the Hows and Whys of Leadership*, 77–102.

8. See, for example, D.E. Yeatts and C. Hyten, *High-Performing Self-Managed Work Teams: A Comparison of Theory to Practice* (Thousand Oaks, CA: Sage Publications, Inc., 1998).

9. See, for example, C. Manz and H.P. Sims, *Business Without Bosses: How Self-Managing Teams Are Building High-Performance Companies* (New York: Wiley, 1993).

10. See, for example, C.L. Pearce and H.P. Sims, "Vertical versus Shared Leadership as Predictors of the Effectiveness of Change Management Teams: An Examination of Aversive, Directive, Transactional, Transformational, and Empowering Leader Behaviors," *Group Dynamics: Theory, Research, and Practice* 6, no. 2 (2002): 172–197.

11. See, for example, J.B. Carson, P.E. Tesluk, and J.A. Marrone, "Shared Leadership in Teams: An Investigation of Antecedent Conditions and Performance," *Academy of Management Journal* 50, no. 5 (2007): 1217–1234.

12. Passenger traffic information from Dubai Airports Media Centre, http://www.dubaiairports.ae/corporate/media-centre/fact-sheets/detail/dubai-airports, July 22, 2018. Number of employees as of date of interview in 2014.

13. J. O'Toole et al., "The Promise and Pitfalls of Shared Leadership."

14. This section was adapted from R. Newton, "Collaborate Across Teams, Silos and Even Companies," *Harvard Business Review*, July 25, 2014, https://hbr.org/2014/07/collaborate-across-teams-silos-and-even-companies.

15. This section was adapted from R. Newton, "How to Co-Lead a Team," *Harvard Business Review*, July 14, 2015, https://hbr.org/2015/07/how-to-co-lead-a-team.

16. This section was adapted from R. Newton, "Strategies for Working Smoothly with Your Peers," *Harvard Business Review*, June 11, 2015, https://hbr.org/2015/06/strategies-for-working-smoothly-with-your-peers.

17. G. Barczak, F. Lassk, and J. Mulki, "Emotional Intelligence, Team Trust and Collaborative Culture," *Creativity and Innovation Management* 19, no. 4 (2010): 332–345.

18. L. Huang and J.K. Murnighan, "What's in a Name? Subliminally Activating Trust Behavior," *Organizational Behavior and Human Decision Processes* 111, no. 1 (2010): 62–70.

19. F. Chiocchio, D. Forgues, D. Paradis, and I. Iordanova, "Teamwork in Integrated Design Projects: Understanding the Effects of Trust, Conflict, and Collaboration on Performance," *Project Management Journal* 42, no. 6 (2011): 78–91.

INDEX

ABOUT THE AUTHOR

Rebecca Newton, PhD, is an organizational and social psychologist and Senior Visiting Fellow at the London School of Economics and Political Science in the Department of Management. She has spent the past two decades researching and teaching on leadership, communication, professional development, organizational culture, change, and management practice. Newton is the CEO of CoachAdviser and has twenty years' experience advising and coaching business leaders and teams in organizations around the world. She writes for the *Harvard Business Review*, was formerly a Visiting Fellow at Harvard University, and has facilitated executive education for the University of Cambridge. Originally from Sydney, Australia, she lives in London with her husband and three children.